YO-AAY-326

ALCOHOLISM

Group Psychotherapy
and Rehabilitation

Publication Number 632
AMERICAN LECTURE SERIES®

A Monograph in
The BANNERSTONE DIVISION *of*
AMERICAN LECTURES IN CLINICAL PSYCHIATRY

Edited by
HOWARD P. ROME, M.D.
Section of Psychiatry
Mayo Clinic
Rochester, Minnesota

ALCOHOLISM
Group Psychotherapy and Rehabilitation

By

HUGH MULLAN, M.D.
Private Practice, New York, New York
Formerly, Medical Director
New York Alcoholism
Vocational Rehabilitation Project
Formerly, Assistant Psychiatrist
Vanderbilt Clinic
Presbyterian Hospital, New York, New York
Past President American Group Psychotherapy Association

and

IRIS SANGIULIANO, Ph.D.
Private Practice, New York, New York
Formerly, Consultant in Group Psychotherapy
New York Alcoholism
Vocational Rehabilitation Project
Formerly, Staff Psychologist
Kings County Hospital

With a Foreword by

Mary E. Switzer
Commissioner, Vocational Rehabilitation Administration
Department of Health, Education, and Welfare

RC 565
M958a
1966
L.C.

CHARLES C THOMAS • PUBLISHER
Springfield • Illinois • U.S.A.

198427

Published and Distributed Throughout the World by
CHARLES C THOMAS • PUBLISHER
BANNERSTONE HOUSE
301-327 East Lawrence Avenue, Springfield, Illinois, U.S.A.
NATCHEZ PLANTATION HOUSE
735 North Atlantic Boulevard, Fort Lauderdale, Florida, U.S.A.

This book is protected by copyright. No
part of it may be reproduced in any manner
without written permission from the publisher.

© *1966, by* CHARLES C THOMAS • PUBLISHER
Library of Congress Catalog Card Number: 65-25743

*With THOMAS BOOKS careful attention is given to all details of
manufacturing and design. It is the Publisher's desire to present books
that are satisfactory as to their physical qualities and artistic possibilities
and appropriate for their particular use. THOMAS BOOKS will be true
to those laws of quality that assure a good name and good will.*

Printed in the United States of America
H-2

DEDICATION

To all those in the many different disciplines who have worked with commitment and devotion toward the greater understanding and treatment of the alcoholic.

CONTRIBUTORS

RUTH FOX, M.D.

Medical Director, The National Council on Alcoholism, Inc.
Member of the Cooperative Commission on the Study of Alcoholism
Member of the Advisory Council on Alcoholism
to the State of New York,
New York, New York

ESTHER J. GRIFFING, M.S.W.

Research Associate and Group Therapist
Mental Retardation Clinic
New York Medical College, Flower-Fifth Avenue Hospital
Lecturer and Field Work Supervisor
Fordham School Social Service
Fordham University
Formerly, Chief Psychiatric Social Worker
New York Alcoholism Vocational Rehabilitation Project
New York, New York

ROSE WOLFSON, Ph.D.

Senior Psychologist, Flower and Fifth Avenue Hospital
Department of Pediatrics
Supervisory Psychologist
Neurological Institute of New York
Department of Psychology
Formerly Clinical Psychologist
New York Alcoholism Vocational Rehabilitation Project
New York, New York

FOREWORD

Redirecting the alcoholic into constructive channels of activity, in other words his rehabilitation, has been a matter of major concern since the dawn of civilization. For the most part, the helping professions have acknowledged defeat. This has resulted in a tendency to ignore this major health problem as such, and has resulted in the alcoholic becoming an outcast of society whose only recourse has been the revolving door between the community and jail.

Undoubtedly the greatest forward movement in combating this social, psychological and physical illness has come about through Alcoholics Anonymous.

Following the steps propounded by this organization many problem drinkers have been helped to total abstinence. Others for a variety of personal reasons have not taken advantage of this opportunity, or found it wanting in meeting their particular needs. As pointed out in this publication, the group approach of Alcoholics Anonymous is not group psychotherapy but the two approaches can and should be used jointly sharing a mutual respect.

One of the most gratifying aspects of our Research and Demonstration Grant Program has been the interest evidenced by various groups in studying and evaluating new methods and techniques which might prove more effective in the total rehabilitation of the alcoholic.

I am delighted that this book containing an unusually comprehensive and informative treatment of the problem was stimulated by the New York Alcoholism Vocational Rehabilitation project sponsored jointly by the National Council of Alcoholism and the Vocational Rehabilitation Administration.

Understandably I have a special interest in the discussion around the role of the vocational counselor but we must heed the emphasis placed on the fact that all therapeutic disciplines involved must coordinate their efforts while respecting the distinct contribution of each.

I like the authors' clear differentiation between group psychotherapy and vocational counseling. "Group psychotherapy is concerned with the inner dynamics of the patient's personality and vocational counseling with the effective reality adaptation of the personality in areas of employment and occupation."

I like too the emphasis placed on the need for follow-up after placement. It is true that the alcoholic disability is lessened when the patient is gainfully employed, but we must remember that his life has consisted of a tangled web of conflicts which must be resolved before he can gain the inner satisfactions from his work which provide the motivation to continue from day to day.

I believe that this should be required reading for all professional personnel working in the field of alcoholism.

As we increase our store of knowledge we shall stand better prepared to intercept the insidious growth of this problem which constitutes one of the greatest threats to our national economy, security, health and social stability.

MARY E. SWITZER
Commissioner
Vocational Rehabilitation Administration
Department of Health, Education, and Welfare

PREFACE

THE alarming rise throughout the world in the number of problem drinkers has made it evident that alcoholism must be met and controlled. In the United States alone, for example, there are over 5,000,000 acknowledged alcoholics, and their numbers are steadily increasing. Although professional workers devote considerable time at international meetings exchanging information on the best ways to prevent, control, and treat alcoholism, usually the only point on which they can all agree is that the alcoholic patient is extremely difficult to rehabilitate. The professional who is trying to help this patient is, at best, unsure about *why* the alcoholic drinks, and what the preferred method of treatment might be. Nonetheless, there are a few valid conclusions that are advanced. The first is that no single therapeutic discipline applied by itself is likely to effect rehabilitation. The alcoholic, it appears, must be treated by a number of coordinated and jointly applied methods if he is to be lastingly rehabilitated. Secondly, the economic, social and psychological problems that arise as the alcoholic patient deteriorates require that the community at large take interest in, and responsibility for, his treatment. This kind of community support is necessary in order to counteract society's usual punitive and damaging response to the uncontrolled drinker, and to insure gaining society's more reasonable and knowledgable attitude toward his illness.

This book, as the title suggests, advocates a systematic truly cooperative approach to the treatment of alcoholism for both the Treatment Center and private practitioner. We describe a broad treatment and rehabilitation program for the alcoholic which meets this patient's unusual needs and which also makes use of all community services that might contribute to his recovery and help him function productively. The conclusions presented in this volume grew out of our three-year experience at the New York Alcoholism Vocational Rehabilitation Project—a Treatment Center where group psychotherapy, social work, psychological evaluation, vocational counseling, and orientation *all* played critical roles in the alcoholic patients' rehabilitation. From December 1959 to November 1962, one of us, Hugh Mullan, M.D., was Medical Director of this project; and the other, Iris Sangiuliano, Ph.D., served as Group Psychotherapy Consultant. This demonstration and treatment project was jointly sponsored by the office of Vocational Rehabilitation, Department of Health, Education and Welfare, Washington, D.C. (Project No. 418) and the National Council on Alcoholism, New York City. Contributors to this volume who were directly connected with the Project are Dr. Rose Wolfson, clinical psychologist; and Esther Griffing, psychiatric social worker. Dr. Ruth Fox, Medical Director of the National Council on Alcoholism was not immediately involved in the Project but nonetheless gave much to it by her continuous support, encouragement and enthusiasm.

Programs for the alcoholic such as Alcoholics Anonymous, that depend upon the guidance and support of nonprofessionals, are a testimonial to the gravity of the alcoholic problem, and to the courage of the layman. The interest and enthusiasm, however, that these leaders and workers display in the majority of cases is motivated by the presence of alcoholism either in themselves or in a member of their families. Frequently, this personal involvement with alcoholism provokes exaggerated and sometimes inflexible attitudes that are best summed up in the often-made statement that "only an alcoholic can cure another alcoholic." While there is no question that A.A., for example, is genuinely fulfilling an urgent need, its effectiveness in "sobering up" the patient seems to encourage members of the professional disciplines to remain on the sidelines. Certainly, there has been a dearth of psychiatric leadership in this field; there have been few treatment concepts and procedures forthcoming, and it is commonplace for a busy psychiatrist or psychologist to immediately refer the recalcitrant and frustrating drinker to A.A. since "they are better equipped to deal with him." One of the reasons for our writing this text is thus to offer administrators and professional workers an integrated system of treatment and rehabilitation for the alcoholic which, although relying heavily upon community resources, still takes the fullest possible advantage of each professional's training, his treatment methods and direction.

The most therapeutic and practical approach to alcoholics occurs in a separate treatment unit devoted exclusively to their group treatment, vocational counseling and rehabilitation. A treatment facility that is separately staffed and operated serves the extraordinary needs and extensive demands of the alcoholic beginning treatment, better than a general psychiatric clinic which also treats other kinds of patients. When the treatment unit must be a part of the larger psychiatric division, its autonomy is especially important. Moreover, the alcoholic's physical well-being must always be a matter of concern, whoever is treating him. Whether it is the staff in a treatment unit, or a therapist in private practice, both must always maintain close and continuous liaison with physicians, hospitals, clinics, and laboratories.

The plans and methods offered in these chapters can also be used in the establishment and the operation of either day or night alcoholic centers. The intensive rehabilitation occurring in this fashion should diminish the need for more formal custodial care in hospitals or rest homes. The private practitioner working alone, on the other hand, will find much in this book to help him contend effectively with the alcoholic patient. He will become aware of the potential aid available to him from social service, vocational counseling and more extensive rehabilitation, medical treatment, psychological evaluations, and such community resources as A.A.

In Part I we outline a systematic treatment approach that is based on a large and specifically-trained professional team working in a center devoted exclusively to alcoholics. The ways in which the center meets and adjusts to the alcoholics' behavior; who the center's staff members are; and what goals they should be working toward, are described. The integrated treatment program offered dovetails with efforts, methods and community resources, especially those of Alcoholics Anonymous, which have proved effective. We suggest significant modifications in the usual "team" approach, to help deal with the pervasive disruptive influence of alcoholism: (1) Adding a vocational counselor to the staff, to help the alcoholic regain his self-esteem through fruitful and satisfying employment commensurate with his capacities; and (2) Promoting an intensive interchange among all staff members, to lessen the usual struggles over status, roles and disciplines; and to help the staff members direct their energies toward helping the alcoholic patient.

In Part II, we describe preparations for motivating and supporting the patient to accept the rigors of psychotherapeutic intervention. It is obvious that alcoholics require help; the *timing* of the specific method of treatment is, however, all-important.

Every professional worker in the clinic must be made aware of the impact that his actions with the alcoholic may have. The initial social worker's meeting, as well as subsequent clinic meetings, color the alcoholic's relationship with the center and may therefore determine whether he stays or leaves. Esther Griffing and one of the authors (Hugh Mullan) suggest that a case worker can properly approach the patient only when he is knowledgeable about alcoholism and the alcoholic's behavior; when he understands the importance of group psychotherapy and vocational counseling for this patient's rehabilitation; and when he is able to withstand frustration, aggressive noncompliance, and extremes of acting out.

In order to prepare the alcoholic for intensive treatment, he and his family must be informed about his condition, its nature, the therapy program, and prognosis. Orientation of the patient and those close to him, therefore, is one aspect of preparing the alcoholic for treatment. The New York Alcoholism Vocational Rehabilitation Project relied upon informal individual discussion about alcoholism; however, we now believe that a carefully planned and executed orientation program serves many ends besides motivating the patient. Dr. Ruth Fox, in Chapter V, illustrates methods of orientation suitable to different settings in which the alcoholic may be treated. The series of lectures on the physical, psychological, and social implications of alcoholism that she describes will help motivate the patient to evaluate himself, reconsider his life, and begin to consider the steps necessary for his rehabilitation.

In Chapter VI, Dr. Rose Wolfson discusses the psychological testing and evaluation of the alcoholic, as well as questions of optimal administrative techniques. The diagnostic material—the patient's underlying personality, the extent of psychological malfunction, his strengths and his vulnerabilities, as well as his response to the test situation—all help the staff members to better know and understand the patient. Dr. Wolfson suggests a modified method of testing for the alcoholic and also discusses those tests which have been found most suitable; in addition, she gives test results as well as the results of some follow-up testing.

In Part III, we focus upon vocational counseling and intensive group psychotherapy, and show how central these two disciplines are to the alcoholic's rehabilitation. Vocational counseling encourages the patient to face his work uncertainties, to get a job and to keep it; group therapy encourages him to face his inner conflicts and stresses, and to modify his behavior.

We discuss the role of the vocational counselor in the Treatment Center for alcoholics. In contrast to working with nonalcoholics, the vocational counselor in the center must be directive, persistent, and careful to individualize both the kind and amount of his support. A method of joint vocational counseling and group psychotherapy, described here for the first time, makes it possible for the patient threatened by vocational guidance on a one-to-one basis, to receive continuing vocational assistance in a group setting.

The last six chapters describe an intensive group therapeutic approach—the core of the rehabilitation effort—modified to fit the *peculiar* needs of the alcoholic patient. This approach can be used by the group psychotherapist working privately, or in a Treatment Center. In Chapter VIII, we suggest the rationale for effective patient selection, methods of evaluation and preparation, and patient placement. Keeping the alcoholic patient in group psychotherapy very often depends upon establishing a strong patient-therapist bond, and placing the right patient in the right group at the right time.

In the last five chapters, we directly address the group psychotherapist treating alcoholic patients, discussing—with clarifying illustration—both theoretical conceptions and practical procedures. We point out that the quasi group cohesion that quickly and easily brings alcoholics together, when they find that they are all "in the same boat," must not be allowed to mislead the therapist into identifying the patients as primarily alcoholic. Quasi group cohesion also acts as a resistance against any psychotherapy which is aimed at treating the person rather than his isolated symptom. The therapist responding to and interpreting the patients' behavior moves the alcoholic group members to become more certainly involved with one another as total human beings. The continuous, destructive, and sometimes bizarre acting out that characterizes the alcoholic must be controlled, interpreted and reduced. We suggest that even though acting out is generally harmful, if it is understood by the therapist, and sensitively responded to *in each case,* it may be used for constructive ends. The group patient is helped, lessening his need to act out, if the therapist neither rigidly prohibits nor unrealistically permits acting out. The intensity and serious purpose of this aspect of group therapeutic intervention is illustrated. The trained and experienced group therapist's use of dreams in a carefully selected group of alcoholic patients clearly distinguishes the psychotherapeutic group from other kinds of groups of alcoholics brought together for the attainment of sobriety and mutual support.

The final chapter deals with another pressing problem in the treatment of the alcoholic—namely, his lack of motivation and his minimal commitment to therapy. The drop-out rate at the beginning of a rehabilitation program and again at the start of group psychotherapy is high. Absences, lateness and abrupt terminations are so characteristic of the alcoholic patient that they seem to describe his way of life. In this chapter, those factors in the patient's personality and behavior which seem to indicate a tolerance for the vicissitudes of rehabilitation and psychotherapy, are identified. A number of different kinds of terminations characteristic of the alcoholic patient are illustrated.

If the alcoholic patient is to change, the psychotherapist must be flexible enough to meet the challenges which this patient presents. The six chapters of Part III will, we hope, both influence the usual group psychotherapist to begin to treat alcoholics; and influence those therapists already treating alcoholics in groups to consider a less didactic approach and to develop an intensive therapeutic relationship with their patients.

HUGH MULLAN, M.D.
IRIS SANGIULIANO, PH.D.

ACKNOWLEDGMENTS

We, THE AUTHORS and the collaborators, wish to express our deep appreciation to the staff members of the National Council on Alcoholism, especially Mrs. Marty Mann, Doctor Margaret Bailey, Mr. William T. Plunkert, and Mrs. Helen Ferguson for their support of the treatment and demonstration project which resulted in this book.

We owe much to our close colleagues in the New York Alcoholism Vocational Rehabilitation Project. This book stems from their willingness to share with us a most rewarding experience, working out various treatment approaches to the alcoholic. Particularly were we aided in this by Doctors Lloyd Delany and Leon Menaker, group psychotherapists, Mr. Robert L. Jacobson, vocational counselor and administrator, Mrs. Kathleen Richardson, social worker, Doctor Jack Cohen, research consultant, and Mr. Terrence Boyle, the original administrative director.

To Doctors Frank Sexias, Stanley Gitlow and Henry Murphy, internists, our thanks for their treatment and care of the Project's patients and their understanding of, and cooperation with, the Project's design and purpose.

We also wish to thank Mr. Fitzhugh Mullan for his research into the field of vocational counseling with the alcoholic, and Mrs. Barbara Fried for her work on the manuscript.

H. M.
I. S.

CONTENTS

[xix]

TABLES AND ILLUSTRATIONS

ALCOHOLISM

Group Psychotherapy
and Rehabilitation

PART ONE

GROUP-ORIENTED REHABILITATION

CHAPTER I

THE CONTENDING FORCES IN THE TREATMENT AND REHABILITATION OF THE ALCOHOLIC

HUGH MULLAN, M.D.

(The alcoholic is a product of a society in which he neither fully participates, nor consistently contributes. Because he has deep-seated characterological difficulties which include compulsive drinking, and because alcohol is so easily procured, the alcoholic patient is difficult to rehabilitate. Group psychotherapy, however, does offer promise in the treatment of alcoholics, particularly when that therapy is offered in a group-oriented treatment center where other dynamic rehabilitation services are also available. At the present time the rivalry that exists between proponents of group psychotherapy and Alcoholics Anonymous, and the consequent confusions of aims and methods used in the attempt to rehabilitate this patient only hinder his progress. For this reason, these differences should be resolved, and proponents of each approach should make a greater effort to understand the others' contributions.)

INTRODUCTION

The Difficult Challenge

Today there is no more challenging problem than the treatment and rehabilitation of the alcoholic. Inexplicable and illogical is the process whereby a man or woman, liked and respected, who has family and friends and who is moderately successful in job and profession, discards all of these assets and through excessive and uncontrollable drinking alienates himself from society and in many instances jeopardizes his very existence.

In describing a treatment approach to alcoholism, it should be said first that the context in which both the condition and the treatment occur are essential. We deal with a culture which produces alcohol and a society which encourages drinking while simultaneously attempting to cure alcoholism when it occurs among some of its members. The issues involved in alcoholism can be faced only if

[5]

there is an understanding of the patterns of behavior which lead to insobriety. In addition, the value and the plausibility of a particular method of treatment or rehabilitation of the alcoholic can only be weighed and tested if the drinking mores of our society are carefully taken into account.

We define alcoholism as the "compulsive need" to drink alcohol. This drinking has deleterious effects upon the person who is so afflicted. Psychologically, his behavior (thoughts, feelings and actions) and physically, his entire organism are involved in this aberrant process. We refer to the patient who suffers from this condition as alcoholic.

Not only is our knowledge of the nature of the alcoholic process meagre; the nature of the most efficacious remedy is still uncertain. Unlike most physical diseases alcoholism defies exact classification; its etiology remains unknown and its definitive treatment obscure. And unlike many psychological conditions, its origins are not specific. Futhermore, the alcoholic's character structure is not radically dissimilar from that of other patients with different symptomatologies. And finally, an alcoholic in treatment as compared to others, is more resistant to the regressive-reconstructive psychoanalytical and less to repressive-counseling methods.

Basic Treatment Problems

The medical and psychological treatments usually employed for the alcoholic, as well as methods for his social rehabilitation, are complicated, time consuming, and, expensive. Just for these reasons, in many instances, they are slated to fail. If we probe more deeply, however, we see that in many cases failure is related not so much to these obvious factors as, instead, frequently, to the peculiar responses that the chronic drinker evokes in the professional who tries to help him. The reverse is also true, for the alcoholic, from his side, often complains most vehemently that he is poorly understood and that in fact he can *only* be cared for and treated by another alcoholic.

In noninstitutional treatment of the alcoholic, a peculiar phenomenon, not present in the treatment of other emotional disorders, is seen to be present, which is that the planned therapeutic meetings between the *nonalcoholic* therapist or worker and the patient with a severe drinking problem seem to be doomed to failure. Many times the patient fails to keep his appointment or turns up inebriated. But even should he appear regularly there are problems in establishing a workable treatment relationship.

Many writers on alcoholism have pointed this out. For example, Lindt implies that the patients through their behavior become inaccessible. "...psychotherapy with alcoholics has never been popular and that includes to some extent the group treatment of patients in this category since many group therapists do not accept alcoholics in a therapy group. One can almost say that alcoholics have become the 'untouchables' among psychiatric patients" (1, p. 43).

The approach to the treatment of alcoholism, especially psychological treatment, is sometimes made extremely difficult if not impossible by factors which alter the alcoholic patient's self-interest and affect his inclination to change. These factors may be summarized thus:

1. The confused social and personal values surrounding the use and effects of alcohol.
2. The ease with which alcohol can be attained.
3. The fact that the complexities of social intercourse, especially those that produce tension and involve competition, can be "handled" more easily when alcohol is readily accessible.
4. The fact that the use of alcohol to alleviate social tensions is sanctioned.
5. The immediate and chronic effects of alcohol consumption on the psyche and the body of the alcoholic.

We do not mean to imply that any, or even all, of these elements cause alcoholism; undoubtedly, however, all play a part.*

The focal point then of alcoholism is the easy availability of alcohol and the great degree of acceptance of social drinking. A secondary point, which is equally significant, but which will only be alluded to in this book, is alcohol's addictive-and-anxiety-alleviating properties. Thus, because alcohol is so easily attain-' because of its gratifying immediate effects, the ~ ~ocus upon the background

---

*The reader is referred to two excellent articl-e Bacon's "Alcohol and Complex of alcohol in our present day society. Tulues and Social Control" (3, p. 31). Society" (2, p. 5), Lemert's "Alco⌐

sets himself apart from the usual run of patients. Moreover, the addictive quality of his symptomatology shared with other addicts makes his resistance to change even greater. As a result, most psychotherapeutic procedures which are effective for others do not induce the alcoholic to seek, accept, or remain in psychotherapy.

The learned use and misuse of alcohol is very much a function of the patient's environment which includes both society at large and, more important, the family unit. Usually, the family, through its child-rearing practices, impresses upon him the parents' concept of acceptable patterns of drinking. This occurs in both a conscious, direct way; yet, also through the machinations of the child-parent ties, and on a purely unconscious level, the child is being directed by his parents' behavior toward or against the neurotic use of alcohol.

The comments of some educators, religious groups, and temperance organizations, as well as the content of certain local laws inveigh against the immoderate or any use of alcohol. Neither these warnings nor those based upon medical investigation are heeded by the compulsive drinker. In like manner, but even more inexplicably, he ignores the deleterious effects of drinking, although he more than anyone else is made physically aware of them.

The Need to Revise Treatment Methods

Because alcoholism seems to be so difficult to treat by the usual mental health and rehabilitation approaches, there is a need to radically revise our concepts of methods. Anyone who is trying to treat the alcoholic must realize that strict adherence to whatever his usual therapeutic set is, no matter how successful it is with other kinds of patients, will not work with the alcoholic. The therapists themselves have to be devoted; furthermore, the treatment form must offer the patient the opportunity to work through internal conflicts and, at the same time support him in the area of reality adjustment and reality testing.

Even though we have still not achieved a kind of treatment *entirely* psycho... the alcoholic, there is promise in the group method of indicated that *group* p. the last decade, a number of reports have chotherapy) has been effective therapy (as contrasted to individual psy-
the alcoholic patient.   Some group

therapists have noted, for example, that this kind of treatment produces not only the attainment of sobriety but also some modest alteration in the patient's personality. In addition, it has been discovered that alcoholic patients prefer a group setting to the traditional private interview with the therapist.

In this book, therefore, we shall describe an approach to the treatment of alcoholism that is characterized throughout by vital, interacting groups. We suggest that whatever is basic in the pathological process of the alcoholic can be interrupted, and perhaps reversed, through corrective psychotherapeutic group action. We believe, furthermore, that once the destructive features in the alcoholic's personality have been brought under control, his consciousness of his inner problems will expand, and his ability to choose will be increased.

THE GROUP AS IDENTIFICATION AND AS PROCESS

The Significance of Group

Since the group approach to the alcoholic is being described, clarification of two concepts is immediately in order. The first is the term *group,* including the large group of alcoholics who require treatment and rehabilitation and the second, the more exact concept, the alcoholic treatment group.

Group is defined variously: "1. *Fine Arts,* Two or more figures forming a design or a unit in a design . . . 2. An assemblage regarded as a unit; a cluster; aggregation. 3. An assemblage of objects having some common characteristic. 4. *Biol.* Any assemblage of animals or plants having natural relationship to each other" (4, p. 439). While these definitions are helpful, they do not emphasize what is essential to a group of people.

More to the point of rehabilitation and treatment are the following definitions which stress the essential ingredients of common identity and purpose. " . . . a collection of organisms in which the existence of all (in their given relationship) is necessary to the satisfaction of certain individual needs in each" (5, p. 20). And, ". . . only that nucleus of persons, each of whom recognizes or remembers each of the others, and is in turn recognized or remembered by each of the others, constitutes the small group" (6, p. 30).

These definitions and many others cannot begin to cover adequately the kinds of groups and organizations, ranging from very simple to highly structured, which exist in our society. Actually, all of us participate in a series of groups every day, in the family, at work, and in recreation. Everyone is required to participate in society in some manner, to share social responsibility, however slightly, and to accomplish some task, however small. This is why group psychotherapists have long been convinced that patients can be most effectively treated in a group. After all, the family is basically a group whose members live together in order to meet their individual needs of sustenance, support, growth and satisfaction; and the kind of life we are accustomed to could not continue if there were to be a breakdown in group formation and function. The use by our society of the one-to-one meeting is unique—limited to intimate relationships: lovemaking, the medical practitioner and his patient (including psychotherapy), the confessor and the penitent. Unified and co-operative gatherings of men and women, either temporary or permanent, who are working not alone for themselves as individuals, but also for a common good are the order of the day.

What is the significance of group interaction *to the individual?* It is quite clear that the group as a whole may complete a task which benefits all; but why is this significant to each participant? The reason is that the co-ordinated action of a group requires that each member mature socially, and at the same time it offers him a milieu in which to risk new behavior.* The unified co-operative activity of the group members as they come together is thus extremely important. The potentiality for persons to work "therapeutically" together has not always been present. Its achievement now rests upon the willingness of human beings in concert to give up some egocentricity while they apply recently discovered psychological understanding to their behavior. Georg Simmel made this clear in his remarks about intragroup co-operation. "The division of a unified group, and more especially, its division not only from top to bottom, in terms of ruling and being ruled, but among its coordinated members, is one of the most extraordinary advances made by mankind" (7, pp. 10-11).

---

*Group psychotherapy's efficacy as a treatment form rests upon this important point "the risking of new behavior". Group psychotherapists have reported that patients long experienced in psychoanalytical (one-to-one) treatment very often have great difficulty entering an intensive interactional treatment group.

The Large Group of Alcoholics

The identification of an aggregate of human beings as a group on the basis of the fact that they all possess a psychological and perhaps physical need to ingest alcohol is both logical and necessary. (The definition of group implied here is "a number of people, large or small, who are related in such a manner that they can conveniently be considered together.") This assumption is reasonable because the alcoholic differs from the rest of society by virtue of behavior that he exhibits in common with certain of his fellows; and he and they can be identified through this behavior.

In the United States alone, where alcoholism is known to be on the increase, there are at least 5,000,000 alcoholics, the products of every racial, ethnic, and social group in our society. Through common circumstances in their past experiences, and possibly too some physical deficiency, they have begun to drink compulsively. Each alcoholic, in common with other alcoholics, behaves characteristically in a self-destructive manner. Their uncontrollable need for alcohol, their persistent insobriety, and their severely limited and damaged lives significantly distinguish alcoholics as a group, and set them apart from others not so afflicted. It is true that some alcoholics do become sober and remain so for varying lengths of time; nonetheless it is rarely that they have achieved sufficient personality and physical changes to warrant removing them from the group known as alcoholic.

Treatment Groups

The alcoholic, who is thus considered as a part of a defined group, requires treatment. Experience indicates that when he genuinely realizes that he is alcoholic he is more likely to accept treatment. As this early and partial identification (for he is much more than alcoholic) takes place more easily in a group with others similarly afflicted, treatment also proceeds more effectively in such a group setting.

The *treatment group* is one of a series of small groups composed of selected alcoholic patients and conducted by professionals with specific methods and goals. Treatment groups are therefore considered to be *primary* because they are characterized by "face-to-face association and co-operation" toward certain definite goals (see Chapter III).

The psychotherapeutic group is a special kind of treatment group. It is conducted by a trained group psychotherapist who carefully selects and prepares the alcoholic patients and proceeds to bring his psychological methodology to bear upon the individual and group psychopathologies.

Two kinds of people participate in the group treatment. One, the staff member who accepts responsibility, conducts treatment groups, and participates with other staff members in the clinic or agency. The second, the alcoholic patient who is very apt to ignore his responsibility and is, at least loath to keep his initial appointments; later, he may resist entering any treatment group, especially the psychotherapy group. This disparity between these two people is emphasized by their vastly different values about drinking. The first kind of person does not need alcohol, and therefore uses it only sparingly if at all. The alcoholic appears to require alcohol in order *simply* to get through daily tasks.

These identifications based upon responsible activity and sobriety may seem to be oversimplified and obvious, but they have deeper implications relevant for all professionals and particularly psychotherapists who have never formed and conducted a group composed of alcoholics. Group psychotherapy with nonalcoholic patients is usually attended regularly. This does not happen with alcoholic patients. The group psychotherapist who is beginning to work with homogeneous alcoholic groups will very soon find out that a member's constancy and sobriety are not easily won achievements. His unreliability at the start and his tendency to "slip" (to start drinking again) are very discouraging to the agency staff, particularly an inexperienced staff; and it is for this reason that we stress the differences in the staff's attitudes from those of the alcoholic's.

In the rehabilitation center, then, one group of professionally trained persons come together daily in a common effort to facilitate change in another group, the alcoholic patients. To the degree that the impasse in the patient group is due to compulsive drinking, the staff member will find it difficult to identify himself with this addictive problem that is foreign to him. Very soon the alcoholic group is found by the staff to be unreliable, unco-operative, inconstant, late, or absent, and it is *this* behavior of the alcoholic, whether drinking or not that begins to characterize him in the minds of the staff. This behavior, which is so unlike that of other patients, *and not the insobriety alone,* at once molds the response of the staff member to the alcoholic patient. The rehabilitation director and the supervisors must be aware of this, so that the staff members may be supported through their original frustrating experiences with the alcoholic and not be allowed to negatively overreact.

All treatment groups used in the rehabilitation of the alcoholic have both individual and common goals which have to do most immediately with mobilizing the alcoholic's inner forces to the point where he will be able to cope with the environment *without drinking alcohol.* In addition to this, there are other goals which have to do with attaining a gradual change in the personality of the drinker so that he will be able to participate consistently and creatively in his environment. This kind of personality modification of the alcoholic is possible through individual psychotherapy, counseling toward adjustment, and the establishment of continuing dependent relationships. However, we believe that both sobriety and personality change of an evolving nature can best be simultaneously gained and sustained through a team approach which includes group psychotherapeutic treatment and continuous vocational counseling. When various staff members use the group format, *in their own specific disciplines* with the alcoholic patients, their aims are more fully realized. In such a system, the psychotherapeutic group becomes the central therapeutic agent, while the other clinic groups of professionals and patients ready the alcoholic for the interacting psychoanalytic therapy group (see Chapter II, Figure 2, p. 51).

THE RECOGNITION OF ALCOHOLISM

Definitions

It is significant that none of the contributors to this book offers a definitive categorization of alcoholism, but instead simply describes the alcoholic's behavior and his response to it. Perhaps an exact definition of this pathological functioning is not necessary for those who are most concerned. Indeed, it is possible that minutely and carefully labeling the patient who is in such obvious difficulty because he drinks would only serve to further separate him from the nonalcoholic professional.

Also, the more detached and objective approach that is taken toward the alcoholic, the less chance there will be of establishing rapport with him, and the greater the liklihood of abrupt termination. A traditional history-taking period of any significant duration and the imposition of arbitrary clinic routines, accepted by other patients, only lessen the willingness of the alcoholic to communicate, and add problems to the already difficult and usually unsatisfactory first meeting between the staff member and the alcoholic (see Chapter III).

There are, of course, certain salient behavioral characteristics which most professionals would agree are pathological and indeed pathognomonic for this condition. Staff members, regardless of their specialty, find the alcoholic patient presents unpredictable behavior (acting out), an absent or dishearteningly meagre inclination to either start or continue therapy, and a lack of responsibility to himself and to any others (family, friends, staff) with whom he is involved. These characteristic behaviors occur so generally that they have become expected norms of conduct and serve to differentiate the alcoholic from other patients who are more reliable (8).

Diethelm states, "A patient should be considered a chronic alcoholic when he harms himself, or his family, through the use of alcohol and cannot be made to realize it, or when he no longer has the will or strength to overcome his habit. The diagnosis does not depend on the frequency of acute intoxications which is merely an indication of his susceptibility to alcohol, but on the development of personality and somatic changes" (9, p. 441).

Alcoholics Anonymous, in a very practical manner, asks ten questions which if answered "yes" spell "danger," and suggest that the person is indeed not a heavy drinker but an alcoholic:

"1. Do you crave a drink at a definite time daily?
2. Do you gulp your drinks, and sneak extras?
3. Do you drink to relieve feelings of inadequacy?
4. Do you drink to escape worry and to dispel the blues?
5. Do you drink, when overtired, to "brace up"?
6. Is drinking affecting your peace of mind?
7. Is drinking making your home life unhappy?
8. Do you prefer to drink alone?
9. Do you require a drink the next morning?

10. Do you lose time from work due to drinking?" (10, p. 7)

The staff member who is attempting to rehabilitate the alcoholic hardly need rely upon these criteria nor the patient's admission of their presence in order to commence therapeutic action. He knows by the patient's behavior and by the fact that he is present in the office or agency seeking help and care that he requires *emergency and prolonged* psychiatric treatment. He should therefore decide to initiate treatment before an exact history, diagnosis, and prognosis have been made, an approach which is similar to Alcoholics Anonymous. For example, in the pamphlet *An Introduction to A.A.*, Alcoholics Anonymous describes how to become a member.

> "If after examining your record honestly and objectively, you admit to yourself that you are an alcoholic and that you sincerely want to stop drinking once and for all, then you have only to attend the meetings, make an energetic, sincere effort to be guided by the advice and experience of those about you, and try with complete sincerity to live according to the A.A. program to become a member" (10, p. 6).

The mere admission that one is alcoholic is enough for membership in A.A. Similarly, when the patient appears at the clinic asking for advice or help, this is tantamount to an admission that he has psychological problems, and experiences himself as an alcoholic, and he should therefore be offered prompt help.

Definitions are apt to be significant for staff members during conferences, consultations, and supervisory meetings, because commonly understood expressions and descriptions will lessen interdisciplinary confusion and the development of rivalries. A task for the rehabilitation team, therefore, quite early in their work together is to come to an understanding of what alcoholism means *for them in their common experience*, (1) see Chapter II, pp. 50 to 54).

In Mark Keller's comprehensive article "The Definition of Alcoholism and the Estimation of Its Prevalence," he defines alcoholism in terms first of *drinking* and then, second, of its *ill effects* (from drinking, on the drinker). "Alcoholism is a chronic disease manifested by repeated implicative drinking so as to cause injury to the drinker's health or to his social or economic functioning" (1, p. 316). Within the term chronic is implied "a repetitive, disabling, uncontrollable behavior—a 'dysbehaviorism.' " Certainly this definition is better than the traditional medical dictionary categorization which fails to suggest the psychological and social factors inherent in the disease process. For example, *Gould's Medical Dictionary* states that alcoholism is "The morbid results of excessive or prolonged use of alcoholic liquors. The term *acute alcoholism* has been used as a synonym for inebriety. The chronic form is associated with severe disturbances of the digestive and nervous systems" (12, p. 49).

It must not be overlooked that the alcoholic has recognizable physical and psychological limitations and difficulties, and is therefore a subject for rehabilitation services. By definition the alcoholic patient is not only impaired* but he usually is both disabled** and handicapped*** as well.

The implications of the alcoholic's limitations are many. The alcoholic patient is usually impaired vocationally, for instance, and should get not only intensive group psychotherapy but direct vocational guidance and support. On the other hand, the patient's degree of initial impairment immediately offers a yardstick against which his recovery rate as well as his long-term rehabilitation goals can be measured (see Chapter III).

Problem No. 1. The Alcoholic Patient's Avoidance of the Treatment Group Responsibility

As has been pointed out, society is composed of many participant groups that interact with each other for beneficial purposes. Some individuals, however, are unable to behave effectively in groups. They neither contribute to the group's vital activities nor are they concerned with the ends considered significant by the others. These persons, by failing to accept their responsibilities to themselves and to the other

---

*"*Impairment*—any deviation from the normal which results in defective function, structure, organization or development of the whole, or of any of its faculties, senses, systems, organs, members, or any part thereof" (13, p. 2).

**"*Disability*—any limitation experienced by the impaired individual, as compared with the activities of unimpaired individuals of similar age, sex, and culture" (13, p. 2).

***"*Handicap*—the disadvantage imposed by impairment or disability upon a specific individual in his cultural pattern of psychosocial, physical, vocational, and community activities" (13, p. 2).

group members (society and culture), endanger the group's over-all purpose. The alcoholic is one such person who, both in a nonalcoholic group such as his family, or even in an alcoholic treatment group led by a professional, fails many times to act in a responsible and committed way. Early in any rehabilitation treatment group the alcoholic presents Problem One. *He fails to be responsible for his inappropriate behavior. He neither trusts the therapist nor the members. And he fails to constructively participate in personal involvements.*

Problem No. 2. The Alcoholic's Exploitation of the Treatment Group

As the severity of the alcoholic's drinking progresses, his responsibile participation in the family group falters. Similarly his social activity and especially his work become more and more ineffectual. From society's standpoint, his impairment is seen as an ever-increasing abandonment of responsibility. But this is not the whole story. In those social groups where the alcoholic does attempt to function, many times his presence is far from beneficial, and instead seems almost "on purpose" to be destructive and ruinous to the other members. He uses the group, family or others, as actors on *his* stage and then proceeds to react against them according to his fantastic version of life. As he falls further and further behind in his work, or acts out on the job, the alcoholic is often the center of bitter controversy that wastes valuable time and creates work blockages. Similarly, by the time the troubled alcoholic finally leaves his family, the hurt he has inflicted on his spouse and children is often so severe as to make any real resolution of their problems almost impossible. It is not only the eventual absence from the family group which is pathological. The alcoholic's exploitative activities before and especially his rejection of his family at the time of separation are always deleterious to the family and the alcoholic alike.

In the rehabilitation agency, the treatment groups (and especially the psychotherapeutic group) suffer from the continuation of this exploitative behavior. The alcoholic who is beginning treatment thus presents Problem Two. *He exploits the therapist and members using them egocentrically. His view of the group is primarily that they are persons to get something from; and if they do not fulfill his expecta-*

*tions, he sees them as people upon whom he either vents his hostility
or people to ignore and to disdain.*

Problem No. 3. The Alcoholic Patient's Use of Alcohol to Avoid the Treatment Group Reality

Perhaps the most characteristic feature of the alcoholic's behavior
is that he uses alcohol to maintain fantasy and to avoid reality. Regardless of the particular drinking pattern of a given alcoholic, and
regardless of the stated and unconscious reasons for his drinking, the
characteristic that he exhibits in common with all other alcoholics is
that much of the time he prefers his fantasy life to his existence in
the real world.

In the alcohol treatment agency the aims of all of the services are
blocked when the patient because of his need to fantasy either fails
to show up since he has been drinking or comes and participates in-
effectively. The alcoholic patient who does either of these is posing
Problem Three. *He distorts the fundamental reality of the group by
either drinking before his appointment or by having a hangover during
the session. In either case, the group cannot face its members' intra-
pyschic and interpersonal problems; instead it is faced with acute alcoholic behavior in one of its members. It is distracted from those activities which are pertinent to psychotherapeutic change.*

Problem No. 4. The Alcoholic Patient Abandons His Treatment Group

One of the difficulties with the exploitative alcoholic is that when it
becomes quite clear that his exploitation will no longer be allowed by
his family, employer or treatment group, he usually abandons, not
his exploitative behavior, but the group.

> A woman patient who married an alcoholic and lived with him
> for twenty-seven years finally decided upon a divorce. Her hus-
> band had not counted upon this step. He opposed it in every way
> possible. When the divorce decree was about two weeks from its
> effective date, the husband drove into a tree on a road "that he
> traveled four or five times a day." His accidental death was con-
> sidered by those who knew him to be a suicidal abandonment
> of his family at the point when he could no longer exploit those
> close to him.

In similar fashion, both at the beginning and later, the alcoholic patient, when he can no longer exploit the staff member and other patients, tends to abruptly depart from treatment (see Chapter XIII, p. 305). Thus he presents Problem Four. *He traumatizes the other group members, patients and professionals alike, by acting as though motivated—by at first appearing to show serious intent, commitment, and interest—only to precipitously leave the group either before or even after having achieved sobriety.*

GROUP PSYCHOTHERAPY AND MEMBERSHIP IN ALCOHOLICS ANONYMOUS

Confusions and Rivalries

Many patients, professionals, and interested laymen confuse group psychotherapy for the alcoholic with Alcoholics Anonymous. This unfortunate misunderstanding has deleterious effects upon the rehabilitation of the alcoholic and may even prevent his continuation in therapy. It is to be expected that the confused, fantasy-seeking patient will distort treatment procedures; those interested in his recovery should, hopefully, be more knowledgeable. Group therapy and A.A. are two distinct approaches both of which have their place in the rehabilitation of the alcoholic.

People who refer to group psychotherapy and Alcoholics Anonymous are very apt to use loose and inaccurate terminology. For example, Alcoholics Anonymous may be referred to as "group psychotherapy." Workers in Information Centers, sometimes refer to Alcoholics Anonymous as a "kind of big group-therapy session." Physicians, hard-pressed for something constructive to do for the inebriate, often say, "You need group living and therapy. You should become a member of A.A. where you can get group treatment." Even established members of A.A. frequently are under the impression that they are in group psychotherapy. If, in their local meetings, they debate the issue of psychotherapy, they are apt to explain, "We have no need to go into therapy, group or otherwise. Why enter therapy when we *are* group therapy?" Many somatically-oriented psychiatrists and psychotherapists, untrained in the group method of treatment, also confuse the issue. They fail to see that group psychotherapy is distinct from all other group get-togethers, and that it has its own techniques and unique goals. Consequently, they do justice neither to the potential of the interacting treatment group nor to the round-the-clock support gained from the trusting fellowships of Alcoholics Anonymous.

In order to succesfully plan and carry out a rehabilitation program for the alcoholic patient, those charged with this responsibility must know the difference between these two approaches so that timely and accurate referral can be made and effective patient support can be rendered. *Any rivalries between the proponents of these two approaches will adversely effect the alcoholic patient.*

The threefold purpose, then, of this section is (a) a description and differentiation between group psychotherapy and Alcoholics Anonymous; (b) an indication of the methods and goals of these two approaches; and (c) a promotion of the co-operative use of *both* methods to alleviate the alcoholic's deep-seated disturbance.

Definitions and History: Group Psychotherapy

Group psychotherapy is the psychological treatment of psychiatric patients in a group. The resources at the disposal of the therapist, and patients, who are sometimes considered to be "co-therapists," are (a) the group process; (b) immediate interaction; (c) confrontation; (d) some nondistorted relationships (appropriate thoughts, feelings and actions); (e) some distorted relationships (transference and countertransference); (f) abreaction; (g) revelation; (h) identification; and (i) analysis.

Group psychotherapy depends for its success upon a careful individual preparation of the patient; the proper selection of patients for any particular group; the appropriate composition of each group; and the careful timing of the patient's introduction into a group. To be sure, some of these procedures will be empirical, decided on the basis of the group psychotherapist's experiences; however, a large body of theoretical knowledge now exists which the trained group psychotherapist will use in determining who is suitable for a particular group, as well as the propitious moment for patient and group to be brought together.

Group psychotherapy began in the United States at the turn of the century with homogenous groups of tubercular patients. Often-successful attempts were made with these patients to get them to accept their illness, to adjust to its severe physical limitations, and to live productive and happy lives even though they remained chronically ill (14, p. 210). Since World War II, group psychotherapy was influenced first by psychoanalysis, and even more recently, by existential philosophy. The group method is at present applied to heterogeneous groups of all kinds of psychiatric patients, and during the last decade has developed a distinct methodology, with goals similar to psychoanalysis centering about the constructive evolution of the patient's personality and specific goals which have to do with increased social responsibility.

In another context, the group psychotherapeutic method has been elaborated upon in detail. The following quote seems particularly pertinent:

> The therapy group, therefore, is a means for persons to communicate intimately, the one with another, while at the same time this very communication is acted upon by a psychologically adept, trained participant (the therapist). Empirically it has been found that the intensity and authenticity of group communication are the results of *proper* group composition coupled with *proper* psychodynamic leadership. To have one of these and not the other vitiates a therapeutic outcome. Both, therefore, should be attained, having equal importance in the therapeutic potentiality of the group (15, pp. 47-48) (italics the authors').

It is just these two developments—an increased control over the composition of groups, on the one hand, and psychodynamic leadership, on the other—that have brought about a new rigor in the standards of group psychotherapeutic practice. Hand in hand with this increased rigor has come, as might be expected, an increased strictness in training requirements for those who would use the group method.

What we still lack today, however, is a systematic course of training for professionals who wish to treat the alcoholic by intensive group psychotherapy.* Very often, the group treatment of alcoholics is

---

*The American Group Psychotherapy Association at its 1962, 1963 and 1965 Annual Meetings implied an acknowledgement of this need by offering workshops conducted for those vitally concerned with the group treatment of alcoholics.

delegated to any member of the staff, regardless of his training and experience, who is the most sympathetic to the alcoholic's plight. Without question, sympathy, diligence and industry are necessary attributes for those who work with the alcoholic; but group therapists would be much more effective if training in group psychotherapy were available, in the forms of didactic lectures, seminars, workshops, and courses in supervision, all of which focus on the alcoholic patient.

Definitions and History: Alcoholics Anonymous

Alcoholics Anonymous, whose origins are more recent than group psychotherapy's, owes its conception and growth to the specific need of the alcoholic patient *to become and remain sober.* In considering the general characteristics of Alcoholics Anonymous, Bailey states:

> From its original two members, who came together in 1935, A.A. has grown to a worldwide total of 8,615 groups with about 300,000 members. In the United States in 1961, there were 5,875 groups with an estimated membership of 216,000. In addition, upwards of 700 groups meet in prisons and hospitals . . . These groups have the advantage of ready availability in nearly all communities except very small ones. There are no dues or fees (though voluntary contributions are collected at meetings), and for A.A., "the only requirement for membership is a desire to stop drinking." In practice, this means that any one is a member who states that he or she is a member (16, pp. 1-2).

Lee also emphasizes sobriety as the single understood goal of Alcoholics Anonymous:

> A.A. has only two purposes: to help its members stay sober and to help others achieve sobriety. In pursuit of the second purpose (normally called carrying the message), A.A. members are eager to be called on for what they speak of as twelfth step work—so-called because the twelfth-step of the program describes this obligation to help others (17, p. 24).

Since every alcoholic is first an individual, it seems quite likely that he seeks out, joins and participates in Alcoholics Anonymous in quite individual and unique ways. Therefore, the dynamics of the drinker as he recovers sobriety in this fellowship are probably different in many particulars while being similar in certain over-all generalities. It is important for each professional who works closely with the alcoholic to conceptualize in his own terms, the process of Alcoholics Anonymous as it pertains to each patient. The staff worker must become aware of the unique dynamics involved because it gives him valuable information concerning the needs of the patient. As the professional gains more experience in working jointly with A.A., his understanding of the interpersonal and intrapsychic dynamics involved with each patient will be found to be different. Hopefully, as time goes on, the staff member will find that his understanding of A.A.'s function increases. However, for this to come about the professional must be open and flexible to new ideas rather than be rigidly doctrinaire; accepting of another approach rather than rejecting; and value A.A.'s contribution because of its feasibility and reality rather than because of its clarity of theory and completeness. In this manner, a full and congenial use of the two approaches, group psychotherapy on the one hand, and Alcoholics Anonymous on the other, is possible. This harmony, when achieved, helps the alcoholic patient immeasurably.

The Psychodynamic Import of Alcoholics Anonymous

Some of A.A.'s general psychodynamics that are effective for many alcoholics, as seen from the psychotherapist's standpoint, are the following:

1. The alcoholic demonstrates the lack of a "real" self; that is, he exhibits a diffused identity, an inability to relate, irresponsibility to self and others, and the need to fantasy rather than act. The alcoholic commences to attain direction when he begins to participate tentatively in Alcoholics Anonymous.

2. Participation in Alcoholics Anonymous immediately challenges him: "If he (another) can do it I can do it"; mitigates some of his self-hatred: "We are all a bunch of drunks together"; and gives him a new identity: that of being a member in Alcoholics Anonymous.

3. The alcoholic does not feel that he belongs to our complicated, highly demanding society, and in Alcoholics Anonymous he finds a relatively simple society to which he can belong and in which he can effectively participate, if he will but remain sober *for twenty-four hours at a time.* He thus becomes a participating

member of a group, although he is ostracized from other groups in society in general—from friends, business associates, family, and so forth. Part of the strength which he feels as a member of A.A. is rooted in group loyalty: a common experience of drinking with asocial behavior, common goals, and a sense of belonging.

4. As he comes to the point of helping others in A.A., his guilt begins to lessen. This guilt emanates basically from his destruction of his own self. He neutralizes this guilt and lessens it through helping others gain sobriety. He does this in many ways, including constant attendance, constant participation, revealing his past alcoholic experiences, continuing sobriety, and sponsorship of others.

5. The alcoholic slowly recovers his self-esteem by virtue of the duration of his sobriety and his association with others who have similar problems. His sponsorship of another inebriate in A.A. and his personal stake in this person's maintainence of sobriety gives him a continuing sense of worth.

Alcoholics Anonymous has been evaluated differently by different psychotherapists. In Ernest Simmel's opinion:

> The alcoholic identifies with the ex-alcoholic which is further reinforced by his curing others. He identifies also with the society in which alcohol, in contrast to our normal society, is taboo. The alcoholic accepts two beliefs: one, that he is powerless against alcohol; that is, he accepts the destruction of his omnipotence fantasies; and the corollary of this, that there is a power greater than himself and he must submit to it to be well. Once there is acceptance emotionally of this universal power the alcoholic compulsion can be expelled. This is the basis of the spiritual experience necessary for cure. The alcoholic's psychopathological formula of destroy and be destroyed (by incorporation) is changed to save and be saved. Identification is substituted for addiction; that is, devouring is replaced by identification. Alcoholics Anonymous, like church groups such as the Evangelical and the Salvation Army, make use of suppressive and repressive mechanisms as well, and proselytization aids this repression (18, pp. 490-491).

It cannot be emphasized too often, that what is of significance for the therapist who treats the alcoholic patient is the therapist's ability to accept and appreciate the "group" process involved in A.A. When the group therapist carefully evaluates the dynamics of A.A., he can combine his own and A.A.'s efforts to benefit the alcoholic most.

This view is in some ways unorthodox. But there is much that the group psychotherapist can learn both from the experience of A.A. and also from his own experience with the homogenous alcoholic group; and this knowledge will be of particular value in his initial response and treatment of the alcoholic. The therapist, for instance, will find that certain alterations may occur in his approach to treatment. The group psychotherapist in the early therapy sessions with the alcoholic should not be primarily interested in the alcoholic's diagnosis and prognosis, in his history, or in having the patient diagnosticaly tested, and this response is borne out by the success of a similar procedure in A.A. The group psychotherapist's concern ought to be directed toward the attendance of the patient, his participation in the group, and his gaining sobriety, and all other procedures can wait. Tiebout tells us why:

> A.A. came along with a program to stop drinking; causation was ignored, the focus was all on treatment. Medicine's insistence on treating causes was disregarded, not wittingly to be sure, but the emphasis was on stopping the drinking and helping the individual to achieve and maintain that end. Like the treatment by surgery, the causes were irrelevant in meeting the immediate issues. Instead of the scalpel, there was the A.A. program. Instead of the infected appendix being removed, the individual was told to stop drinking, or, stated in another way, liquor was removed from his life (13, p. 5).

FUNDAMENTAL DIFFERENCES—
GROUP PSYCHOTHERAPY AND ALCHOLICS ANONYMOUS
Similarities and Differences

If these outlined dynamics of A.A. benefit the patient who participates in its fellowship, why should he, in addition, engage in group psychotherapy? Does not A.A. alone offer sufficient reward? Is he not changed sufficiently through gaining and maintaining sobriety?

Before we can answer these questions, we have to have an understanding of the similarities and differences between group psychotherapy and A.A. Although both methods make the patient's sobriety an immediate goal, their means for the patient's eventually maintaining sobriety permanently are dissimilar. Both consider that abstinence from alcohol is a primary requirement for the duration of the person's life; but each group sets about to accomplish this goal in a different way (see Chapter III).

From the start, the psychotherapist asks that each member in the alcohol-patient group involve himself in his own intrapsychic struggle to the end that, through this activity, he will become responsible for his inner emotional life and, therefore, for his life in general. The emotional content of the group changes as patients begin to question their own motives and evaluate themselves. Search for a solution to the drinking problem and for a "miracle" gives way to a growing self-awareness and a lessening in self-deception. At about four to six months later the group patient no longer ruminates about his wasted life, about his cruel fate, or about his latest drinking bout. Instead, he focuses upon his newly discovered self, his ever-recurring anxiety, and his keenly-felt despair. Naturally it is desirable for these changes to be achieved without recourse to the patient's drinking, if it is possible. However, in many instances, these beginning signs of an expanding and developing self indicate risks are being taken not only in treatment but in the patient's social and marital life, and "slips" which do occur at these times do not necessarily indicate a poor prognosis.

The therapist also continues to request that the members involve themselves more with one another. Patients will respond to this request by being on time for sessions, being absent less, and, in general, by offering fewer obstacles to treatment. The patient's sobriety, as with all of his other growth strivings, must be motivated by constructive forces within himself; and as he begins to relinquish some of his defensive armor, when risk, responsibility, and choice have been activated, abstinence from drinking becomes a total commitment. Toward the last part of treatment, the patient exhibits a growing capacity for responsibility to himself and to others. His life, both inside the treatment group and out moves in the direction of ever more meaningful relationships.

The following question and answer from an A.A. pamphlet indicates that A.A. uses a very different method.

Why can A.A. help me where others could not? *Because A.A. has a sound and simple solution to the alcoholic problem and the greatest recommendation of our program is—IT WORKS!*

A.A. combines the basic and essential elements of sound alcoholic therapy. A.A. advises you to seek medical help for your physical deficiencies, if any; a belief in a Higher Power for your spiritual well-being; and the righting on your part, in so far as possible, of all past wrongs in order to relieve your mind of inner conflicts.

A.A. furnishes you with social and physical activities for the release of nervous energy and the correction of introvertive thinking. A.A. offers friendship and understanding such as you have probably not known in years. It gives opportunity for sympathetic mutual discussions to give relief to your complexes, repressions, and self-recriminations.

Finally, and most important, A.A. gives you an opportunity to help others in the same way you will be helped (10, p. 4) (Italics the authors').

Although both A.A. and group psychotherapy focus on the immediate attainment and maintenance of sobriety in the patient, the total and ultimate end of psychotherapy is not sobriety alone. Sobriety and its maintenance are instead valued as crucial for the patient's attainment of freedom, his freedom to choose and to be (20, 21). Without a doubt, the immediate aim of group psychotherapy must be directed toward sobriety, but this aim cannot be separated from the therapist's ultimate intention, the patient's attainment of freedom of choice which will enable the alcoholic eventually to leave his psychotherapeutic group, Alcoholics Anonymous, or any other group which assists him in his struggle. An exclusive emphasis on the limited goal of sobriety restricts the scope and depth of psychotherapy; in addition, it often means that the patient will prematurely terminate treatment because an alcoholic patient who has attained sobriety will frequently stop abruptly rather than risk new experiences and new meanings.

A comparison between these two approaches suggests that only in the broadest sense are they actually at all similar. Table I below compares these two methods indicating marked differences in the ad-

TABLE I
GROUP PSYCHOTHERAPY AND ALCOHOLICS ANONYMOUS
DIFFERENTIAL CHARACTERISTICS

Administration	*Group Psychotherapy*	*Alcoholics Anonymous*
Responsibility	Defined directly. Held by each group psychotherapist by virtue of his training and professional status.	Defined loosely. Held loosely by each local leader by virtue of his sobriety, length of sobriety, and talent and ability to lead.
Fee	Required in private practice. Fees in private practice range from $5.00 upward per patient. In clinic and agency minimal fee based upon ability to pay or no fee.	No fee. Donations encouraged but not required.
Place of meeting	The professional's office, the agency, clinic, hospital and so forth.	Usually, a non-psychiatric setting. A hall, church, school and so forth. For in-patients, a hospital.
Overall structure	Therapist as an acknowledged clinician, and patients together.	Alcoholics together.
Hierarchical communication and responsibility	None. No connection with another group. Great diversity, with many different theoretical orientations.	Some but minimal. Fellowship shared with other local groups. Quasi-direction from "national headquarters." Inter-group offices which come together to form a steering committee.
Milieu	Therapeutic, therapist and patients together. Non-social. Free milieu to permit the emergence of individuality and therapeusis.	Quasi-social. No acknowledged person as authority, oriented toward a fixed agenda and goals.
Race	Heterogeneous (by design).	Heterogeneous (self-selection). Members gravitate toward same race.
Economic status	Heterogeneous (by design).	Heterogeneous (self-selection). Members gravitate toward same socio-economic level.

	Group Psychotherapy	Alcoholics Anonymous
Administration		
Autonomy	Originally the psychotherapist's then the group's and finally the individual patient's. A personal re-evaluation of all values and all systems including psychotherapy.	Each local group is thought to be autonomous. However, there is adherence to the 12 step tradition as a guide to belief, policy and functioning.
Organization		
Sponsorship and introduction	Not required. Group psychotherapy is offered the patient because he has emotional problems.	Preferred but not required.
Constancy of attendance	Usually high.	Inconsistent. Considerable change.
Commitment to attend and participate	Required.	Open meetings: Not required Closed meetings: Required.
Number of persons	6 - 9.	Unlimited; dependent upon the size and activity of the local group.
Visitors to sessions	None allowed	Open meetings: Allowed Closed meetings: Only alcoholics.
Contact after meetings	Permitted but *discouraged*.	Sanctioned and encouraged.
Sex	Heterosexual.	Heterosexual.
Operation		
Group selection	Patients carefully selected for any particular group by a group psychotherapist.	No selection other than a self-selection "The only requirement for membership is a desire to stop drinking."
Preparation for group experience	Careful individual preparation for weeks or months by the group psychotherapist.	No preparation. The sponsor or Beginners Group may serve as an orientation.

TABLE I (cont'd.)

Operation	*Group Psychotherapy*	*Alcoholics Anonymous*
Leadership	A trained group psychotherapist. Usually a psychiatrist, psychologist or social worker.	Group leaders arise from the membership and need no formal training other than A.A. experience.
Status of leader	Degree in medicine, psychology or social work. Training in individual and group psychotherapies.	An alcoholic in remission.
Means of treatment	Spontaneous group interaction interpreted in the framework of psychological and psychoanalytic constructs. The nonrational and fantastic life theme of the alcoholic patient is uncovered, accepted by him and altered.	Identification is a major factor in an essentially inspirational and educational approach. Structure is quasi-religious in which catharsis and reparation are intended to alleviate guilt. Emphasis is placed on the rational and logical solution.
Content and aims	Evolving personality change. *Sobriety* concommitant with a greater freedom to choose.	*Sobriety* and its maintenance; living in a manner in which sobriety is always the primary concern.
(1) Original	*Sobriety.* Repetitious verbalizations of experiences with the problem of drinking. Encouragement of the patient to more fully relate to the others.	*Sobriety.* Witness to, and expression of repititious verbalizations of experiences related to the problem of drinking.
(2) Middle period	*Sobriety.* The deepening of relationships among the patients in the group. The development of a responsibility for self and others. The realization that one has many problems and strengths. Increase in the immediate affective response.	*Sobriety.* Gradual bringing to bear the full potential of fellowship. Introduction to and participation in the 12 Step program. Development of sponsorship capabilities.
(3) End phase	*Sobriety.* The alcoholic patient eventually leaves his psychotherapy group. His terminal phase similar to other patients. Termination from a nonalcoholic therapy group for this reason is preferable to leaving a homogeneous alcoholic therapy group.	*Sobriety.* It is suggested that the A.A. member remain indefinitely as a supportive measure. "Life membership" is encouraged.

ministration, organization, and operation of psychotherapy groups and those of A.A.

The Need for Co-operation

Even though, as Table I shows, there are marked differences between group psychotherapy and Alcoholics Anonymous, it does not follow that these two methods should be mutually exclusive. As both are dedicated to helping the alcoholic, though in different ways and at different depths, and at times, both, where the attainment of sobriety is concerned, may use similar means, they should be used jointly.

Careful and sensitive appraisal of the differing means and goals by each may lead to better understanding between staff members whose responsibility it is to treat and rehabilitate the alcoholic and the members of Alcoholics Anonymous. On both sides, there must be a curiousity as to the other's procedures, a respect for the other's activity and effort, a fairness in the evaluation of the other's work and finally a noncompetitive attitude. The primary result of a closer collaboration between group psychotherapy and Alcoholics Anonymous would be a beneficial improvement in the treatment of the alcoholic.

A secondary gain, perhaps not immediately discernible, but nonetheless of lasting significance, would be the modification of the treatment approach of the group psychotherapist, based on an understanding of the dynamics of A.A. From a different point of view, Bailey suggests the same idea. "The current interest in professional group therapy for alcoholics, which many people believe to be superior to individual therapy for these patients, appears to have caught hold in large measure because of the marked success of A.A.'s methods" (16, p. 3).

Many other statements indicate how important a closer tie and understanding between the group therapist and the members of A.A. can be. Three are quoted here that reveal shifts in the therapist's ideas and changes in his methods.

> Since becoming a side-line observer of Alcoholics Anonymous in 1939, my approach to alcoholism has undergone an almost total reorientation. For the first time, I saw what peace of mind means in the achievement of sobriety and I began to consider the emotional factors involved from a very different viewpoint. In A.A. meetings, the role of resentments was a recurrent theme.

This seemed significant. Continuing this line of observation, I found that another enemy of sobriety was defiance, which Sillman had already described as "defiant individuality," a major hallmark of the personality of alcoholics.

Another significant emphasis in A.A. was humility and "hitting bottom," completely new points of emphasis for me. It was clear that if the individual remained stiff-necked he would continue to drink, but I could not see why. Finally, the presence of an apparently unconquerable ego became evident. It was this ego which had to become humble. Then the role of hitting bottom, which means reaching a feeling of personal helplessness, began to be clear. It was this process that produced in the ego an awareness of vulnerability, initiating the positive phase. In hitting bottom the ego becomes tractable and is ready for humility. The conversion experience has started (22, p. 1).

No one can really understand the A.A. program by merely reading about it. The social worker who is interested should inquire as to the location of an A.A. group and learn when it will have an open meeting he can attend. It is likely that he, as all others that come in contact with the group, will be stimulated, excited, and deeply moved by what he sees going on in the group (17, p. 24).

Liaison like this can do far more than simply help the destitute. Of the agencies cited, Alcoholics Anonymous stands apart because of its frequent success and broad scope, the alcoholic and his family being able to participate in several ways. Many physicians are ignorant or only superficially informed about this fellowship and do not even know how to make referrals. Through a day-care service, however, physicians and Twelfth-Step workers can get acquainted to mutual advantage. A physician does well to develop and maintain rapport with several A.A. sponsors so as to choose someone suitable when one of his own patients shows interest; correspondingly, many in A.A. can usefully learn more about the role of professional help. In short, an outpatient unit of the type described can make friends of fellow workers and promote a more unified effort in this field (23, p. 464).

Although the conflict which exists between some of the A.A. membership and some group psychotherapists is not only the result of distorted attitudes on the part of the group psychotherapist, he is still partly at fault. Bailey suggests that the professional may either be too dependent upon A.A., or, at the other extreme, have so little trust in A.A. that he neglects it as a resource.

I have occasionally heard professional people express attitudes which attributed almost magical powers to A.A. and which perhaps reflected a sense of relief that responsibility for a difficult alcoholic could be transferred to the members of the A.A. fellowship, once a referral had been effected. On the other hand, there are those who question the wisdom of referring alcoholics and their families to such entirely non-professional groups (16, p. 1).

The problem of whether or not to trust this nonprofessional group of alcoholics is at the center of the professional's dilemma about A.A. How can a psychotherapist trained and experienced in individual and group psychotherapy acknowledge that a group of alcoholics, members of A.A., might actually determine the outcome of his entire treatment effort? Yet this is what is required of him if he is to co-operate with A.A. Interestingly enough, Hayman, in an article entitled "Attitudes Toward Alcoholism," points out that of a sample of psychiatrists in Southern California, only a few treated alcoholics and they, in turn, limited the number they treated. Among these few psychiatrists, however, 99 per cent approved of A.A., 97 per cent knew the A.A. procedures, and 77 per cent referred patients to A.A. (18). These very high figures are apt to obscure the rejection of the alcoholic implied in Hayman's data: that 66 per cent of the psychiatrists he interviewed do not treat alcoholics at all, and that the others (34 per cent) limit their practice to a very few alcoholics. The great use of A.A. therefore might well indicate only a desire to unload difficult patients rather than a real wish to share the curative function with a nonprofessional group.

Bird, as early as 1948, summarized our point of view concerning co-operation with Alcoholics Anonymous. He states:

There are many more factors in Alcoholics Anonymous that contribute to its success and those who are interested in alcoholism may well study the A.A. program intimately. We should use A.A. freely and without assuming a competitive attitude toward its work. Too commonly, professional people in social agencies, courts, hospitals and churches are suspicious or openly critical, or even somewhat contemptuous of Alcoholics Anonymous. There is, of course, cause to criticize some part of what A.A. does, to criticize certain A.A. groups or members; but to apply such criticism to Alcoholics Anonymous generally is unjustified. From the other side of the fence, we often observe A.A. members assuming Godlike roles in the treatment of alcoholism: they brook no interference; they highhandedly tell people what to do and how to do it; they antagonize nonalcoholic workers unnecessarily. The impatience of A.A.'s with other groups is often justified but they do not serve their own interest well by provoking or continuing disagreeable disputes (24, p. 541).

In a task as difficult and at times as unrewarding as the treatment and rehabilitation of the alcoholic, the worker in this field and particularly the group psychotherapist must rely heavily upon all of society's resources, including Alcoholics Anonymous. The chapters that follow therefore outline an empirical method for the rehabilitation of the alcoholic which is truly a co-operative effort.

REFERENCES

1. Lindt, H.: The rescue fantasy in group treatment of alcoholics. *Int. J. Group Psychother., 9*:43-52, 1959.
2. Bacon, S. D.: Alcohol and Complex Society. In *Society, Culture, and Drinking Patterns.* Edited by D. J. Pittman and C. R. Snyder. New York, Wiley 1962, 78-93.
3. Lemert, E. M.: Alcohol, Values and Social Control. In *Society, Culture, and Drinking Patterns.* Edited by D. J. Pittman and C. R. Snyder. New York, Wiley 1962, 553-571.
4. *Webster's Collegiate Dictionary,* Third Edition of the Merriam Series. Springfield, Mass., Merriam 1929.
5. Cattell, R.B.: New Concepts for Measuring Leadership in Terms of Group Syntality. In *Group Dynamics, Research and Theory.* Edited by D. Cartwright and A. Zander. New York, Row Peterson 1953, 14-27.
6. Bales, R. B.: A Theoretical Framework for Interaction Process Analysis. In *Group Dynamics, Research and Theory.* Edited by D. Cartwright and A. Zander. New York, Row Peterson 1953, 29-38.
7. Wolff, K. H.: The Sociology of Georg Simmel, New York, *The Free Press of Glencoe,* 1950.
8. Mullan, H. and Sangiuliano, I.: Group psychotherapy and the alcoholic: Early therapeutic moves. Presented in part at the *World Congress of Psychiatry,* Montreal, Canada, June 4-10, 1961.
9. Diethelm, O.: *Treatment In Psychiatry,* New York, MacMillan, 1936.
10. An Introduction to A.A., Intergroup Assoc. of A.A., 133 E. 39th St., New York 16, New York.

11. Keller, M.: The Definition of Alcoholism and the Estimation of Its Prevalence. In *Society, Culture, and Drinking Patterns.* Edited by D. J. Pittman and C. R. Snyder. New York, Wylie 1962.
12. Gould's Medical Dictionary. Philadelphia, Blakiston's 1935.
13. Riviere, M.: Rehabilitation codes, five-year progress report, 1957-1962. Special Project RD-788. Office of Vocational Rehabilitation, 1961-64.
14. Pratt, J. H.: The home sanatorium treatment of consumption. *Boston Medical & Surgical J.,* 154:210-216, 1906.
15. Mullan H. and Rosenbaum, M.: *Group Psychotherapy: Theory and Practice.* New York, The Free Press of Glencoe, 1962.
16. Bailey, M.: A.A. and Al-Anon as Resources. Delivered at the Workshop for the Family Agency Supervisors and Executives by the Illinois Division of Alcoholism, The Nat'l Inst. of Mental Health, and the Chicago Committee on Alcoholism, Aurora, Ill., Mar. 1-3, 1962.
17. Lee, J. P.: Alcoholics anonymous as a community resource. *Social Work,* Oct., 1960, 20-26.
18. Hayman, M.: Current attitudes to alcoholism of psychiatrists in Southern California. *Amer. J. Psychiat.,* 112:485-493, 1956.
19. Tiebout, H. M.: Perspectives in alcoholism. The keynote address, 1955 Nat'l States' Conf., Distributed by Nat'l. Council on Alcoholism.
20. Mullan H., and Sangiuliano, I.: Group psychotherapy and the alcoholic: 2. The phenomenology of early group interaction. Presented in part at the 5th Internat'l Congress for Psychotherapy, Wien, Austria, Aug. 21-26, 1961.
21. Mullan, H. and Sangiuliano, I.: *The Therapist's Contribution To The Treatment Process: His Person, Transactions and Treatment Methods.* Springfield, Thomas, 1964.
22. Tiebout, H. M.: Conversion as a psychological phenomenon. Read before the New York Psychiatric Soc., Apr. 11, 1944.
23. Ruprecht, A. L.: Day-care facilities in the treatment of alcoholics. *Quart. J. Studies Alcohol,* 22:461-470, 1961.
24. Bird, B.: One aspect of causation in alcoholism. *Quart. J. Stud. Alcohol,* 9:532-543, 1949.

CHAPTER II

THE CLINIC'S ACCOMMODATION
AND THE STAFF'S ADJUSTMENT
TO THE ALCOHOLIC

HUGH MULLAN, M.D.

(For a group-centered clinic or agency to accommodate the alcoholic patient, the entire staff must adjust to two facts:
  (a) The alcoholic patient is extremely vulnerable to hurt, and
  (b) the alcoholic lacks almost all motivation for treatment. Even though both these things are true, the psychiatric institution must not give up its psychotherapeutic goals, or the rehabilitation team abandon its specific technical methods. Proficiency in treatment skill, dedication to the task at hand, interdisciplinary unity and co-operation, plus the willingness to allow new concepts and methods to evolve are necessary if the staff is to meet the bizarre behavior of the alcoholic and to keep him in treatment.)

INTRODUCTION

The period of referral and clinic accommodation is crucial in the rehabilitation of the alcoholic patient, for it is the time that the usually unmotivated drinker becomes momentarily receptive and simultaneously receives sufficient stimulation to seek help. Regardless of the source of the impetus that sends him to the clinic—a threat from those near him, or an inner despair at "hitting bottom," or even a psychiatrically oriented judge's stipulation that "he go to the clinic or face jail"—this belated action when set in motion must be capitalized upon. The patient must be met by staff members who are acquainted with the problems of alcoholism, who realize the importance of their *personal* relationship to the inebriate, and who are willing and able to give generously of their time, effort, and feelings. This support must continue unabated all along the line, from the initial referral and even after final group psychotherapeutic placement in the alcohol clinic.

[36]

THE REFERRAL OF THE ALCOHOLIC*

Referral Practices and Insufficient Motivation

The patient suffering from alcoholism seeks help because of an emergency in his life. In most instances, however, the emergency is identified by others, and only rarely is it experienced by the patient himself. Most frequently, the patient comes to an agency because of extreme external pressure to change his behavior. Often, he is threatened with severe reprisal unless he does change—for instance, the loss of family, wife, or job. Or, the fact that his physical and financial resources are exhausted may force him into coming to the clinic. Whatever brings his crisis to a head makes him realize that the realities of the world about him and the irreversible physical changes within him no longer permit him to continue his mode of life.

The fact that he appears at a group oriented alcoholism treatment agency suggests that he and the referring person have two significant ideas. The first is that his problems are caused by his ingestion of alcohol; and the second is that he can be helped through treatment with others similarly afflicted. The patient's tendency, however, is to equate "help" with advice, and so he usually comes to the agency looking only for information and suggestions. Therefore, it is crucial that both the referring person and the staff members who receive the alcoholic attempt to stimulate his motivation for more extensive rehabilitation and group psychotherapy.

The alcoholic, it must be remembered, whether sober for many months or actively drinking, has no genuine desire for intensive rehabilitation; and once he's started in treatment, he will not cling firmly to his decision to accept help. As compared to other newly-admitted patients he is, at best, a lukewarm participant in the center with no strong relationships to staff and little sympathy or understanding of the various resources open to him. Occasionally, however, after a serious drinking crisis, when he faces despair, isolation, and abandonment, he is able to identify the emergency directly as *his* own and seek rehabilitation. But even under these optimal circumstances, his resistance to change is great. Those involved with the alco-

---

*The referral of an alcoholic to an agency for treatment is no different from his referral to a private practitioner, and what is said in this chapter has equal validity for both instances.

holic, professional and nonprofessional alike, must realize this fact. The alcoholic person who gets psychiatric help has to enter an entirely new world, a world which he has attempted to avoid for the many years he has been drinking. And it is this newness, which he construes as a threat, that he cannot tolerate.

In a group-oriented treatment center, this threat is offset to some extent because he is apt to be involved in a group composed of other patients who are similarly troubled. This is less threatening to an alcoholic than the one-to-one contact with a counselor, social worker or therapist. This is borne out in the group psychotherapetic setting, where these patients appear to quickly and easily develop a sense of identification and of belonging. Although this is viewed as a kind of quasi-cohesiveness, and, therefore, not productive of change, nonetheless, it serves the purpose of bringing the group together and maintaining it initially (see Chapter IX).

Professional and Family Referrals

Psychotherapy commences at the moment of referral. The professional person, therefore, who first suggests some form of treatment is many times the crucial stimulus in the patient's acceptance of the agency's rehabilitation plan and particularly of group psychotherapy. The responsibility of the one who refers includes taking an interest in the person and his problems, having an awareness of the character structure of the alcoholic, an understanding of the method and the aims of rehabilitation and particularly of group psychotherapy, and, most important, being willing to support the patient, if need be, in his struggle to become integrated into the center's program and the therapy group. This kind of support is essential when the upset, discouraged, anxious or despairing patient is reluctant to continue in his group and he has to be encouraged nevertheless to return. A knowledge of the method and aims of group psychotherapy is essential. If the referring person realizes that group psychotherapy, similar to psychoanalysis, is a long term and highly involved process, he will realize that there will be many moments of intense anxiety and indecision on the part of the group members (1, p. 55). If referral is mostly a way to get rid of a difficult patient, and the necessary encouragement and understanding are lacking, it bodes ill for the success of the group treatment approach.

Referrals from members of the patient's family and close friends, although well meaning, are frequently doomed to failure. Since these people lack an awareness of the complexities of the alcoholic and know little of rehabilitation methods, their positive influence wanes as the patient becomes embroiled in the group interaction. Paradoxically, the intense emotional tie between, for example, a wife and her sick husband, may initiate the original therapeutic contact; but this same tie also prevails to disconnect the patient from his group. When intimates of the alcoholic patient are threatened by sudden changes in his overt behavior, many times, quite unconsciously, they try to return to the earlier situation where the patient drank, for the sake of their own neurotic satisfactions which are neither apparent nor admissable. *

> Robert, a prominent entertainer, was referred to the therapist for a long existing drinking problem. During the period of preparation for the private practice therapy group this patient's wife was seen with the patient and two therapists, and this was Robert's last visit for a long while. He went away for "the cure." Neither his wife nor the new found "therapists" at the rest home wanted him to continue intensive psychotherapy.

Frequently, patients referred by family members can be sustained in treatment better if the referring relatives are brought into the rehabilitation program at either the orientation level (see Chapter V), where they are offered supportive case work, or even are persuaded to become involved in group psychotherapy for themselves. In this latter instance the nonalcoholic spouse may become a part of a treatment group consisting of married couples in which one partner is alcoholic.

THE GROUP-ORIENTED ALCOHOL TREATMENT CENTER

Introduction

Mental health treatment agencies and particularly psychiatric clinics of general hospitals which treat many kinds of patients have a

*This dynamic is similar to that of another situation—a mother who originally enthusiastically consults a therapist concerning her child, then much too soon withdraws it from therapy when her own neurotic attachments to the child are threatened.

difficult time with the patient who drinks compulsively. Almost any other patient is more reliable and responsive, and therefore, admitting personnel and those who diagnostically interview the alcoholic may unknowingly convey to him their preference for more committed and less defensive patients.

Fink bases this difficulty which he sees as the therapist's reluctance to treat alcoholics on the peculiar resistance of the alcoholic:

> Many psychotherapists are unwilling to work with alcoholics. They refuse to accept referral of alcoholics because of the intense and persistent resistance such patients typically exert toward progress and health, and remaining dry (2, p. 48).

It may well be that in order to treat alcoholics, an agency or clinic should keep the treatment function separate, and staff this unit with competent and especially interested people. In this connection Armstrong maintains:

> . . . experience has demonstrated that there are sufficient patients with alcoholism problems who are willing to accept help and that results are sufficiently encouraging to warrant special attention for them. Furthermore, those units especially set up to deal with the problem see a sufficient variety of cases coming under various conditions to be able to formulate more clearly the clinical picture of the problem (3, p. 1359).

Similarly, the National Council on Alcoholism suggests that the community participate in the treatment and prevention of alcoholism by augmenting already-existing institutions so that they may engage in this work. The need for special training and education for all those involved in this special task of treating the alcoholic is emphasized by the Council.

Advantages and Disadvantages of an Autonomous Clinic

There are both advantages and disadvantages to having the alcoholic clinic either a part of a general psychiatric agency or an integral section of a general out-patient, psychiatric department.

In the first case, for example, a community mental health clinic is established and staffed to take care of the out-patient treatment of psychiatric patients. To include alcoholic patients in this program would prevent wasteful duplication. In addition, if alcoholics could be encouraged to use this facility, their medical consultations and laboratory tests would be performed by the already established panel of physicians and technicians. Frequently, also, it would be advantageous to treat the alcoholic members of families of patients who are already receiving psychotherapy at the clinic.

Disadvantages in including the alcoholic patient in a community agency, which we believe outweigh the advantages, stem from the difficulties inherent in encouraging the alcoholic patient to present himself for treatment. He is much more likely to look for aid in a center known to him as specializing in alcoholism. This fact coupled with his hard-to-take drinking behavior which upsets the usual staff and nonalcoholic patients alike suggests to us that he be treated in a separate setting.

In the second case, the advantage of treating some alcoholic patients in a general hospital, either as out-or-in-patients, is that it allows the medical specialists to work closely with the rehabilitation staff. It should be stated here that the alcoholic must get frequent medical attention and physical examinations, care which is imperative because the chronic drinker usually suffers from systemic disease.

The disadvantages of having the group-oriented alcohol treatment center part of a more general medical center come from the asocial and exploitative tendencies of the alcoholic and from the human frailties of those who care for and treat him. The alcoholic is prone to act out, and uses everybody he can to serve his neurotic needs. He often sets one staff member or department against another, so that the spirit and purpose of the staff are divided. Furthermore, when the alcohol treatment staff is under the supervision of a general psychiatric department its morale may suffer. So few persons want to work with the alcoholic to begin with, and even they can become hopelessly discouraged if, for example, the head of a psychiatric department unconsciously suggests to them that alcoholics are "willful and bad" or that their pathology is irreversible. Ideally a group treatment staff concerned with alcoholism works best as a *group*— utilizing to the full its common points of view, common methods, common understandings, and common supports. This is why, when the alcohol treatment unit is part of a larger psychiatric institution, it should, as far as possible, be autonomous.

The Organization of a Professional Staff

It is most desirable of course to have genuine co-operation among the various services involved in treating the alcoholic, based upon equality of treatment function and mutual respect. However, medical responsibility and administrative needs usually require the kind of clinic organization illustrated in Figure 1.

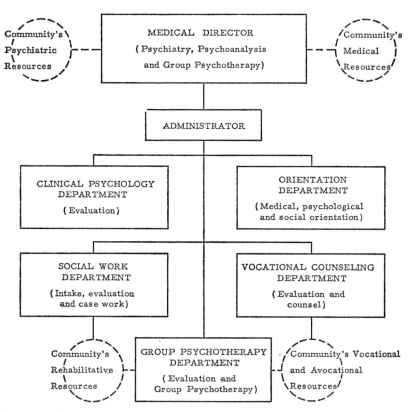

FIGURE 1. This figure shows the lines of administrative authority and communication and the departmental functions as well. Circles include other resources essential to the treatment and rehabilitation of the alcoholic which are to be found in the community. Continuous and efficient liaison is important between the various departments and these facilities.

Here, three points are to be noted: (a) The Director of the Center should be a physician, and ideally one trained both in psychiatry and in group psychotherapy; (b) Medical attention, including diagnosis and treatment, can occur *outside* the limits of the rehabilitation center; and (c) The department of Social Service, Vocational Counseling, and Group Psychotherapy should all utilize the community's many resources. The first point is in keeping with the fact that alcoholism is a multifaceted disease which many times requires medical supervision, care and treatment. This was borne out when, in 1956, the American Medical Association's Council on Mental Health and its Committee on Alcoholism submitted the following statement quoted in part, to the House of Delegates:

> Among the numerous personality disorders encountered in the general population, it has long been recognized that a vast number of such disorders are characterized by the outstanding sign of excessive use of alcohol. All excessive users of alcohol are not diagnosed as alcoholics, but all alcoholics are excessive users. When, in addition to this excessive use, there are certain signs and symptoms of behavioral, personality and physical disorder or of their development, the syndrome of alcoholism is achieved. The intoxication and some of the other possible complications manifested in this syndrome often make treatment difficult. However, alcoholism must be regarded as within the purview of medical practice. The Council on Mental Health, its Committee on Alcoholism, and the profession in general *recognizes this syndrome of alcoholism as illness which justifiably should have the attention of physicians* (4, p. 750, II). (Italics the author's.)

The Over-all Staff Treatment Group

The entire staff group, working together, to rehabilitate the alcoholic is the essential agent for therapeutic change in the patient. It consists of those workers in the various mental health disciplines who offer group psychotherapy and vocational counseling, and who offer case work, examine, diagnose, and evaluate the patient.

Since group treatment implies a psychological intervention, the staff group consists of a medical director (psychiatrist and group psychotherapist), group psychotherapist(s), clinical psychologist(s), social case worker(s), and vocational counselor(s). The staff group must consult from time to time with physicians. It is important also that the staff understands alcoholism from the point of view of social psychologists, anthropologists and other social scientists.

Because the alcoholic is at first unable to be responsible in clinic group participation, his noncommitment must be counteracted by the commitment of the members of the staff. Staff workers of the various specialities selected to treat the alcoholic must therefore be highly motivated and able to withstand the frustration and hostility which they most certainly will meet.

The Dynamic Treatment Groups

The rehabilitation staff group is of course divided into departments for administrative reasons; it is also separated into dynamic treatment groups, that are led by the representatives of various services. These groups consist of one or more professionals, alcoholic patients, and in two instances, members of the patients' families. Below are listed treatment units whose function is to interrupt the alcoholic's way of life, to intervene against his destructive personality, and to rehabilitate him so that he can either return, if estranged, to his family and community, or if at home, more productively meet his current responsibilities.

Psychotherapeutic Groups:

A group of seven to nine members conducted by a trained group psychotherapist. Groups consist of men and women who meet once or twice a week. Sessions last one and one half hours. Patients are carefully selected, prepared and introduced. The duration of therapy is indefinite and individually determined. (See Chapters VIII to XIII.)

Vocational Evaluation Groups:

A group of three to ten members led by a vocational counselor. Membership consists of alcoholic patients and the counselor. In "class-room" fashion vocational and avocational performance and interests are determined. The tests are administered on one or two evenings in one and one half hour sessions. After their completion and scoring the test data is used to guide future individual and/or group vocational counseling. (See Chapter VII.)

Vocational Counseling Groups:

A group of three to ten members led by a vocational counselor.

Membership consists of evaluated and selected patients and the counselor. The group meets weekly or bi-weekly for one and one half hours. The content of the sessions centers about the realities of vocation and avocation. In addition to this kind of counseling in groups, it is advantageous for the counselor to enter the group psychotherapy group at a regular time once a month to confront the patients with their social responsibilities in the community and to determine how they are meeting them. (See Chapter VII.)

Social Case Work Groups:

A group consisting of a case worker, the alcoholic, and sometimes his spouse or other members of the patient's family. The social worker must be well versed in alcoholism and be personally able to withstand frustration and hostility. The social worker's purpose is to get a detailed social history, encourage and support the patient and to stimulate him to enter group psychotherapy. (See Chapter IV.)

Orientation Groups:

A group of ten to 30 members led by a physican or another professional who understands the physiological, sociological and psychological disruptions of alcoholism. Membership consists of the alcoholic himself, family, and intimate friends. Teaching aids and guest speakers are used. Orientation precedes more formal aspects of the center's treatment, that is, group psychotherapy and vocational counseling. (See Chapter V.)

Clinical Psychological Groups:

A group of three to ten members conducted by a clinical psychologist trained in group-testing techniques. Membership consists of the patients and the psychologist. Standard individual and group-test forms are used. The psychologist should be aware of the alcoholic's difficulties about commitment and responsibility. (See Chapter VI.)

THE SCHEME OF REHABILITATION

Introduction

Rehabilitation begins with the patient's successful referral to the agency. What attitudes, purposes, and behaviors of the staff toward the alcoholic patient will induce him to commence and continue his rehabilitative effort? What are some of the pitfalls to be avoided by the inexperienced worker in this field? What climate must the staff provide to receive and accommodate the alcoholic patient?

The Alcoholic's Reception by Staff

After the patient has been referred to the agency and before he is evaluated for group psychotherapy he will have chance meetings with the clinic's nonprofessional workers, that is, the telephone operator, the elevator man, and so on. The first relationship that must be established by the alcoholic is between himself and the agency, and it has singular importance. Should these first encounters fall short of the alcoholic's expectations, which can easily happen if he gets a careless word from the receptionist, he may turn away from seeking help. Therefore, these beginning meetings, regardless of how irregular and informal they are, must be filled with interest, care, and warmth. Nonprofessional workers should be made aware of the importance of their roles in regard to the newly referred alcoholic patient. The medical director or a designated person should be responsible for the careful and continuous training and orientation of the nonprofessional personnel. When these people are first hired they may even be given orientation sessions, during which they may profitably be instructed in their specific roles and also learn about alcoholism in general.

Alcoholic patients are conditioned by society's mistrust and dislike. When they come for psychiatric help they anticipate rejection and are acutely sensitive to its presence. Thus, mere interest and curiosity will not be sufficient to win them over to the rigors of rehabilitation. They must receive genuine acceptance and understanding. All too often there is an over-reliance upon techniques, and the agency personnel will seem to accept the alcoholic patient; at another, perhaps quite unconscious level, however, they will express their hidden contempt.

In order to minimize rejecting attitudes toward the alcoholic, the clinic worker, regardless of his specialty, must: (a) be aware of his own feelings and behavior (see group consultation of staff), and (b) indicate that he has certain minimal expectations that the patient must meet. The worker requires the patient's attendance, his promptness, and his eventual participation in group psychotherapy and vocational counseling sessions. If the worker does not make these minimal demands, the patient may feel even more contemptible and despairing than ever. Moore points out the disadvantage of an unreal, unfeeling, and technical approach to the alcoholic.

> A defense frequently used by professional people dealing with alcoholics is reaction formation, the adopting of an attitude opposite to that actually felt. Rather than experiencing and expressing disgust with the alcoholic, a therapist is overly kind, overly permissive and indulgent, unable to deny his patient any request, and so thoroughly on the patient's side as to view with the patient the rest of the hospital staff, the public, and the patient's family as cruel, restrictive and unreasonable (5, p. 483).

The staff member who works with the alcoholic patient must be more steadfast in purpose than perhaps he need be with any other malfunctioning individual. Inordinate in his expectations and skillful in bringing about rejection, the compulsive drinker continuously tests staff members. Many writers allude to this almost unbearable behavior on the part of the alcoholic patient. For example, Fink describes this characteristic mode of behavior as follows:

> The therapist, then, can expect less cooperation from the alcoholic, more tardiness, more excuses, more whining about the bill and the time required for sessions, and attempts to be taken at a lower fee than his income justifies, or even gratis, "because I'm such an interesting case, and you can write me up in a big magazine and make lots of money." The alcoholic will try all the tricks in the book to test the therapist's acceptance and frustration tolerance, skill and objectivity. He can make a fool out of the inexperienced and unsuspecting worker who allows himself to be drawn into the alcoholic's maneuvers, allegations, fantasies, and purposeful lies (2, pp. 48-49).

From the very first contacts, therefore, an atmosphere of mutuality must be created. The alcoholic needs to experience a genuine give-and-take in which he and the other can exist together, in contrast to his pretherapy behavior in which either he exploited the other or was himself exploited. It is true, however, that at the beginning the intake worker, other staff members, and later the group psychotherapist will do more of the giving than the patient. Lateness, cancelled appointments, and even insobriety are not sufficient reasons for excluding the patient from either the particular service or clinic. These testing maneuvers as well as other antisocial acts are to be viewed dynamically, and responded to, particularly by the intake worker, as indications of a lack of commitment, an irresponsibility, and a destructiveness that are, simply, characteristic of this kind of patient. Once the patient enters the psychotherapy group and identifies it as *his* group, the therapist will be able to respond more personally to this lack of commitment by indicating its meaning to himself, to the other group members, and to the patient.

It is similarly unwise early in the rehabilitative relationships to try to control a tardy or inebriated patient. Making another future appointment while refusing to see him when he does come in may so interrupt his already tenuous motivation that he will fail to return. Personality changes in the patient which would allow more attention to clinic routine can only be expected after he has achieved greater involvement with the treatment program, and feels more at ease with the staff and the therapy group members.

It can readily be seen, therefore, that initial appointments by the staff must include a genuine and an immediate interest, and an acceptance of acting out, and that the worker can expect a deeper sense of responsibility on the patient's part only in the future. In a way, the very first agency meetings are comparable to an infant on a self-demand feeding schedule: the staff attempts to maintain a continuing day-to-day relationship, and the patient comes as frequently as he must. This elastic plan, however, eventually merges into a more realistic and appropriate demand system: the staff maintains regular appointments, carefully scheduled to meet the patient's community commitments and the realities of clinic operation, and the patient comes for treatment and counsel at appointed hours. In general then, the imposition of limits is to be thought of as therapeutic. The limits are, therefore, the function and the responsibility of the group psychotherapist who develops the strongest bond with the patient throughout his rehabilitation.

After the initial appointment, and during the social intake evaluation and group therapy selection period, the psychiatric social worker plays a key role. (See Chapter IV.) Since he is a professional, the alcoholic patient expects much from him. The social worker's attitude and behavior usually have much more influence on whether or not the patient continues in rehabilitation than those of the nonprofessional agency personnel. His usual role of intake worker with other kinds of patients must be extended so as to more certainly contain the poorly motivated alcoholic. (See Chapter IV.) The manner in which the social worker advises group psychotherapy and vocational counseling is crucial, and the case worker must understand and believe in what he is offering. The social worker suggests the group treatment not as a substitute for individual therapy, but rather as the *preferred* method of treatment. Unless this preference is communicated to the patient the alcoholic may either refuse group treatment or else, if he does enter the involved and intense therapy group, he will leave it immediately. The social worker should suggest vocational counseling neither in a critical nor a condescending manner. The social worker must get across to the patient the idea that the staff, like the community, *needs* him to participate in interesting and gainful activity.

This supportive atmosphere must be created with the very first meeting and continue to develop through to the initial treatment group sessions. The staff's purpose initially, then, is neither to permit nor prohibit destructive acting out. Rather it is to attempt to see the patient through this upsetting period, until constructive rehabilitative forces gain some headway.

Introducing and maintaining the alcoholic patient in this program will be doubtful at best unless the staff members are flexible and willing to alter their points of view to the alcoholic's special needs. This means that the staff member must do the following things:

(1) Use the same practice as he does with other patients, but delay the timing of his interpretations, and not expect the patient to be *fully* co-operative. Must realistically reappraise his goals so as to emphasize the immediate results of each meeting.

(2) Be keenly aware of and focus upon the necessity for the day-to-day adjustment of the alcoholic patient.

(3) Realize that his work with the alcoholic patient will be even more difficult, if not impossible, if he does not utilize the other members of the rehabilitation team and the community's resources as well.

(4) Realize that it is only through sometimes difficult, interac-

tional meetings with his co-workers that the usual sources of interdisciplinary discord, egocentric strivings, and competitiveness can be lessened or even eliminated; and that this achievement contributes to the benefit of the patient, primarily, and secondarily to the satisfaction of the clinic personnel.

The Rehabilitation Process

Most patients enter a treatment center under some pressure but more or less voluntarily, although some are actually coerced into beginning rehabilitation by outside forces, as, for example, a court order. In the main, however, this text describes a rehabilitation center that is not part of a custodial institution where patients would be made to participate.*

Upon his arrival at the treatment center, and for many months thereafter, the alcoholic patient enters and participates with other patients similarly troubled, in treatment groups, each of which has its own clearly-defined goals. (See Chapter III.) He terminates the formal aspects of his rehabilitation then, when, on an entirely individual timetable, he departs from the center. The schematic presentation of this process offered in Figure 2 is an idealized and therefore an unusual representation, and is included simply as a guide for the establishment of group-oriented centers for the alcoholic patient. It must be stressed again, however, that there can be no rigidity in the rehabilitation program. The program must be organized so as to fit the needs of the individual patient, the abilities of the total staff, and the talents of each worker. The community's requirements and ability to support rehabilitation should and must color the entire program.

THE STAFF KEEPS ITS OWN HOUSE IN ORDER

The Group Consultation of Staff

At first the staff members, new to each other, may compete at-

---

*This is not to say that the method of group rehabilitation which centers around the dynamic interplay of treatment groups and which is based upon the crucial intensive interaction of group psychotherapy cannot be applied with alcoholics in a closed institution. The system of rehabilitation described in this book is most conducive to out-patient treatment; it is, however, flexible enough to be used successfully in in-patient situations, including psychiatric hospitals, custodial farms, and half-way houses.

THE GROUP REHABILITATION PROCESS OF THE
ALCOHOLIC PATIENT

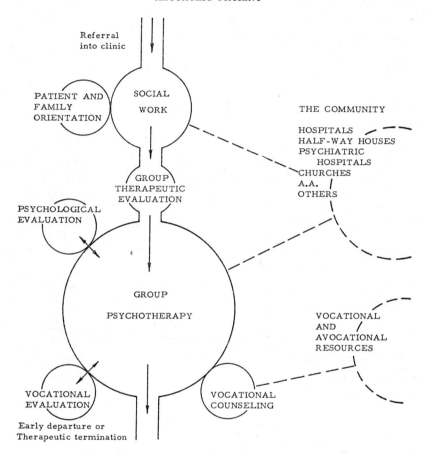

FIGURE 2. This figure describes the patient's rehabilitation process, the disciplines involved in rehabilitation, and the central position of group psychotherapy in the clinic operation. The dotted lines show how the staff must rely upon community resources both in actively treating the patient and in supplementing the group rehabilitative effort.

tempting to justify their particular approach to the treatment and rehabilitation of the alcoholic. What is required to offset this tendency is the development of a mutual bond holding the staff together based upon the staff's common efforts toward the understanding and the treatment of alcoholism. The aim of the kind of clinic that is being discussed in this book requires the early establishment of close-working relationships among the staff. When this occurs, and only then, will a consistent, all-embracing program that presents a solid treatment front to the alcoholic, be possible.

To accomplish this aim in the rehabilitation of the alcoholic more than a "team approach" is required. The internist, psychiatrist, group psychotherapist, psychologist, social worker and other personnel must work individually but also *together* to find a common understanding of the problem of alcoholism. Putting it another way, the staff must find an interdisciplinary personal identification with the many problems presented by the alcoholic's behavior. It is this personal identification with the problem *in concert with others* which allows all staff members to approach, reach and effect change in the alcoholic. This understanding cannot be achieved if each staff member views the alcoholic only in terms of his special discipline, rather than with the perspective of the alcoholic gained from a truly co-operative staff participation.

In order to broaden the basis of both the interdisciplinary and personal communications, weekly meetings are held by those involved and responsible for the treatment and rehabilitation program. These staff meetings, in which spontaneous expression is encouraged, center upon the ways the entire staff can achieve effective treatment for the elusive alcoholic patient, the staff's inner motives for wanting to be involved with alcoholics, and finally, how the treatment situation can help the staff mature both professionally and personally.

These meetings, unlike the usual staff conference in which a particular case or topic is selected for discussion, are similar to the more dynamic interactional consultation of staff that occurs in other settings (6, 7). If the medical director of the alcoholic treatment center suggests that the staff come together and yet gives it no scheme of action and no subject to consider, staff members become some what anxious and begin to ask why they are present and what they are doing. These questions apply not only to the staff meeting but even more significantly to their presence in the treatment center. Very soon even though there may be rivalries present each staff member begins to investigate and discuss his personal interest in the problems of alcoholism and his preference for treating this kind of patient. Gradually, certain experiences with alcoholic patients will emerge and the staff member's sense of achievement or frustration will be acknowledged. Others with similar and different experiences will broaden the factual and emotional content of the staff's meeting. Naturally, in discussing the alcoholic patients in this personal way, the staff members' personalities will be to a degree revealed. The more reticent will be encouraged to speak out.

As an example of the kind of information elicited in these meetings, it is often discovered that a staff member by his professional duties is attempting to prove something to himself. Rather than allowing himself a range of emotional contact with the patient for the purpose of lessening the alcoholic's isolation, he views the treatment session as a challenge to his status in his particular discipline. If such a professional tries to prove his omniscience and omnipotence by enforcing sobriety on an alcoholic he may lose the patient. The staff person with this particular problem will more successfully maintain a relationship with the patient if he understands his own behavior better. If for example this man can express his feelings of helplessness, hopelessness, his dilemmas and even his despair during the interactional staff meetings, it will strengthen him in his efforts with recalcitrant patients and in addition it will bring this staff member closer to the other professionals.

Interdisciplinary cohesion which results from this kind of staff effort, is particularly important to those who are treating alcoholics, because these patients' life histories are full of instances in which they have divided and conquered and suffered considerable guilt for such operations. In the clinic, alcoholics will frequently complain to one staff member about another; ignore the group psychotherapist and call the social worker to cancel his therapeutic session; and in general play one member against another. The interactional staff meeting, seen in this light, is therefore an attempt to offer to the alcoholic a consistent, accepting, and correcting environment which is dissimilar to most of his previous experiences. After a few of these interactional staff meetings a new atmosphere begins to permeate the treatment center; the staff members are more trusting and close, they are more frank and aware of the treatment and rehabilitation potential of other disciplines, and they are much more united in purpose and much more effective.

Any transaction between persons whether we conceive some as

professionals and others as patients involves mutual growth. In this kind of interactional staff meeting, we ask of the professional no more than we ask of the patients. Both groups are being asked to dedicate themselves to constructive change. However, this kind of group consultation of the staff is not to be confused with group psychotherapy of the staff. The goal for group consultation is to achieve greater adequacy in the clinic treatment of the alcoholic in which many people and many disciplines are involved. Group psychotherapy differs markedly in that it focuses upon the psychological need of each staff member which realistically is neither the responsibility nor the scope of the treatment center.

The Benefits of Group Consultation of Staff

The purpose of the interactional consultation of the staff is, in the final analysis, to change the structure and the climate of the over-all staff treatment group. It is suggested that the spirit, point of view, and operating procedures of the clinic charged with the treatment of alcoholics must in some respects be different from that devoted to the treatment of other kinds of psychiatric patients.

The primary benefit to be derived from this kind of consultation is the modification of the relatedness pattern of the Center's staff so that the treatment and rehabilitation of the alcoholic can be more effective.

More particularly, the benefits of this kind of consultation are: (a) new depth of communication between staff members, and (b) a greater commitment by the staff to the treatment of the alcoholic and (c) a greater involvement in the clinic's program. Once the staff's interactional consultations have become routine each staff member will approach his own work with new vigor, and his colleagues with a new respect.

REFERENCES

1. Mullan, H., and Rosenbaum, M.: *Group Psychotherapy: Theory and Practice.* New York, The Free Press of Glencoe, 1962.
2. Fink, H. K.: To accept the alcoholic patient or not: problems in psychotherapy with alcoholics. *Samiksa, 13*(2):47-74, 1959.
3. Armstrong, J. D.: The special clinic for alcoholism. *Canad. Med. Ass. J., 2*:1359-1361, 1960.

4. Report, The Council on Mental Health and its Committee on Alcoholism, *A.M.A. Journal, J.A.M.A., 2*:750, 1956.

5. Moore, R. A.: Reaction formation as a counter-transference phenomenon in the treatment of alcoholism. *Quart. J. Stud. Alcohol., 22*(3):481-486, 1961.

6. Mullan, H.: Trends in group psychotherapy in the United States. *Int. J. Soc. Psychiat., 3*(3):224-230, 1957.

7. Mullan, H., Delany, L., and Harari, C.: Mental health consultation: Similarities and differences with group psychotherapy. Presented in part at the American Group Psychotherapy Association Conference, January 1959, New York. Unpublished.

CHAPTER III

AIMS, GOALS AND DIRECTIONS
IN THE TREATMENT AND REHABILITATION
OF THE ALCOHOLIC

HUGH MULLAN, M.D.

(Because confusion exists about the direction that the treatment of the alcoholic patient should take, and because the workers in each mental health discipline seek to alter the alcoholic in distinct ways, this chapter defines the specific aims of the social worker, the "orientator," of the patient and family, the group psychotherapist, the vocational counselor, and the clinical psychologist.)

INTRODUCTION

The Alcoholic is a Patient

It is easy enough to say that the over-all purpose of the group approach to the alcoholic is his treatment and general rehabilitation; but this remark neither suggests specific aims nor hints at this patient's peculiar resistance to, or acceptance of, the ends designated by his physician, counselor, or therapist. This chapter, therefore, describes and appraises treatment and rehabilitation aims with the alcoholic patient; and emphasizes the difference between treatment goals for him and for others not addictively afflicted.

The alcoholic is a *patient*. The group approach to him as an ill person is a treatment method directed toward the eradication or amelioration of his deep-seated emotional problems. The basic goals of this psychotherapy, therefore, are psychological, although in many instances they are supplemented by medical aims as well. It is necessary to stress this point here because of the presence in the field of alcoholism of large numbers of "non-professional" helpers with separate methods and goals. Membership in A.A., for example, brings home to the alcoholic the need to control his drinking and to maintain sobriety; but, unlike group psychotherapy, an association of alcoholics does not require that he continuously and systematically

[56]

evaluate himself psychologically, in order that his underlying intra-psychic conflicts be resolved, with a marked change in his total personality.

In a radio broadcast,* this distinction between psychotherapy and membership in a fellowship was made clear, when the purpose of Alcoholic Anonymous was given as follows:

The primary purpose of this fellowship is for the alcoholic to stay sober.

The secondary purposes are as follows: (a) To prevent the alcoholic from taking the first drink. (b) To help him stay sober twenty-four hours at a time rather than plan for the years ahead. (c) To have one alchololic talk to another alcoholic because "alcoholics understand each other." (d) To help the alcoholic use the "power within." (e) To help the alcoholic use the example of the sober alcoholic; that is, "If he can do it so can I." (f) To help the alcoholic use "faith." (g) To help the alcoholic use the "twelve steps.**"

Nowhere in this outline of aims is there the recognition that the alcoholic is a *patient* or that his illness requires a formal therapeutic

---

*WNYC, New York City; April 15, 1962; 9 P.M.

**"Here are the steps we took—which are suggested as a Program of Recovery:
1. We admitted we were powerless over alcohol—that our lives had become unmanageable.
2. Came to believe that a Power greater than ourselves could restore us to sanity.
3. Made a decision to turn our will and our lives over to the care of God, *as we understood Him.*
4. Made a searching and fearless moral inventory of ourselves.
5. Admitted to God, to ourselves, and to another human being the exact nature of our wrongs.
6. Were entirely ready to have God remove all these defects of character.
7. Humbly asked Him to remove our shortcomings.
8. Made a list of all persons we had harmed, and became willing to make amends to them all.
9. Made direct amends to such people wherever possible, except when to do so would injure them or others.
10. Continued to take personal inventory, and when we were wrong promptly admitted it.
11. Sought through prayer and meditation to improve our conscious contact with God, *as we understood Him,* praying only for knowledge of His will for us and the power to carry that out.
12. Having had a spiritual awakening as the result of these steps, we tried to carry this message to alcoholics, and to practice these principles in all our affairs" (1, p. 8).

plan of intervention. But alcoholism *is* a disorder involving a complex malfunctioning, and therefore does require the attention of trained mental health specialists. In addition, the treatment should bring about not only the end of drinking, but also cause an evolving personality change with a reduction in the patient's neurotic, or even psychotic, adaptations. The alcoholic differs from other psychiatric patients and requires a different treatment approach; nevertheless, through treatment, his personality can be sufficiently modified so that he will be able to leave the supporting confines of the clinic. In contrast to the goals of A.A., group rehabilitation of the alcoholic is directed toward the patient's eventual ability to make a rational decision, to give up his protective environment and to leave both group therapy and vocational counseling. Many times this ideal aim is difficult to realize. However, the closer this goal is approximated, the more lasting and constructive is the resulting personality change.

Extra-therapeutic Goal Considerations

Anyone working with an alcoholic is overcome by feelings of frustration and helplessness when the patient starts drinking again and gets into more trouble. And at these times the worker becomes keenly aware of what the patient's children, spouse, friends, and employer must endure. It is obvious then that an important purpose in the treatment of the alcoholic must be the development of stable and rewarding relationships between the alcoholic and those important to him. In this connection, from the public health point of view, the one relationship that is particularly significant is that of an alcoholic parent to his children. If there is no significantly beneficial alteration of this relationship, the children will be deeply and irreversibly scarred by the alcoholic parent's aberrant behavior. Joan K. Jackson writes about this:

> Personalities (of children with alcoholic parents) are formed in a social milieu which is markedly unstable, torn with dissension, culturally deviant and socially disapproved. The children must model themselves on adults who play their roles in a distorted fashion. The alcoholic shows little adequate adult behavior. The non-alcoholic parent attempts to play the roles of both father and mother, often failing to do either well . . . His (the child's) alcoholic parent feels one way about him when he is sober, another when he is drunk, and yet another during the hangover stage.

What the child can expect from his parents depends on the phase of the drinking cycle as well as on where he stands in relation to each parent at any given time (2, p. 477).

One of the first steps toward correcting the faulty tie that the alcoholic has with other people with whom he is closely involved, is to support and encourage his sobriety. However, this step does not go far enough. Continuous group psychotherapy during the period of beginning abstinence from alcohol helps the patient to express appropriate feelings to other group members. It also helps him express them to his family, as well as to other significant persons. Indeed, some alcoholic parents tend to behave during periods of sobriety, if corrective psychological intervention is lacking, in a way that adversely affects their children. As one child remarked about his alcoholic father: "I liked him best when he drank. He was kind and would play with me. I guess he was more human when he was drunk. When he was sober he would beat me and my brother up. Maybe he drank so he could love us."

Society's Methods and Goals in the Prevention and Control of Alcoholism

Society attempts to control drinking and intoxication, since these conditions are deemed disrupting and costly to the community. Edwin M. Lemert (3,) lists four social controls now in use to some extent; we add a fifth possibility, "compulsory hospitalization." These five methods are as follows:

1. To reduce or completely limit the manufacture, distribution, and consumption of alcohol—that is, prohibition.

2. To reduce or completely eliminate the consumption of alcohol by educating the public on the consequences of over-drinking, through information and orientation centers.

3. To reduce or partly limit the distribution and availability of alcohol by regulations covering the kinds of beverages which may be sold, for how much and to whom; and where and when public drinking is allowed: all of these usually enforced by local laws.

4. To reduce or partly limit drinking by offering various, healthier, substitutes: sports, gardening, games, and other pursuits, vocational and avocational. This sort of diversion is offered by both religious and secular groups.

(Society's concern about the possible consequences of drinking, including alcoholism, is indicated by these governing restrictions. The societal attitude tends to benefit the alcoholic patient and to support his rehabilitation. For example, our cultural attitude would never permit a treatment team in an alcoholic-treatment center to remain passive, permissive, and non-judging about compulsive drinking, even if they wanted to. Society expects that the patient will either remain in the clinic for treatment, or—having regained his sobriety—will return to his family, a productive member of the community. Although these ends are similar to the professional worker's, society will use methods vastly different from those considered correct in psychotherapeutic procedures. For example, society may resort to involuntary commitment of an extreme case of chronic alcoholism.)

5. To stop drinking completely, by separating the drinker from alcohol—through compulsory commitment, voluntary hospitalization, or legal confinement in jail.

In such cases, society quite directly influences the kind and amount of therapy for the alcoholic patient. The inpatient treatment of alcoholics, for instance, may differ according to the patient load, availability of therapists, physical facilities, and the yearly budget. These factors all help determine the realistic and feasible endpoint of treatment. Just how important social pressures are in the recovery of alcoholic patients is clearly indicated in the following remarks, made by Commissioner H. L. McPheeters of the Kentucky Department of Mental Health:

> . . . the staff of the Department of Mental Health (Kentucky) met with members of the Kentucky Commission on Alcoholism to draft an Alcoholic Commitment Act which was submitted and passed by Kentucky's Legislature in the Spring of 1958. The new law, which became effective that June, provides for a hospitalization petition which can be signed only by the patients themselves, by a member of their immediate families, or by their licensed health officers. A friend, a landlady, a public official cannot sign the petition. At the discretion of the judge, alcoholics are committed to a state mental hospital as *alcoholics* for a period not to exceed six months. Important is the fact that they do not lose their civil rights. Western State is the only hospital designated by the department as one to which alcoholic patients

are to be admitted . . . Some have questioned the department about the reason for an involuntary commitment procedure when it plans to discharge patients who show no inclination to be re-habilitated. The department feels that this procedure is needed for those persons who have a problem, who admit that they have a problem, but who will not seek help voluntarily. We have found that after such patients have been committed by their families, they generally probe to be cooperative in the hospital (4, pp. 41-42).

ABSTINENCE AS A GOAL

Rehabilitation's All-pervasive Goal: Abstinence

From the earliest meeting with the alcoholic patient through the orientation period; social and vocational evaluation; preparation and introduction into the therapy group; physical examination and treatment; psychological evaluation; and, finally, throughout his vocational counseling, abstinence from alcohol is always a goal of rehabilitation. Whether the uncontrollable drinking of alcohol is considered a symptom or the basic disease, if the professional worker is to be *with* the patient, the disruptive effects of alcohol on the patient must be attenuated.

Sobriety, then, is an absolute necessity for meaningful communication between patient and worker. Anything less than sobriety diminishes the degree of communication, and brings to the therapeutic situation grave distortions. Dynamic psychological aid is blocked; and, moreover, the alcoholic's fantasy life, characterized by acting out, would be allowed its full range of expression: not only while he is drunk, but also during the hangover state, between drinking bouts.

Abstinence is required also because without it, relevant relationships cannot be established. Since members of the rehabilitative team function through effective emotional ties—at least to a degree—it is clear that rehabilitation will never be achieved until the patient stops drinking. This point of view is held by all workers in the field of alcoholism. Ruth Fox, writing about the goals of therapy, says:

> To attain a state of complete abstinence from alcohol (for the alcoholic can never become a controlled drinker) is but the first step in therapy. Compulsive drinking, though merely a symptom of a deep-seated personality or social maladjustment, has to be

brought under control before any attempt at deeper therapy can succeed (5, pp. 809-810).

Harold K. Fink asserts the need for abstinence even more strongly:

> Most alcoholics, unfortunately, are not really looking for a way to stay well, but trying to prove to themselves and others that they can drink without getting drunk. "Cure" requires permanent abstinence from the drug in any form, for once someone has passed from normal to abnormal drinking, he can never again learn to control it. There can be no exception in his case, no "just one more little drink," since that first drink is never the last in an alcoholic. (Even fish cooked in sherry wine may provide a psysiological temptation that pushes him into resuming the old habit.) When drink serves many supportive functions, it is understandable why so few alcoholics volunteer for treatment and stay with it long enough to get well. Only when the alcoholic accepts and acts upon the fact of never being able to drink again, can he get and stay well. Brief, sobering-up periods in hospitals or sanitoriums produce little permanent benefit unless followed by supportive psychotherapy, in conjunction with serious participation in A.A. meetings and activities (6, pp. 67-68).

Sobriety as an Essential Value in the Treatment Group

Quite apart from its value to the *individual* patient, sobriety is most important in the treatment of a *group*. One of the primary needs of the therapy group is stability; and stability cannot be maintained unless its members give up drinking, with the fewest possible relapses. As Vogel states:

> As for repeated relapses, one must question whether such a patient should be permitted to continue in therapy. Certain patients use the group for secondary gains. Where the group itself has not detected and explored this, the therapist should guide them in this direction. If after this no change occurs in the patient's alcoholic status, it is best to consider termination of therapy as the situation is potentially too destructive to the group (7, pp. 308-309).

The group is a vital force, whose curative strength depends upon healthy interaction. Therapeutic groups whose members continue to drink become psychodynamically destructive because of the persistence of mutually distorted behavior. This makes each individual patient's attainment and maintenance of sobriety essential, not only for himself and for the other members of the group, but also for the psychotherapy group as a whole.*

Extrinsic and Intrinsic Sobriety

Sobriety is at first achieved mainly as a result of extrinsic forces: that is, in response to pressures from without. Later, the patient himself plays a greater part in maintaining his new physical and psychological condition. As soon as he is able to acknowledge his new freedom from alcohol by choosing not to drink, sobriety becomes an intrinsic operation, internally conceived and self-directed toward his own good. Society's immediate aim of sobriety for the drinking alcoholic is vastly different from sobriety as an ultimate end of treatment. The former may be realized through any number of methods: prohibitions, threats, explanations, or restrictions. The latter control, occurring late in therapy, must replace the earlier external sanctions with a choice: *not to drink*.

Most patients will not achieve sobriety immediately. As a matter of fact, should any member of the rehabilitative team restrict the scope and depth of his activity with the patient, by insisting upon sobriety first and foremost, he may find that his only result is premature termination of treatment by that patient. The unfortunate development may occur not only at the beginning of treatment, but later on as well, if the therapist is too controlling and too restrictive. As the alcoholic patient becomes stronger, he begins to move out of the constricted patterns of his former life, into strange territory. This means that he is assuming greater responsibility for himself and, at the same time, also exposing himself to the possibility of slipping back. In this connection, Martha Brunner-Orne has suggested that alcoholic relapses may be the unfortunate (but not entirely regrettable) result of a patient who attempts new growth and finds the experience anxiety-provoking.

---

*Group psychotherapy is considered to have three interrelated agents of treatment: (1) the psychotherapist: (2) the group as a *gestalt,* and (3) the patient himself. (8, p. 55).

Key Role of the Group Therapist in the Enforcement of Abstinence

For the patient to stop drinking successfully, first by enforced abstinence and—later—upon recovery of his freedom to *choose not to drink*, he must consistently participate in his rehabilitation program. But constancy of purpose is difficult for the alcoholic. Therefore, it is up to the various workers in the treatment center, professional and nonprofessional, to encourage the patient to return for continuing treatment; and at the same time, perform their distinctive functions promptly and adequately. This point is particularly pertinent for the physician and the clinical psychologist, who usually see the patient only once or twice, and consequently do not form intensive and involved relationships. Unless they are aware of and sensitive to the alcoholic's chronic lack of motivation, a careless word or indifferent gesture may be sufficient excuse for the patient to break off treatment, early and entirely.

The situation is somewhat different for the social worker, the vocational counselor, and the group psychotherapist. Here, in ascending order, more and more is expected (and can be required) of the patient. The realities of the alcoholic's unhappy condition, and the part he himself plays in it, can be suggested by the social worker. The vocational counselor can discuss his lack of motivation, his responsibility to his own career. And, finally, the group therapist can delve into the unconscious conflicts relevant to the patient's present and past behavior, analyse his dreams and fantasies, and set limits to protect him and the group.

While it is in the interest and concern of all professionals for the patient to attain sobriety, it is up to the group therapist, eventually, to prohibit drinking. If this requirement, made after all else has failed, is not met, the inebriated patient must be expelled from the treatment group. When a patient continues to drink, he quickly becomes more and more resistant to an interpretive psychological intervention and demoralizes himself, other patients, and the staff.

Imposition of Limits
Based upon the Supposed Etiology of Alcoholism

In talking about the therapist's imposition of limits, it is interesting to note (9, p. 1) that the therapist's concepts concerning the etiology of alcoholism may prevent him from requiring sobriety of his alcoholic patient. When the therapist considers alcoholism *only* as a symptom of an underlying psychopathological state, he usually insists upon a treatment suitable for other kinds of patients, and does not attempt to openly and directly control the drinking. It is essential to understand that the alcoholic patient is more than neurotic; and that, this being so, sobriety is absolutely necessary for treatment. Robert A. Moore supports this view:

> Differences of opinion as to the need for abstinence in the treatment of alcoholism may partly reflect uncertainty concerning its etiology. A major reason for the controversy, however, rests in the viewing of alcoholism as a neurotic disorder. When it is seen as a manifestation of a deeply ingrained, hedonistically oriented, egosyntonic disturbance, protected from detection through the defense mechanism of denial, the controversy seems more academic. Abstinence as the first step in the treatment of alcoholism is desired, though often difficult to obtain, and is based on the psychological understanding of alcoholism (10, p. 111).

GOALS: SOCIAL CASE WORK

Introduction

The confused, belligerent, and unmotivated alcoholic is perhaps the most difficult patient that the social worker encounters. Asocial and self-destructive behavior, plus an ability to engage both individuals and entire agencies in fruitless and frustrating efforts on his part, makes the alcoholic a primary target for resentment from social workers. Many of these professionals may have residual tendencies to misunderstand, mistrust, and personally resent the alcoholic's behavior. As one author says:

> Alcoholism is known to social work today as one of the most complex and baffling problems the worker faces as he attempts to face families and their problems (11, p. 20).

With such a challenging and difficult kind of patient, the social worker might find that rehabilitation is less of a problem in a setting where group psychotherapy is the primary treatment. (For the case worker's overall function in this sort of program, see Chapter IV.)

Ordinarily, the social worker/alcoholic relationship begins when the patient—or other people interested in his welfare—makes the first hesitant inquiry about help; and it continues until after the patient has concluded his more general rehabilitation in the agency. This means that the social worker along with the group psychotherapist and vocational counselor, performs direct, major therapeutic intervention in the patient's struggle. But, in addition, social work duties include direct aid to, and psychological support of, the patient's family, substantially increasing his value in the total plan of treatment. It cannot be stressed too strongly that the entire program rests upon the social worker's effective and reassuring presentation of the agency or clinic's "image" to the patient and—often—his family, too. This image, based upon factual operation and staff spirit, must portray acceptance of the alcoholic and his plight. All too often this is not the case and, as a result, ". . . the patients themselves associate the clinics with something offensive, and the staff often comes to think of them in a similar vein" (12, p. 414).

Upon intake, the acoholic seeking assistance usually describes his reasons for initiating treatment in one of three general ways: (a) that he has a fear *of becoming alcoholic* but really has no drinking problem *yet;* (b) that his problem is *only* a drinking problem; or, (c) that he has many problems, of which drinking is only one. Implicit in each of these reasons are his expectations about, or goals for, therapy. So the social worker's first job is to determine whether the patient's perception of his own problem is correct or faulty; and, if the latter, point out, adroitly and sensitively, the real extent and severity of the drinking problem.

As for specific social work goals with an alcoholic patient, these will depend in large measure upon the clinic's overall functioning and the disciplines represented within the staff. Thus, if vocational counseling is not available, either on an in-clinic or out-clinic basis, the social worker may well find himself concerned with job and educational evaluation, and vocational counseling. If the agency has insufficient group psychotherapists, and the social worker has been trained in group psychotherapy, then it may be appropriate for him (under supervision, of course) to establish groups and to conduct psychotherapy (13). The outline of goals which follows is based upon traditional social work functions—modified in this case by the particular needs of alcoholics—in a setting where other mental health services are amply present.

Immediate Social Work Aims

(a) To establish continuous communication and observation (See Chapter IV, p. 102).

(b) To form a positive relationship.

(c) To establish continuous contact with the patient's family and (in the absence of a vocational counselor) with his employer.

(d) To give immediate support and encouragement to the patient.

(e) To begin orienting the patient to clinic routine.*

Long-term Social Work Aims

(a) To point out the benefits of *evaluation:* medical, social work, psychiatric, group psychotherapeutic, psychological, and vocational.

(b) To point out the benefits of *continuous attendance and effort* in medical examinations and treatment, case work, psychiatric and group psychotherapeutic treatment, psychological testing, and vocational counseling.

(c) To point out the benefits of pastoral counseling where such is indicated.

(d) To point out the benefits of continuous membership in Alcoholics Anonymous.

(e) To screen incoming patients for proper referral.

(f) To refer certain patients to the group psychotherapist for evaluation.

(g) To refer such patients as may not respond to this agency's treatment, to other agencies.

(h) To act as liaison between the agency and patient's family or (where there is no vocational counselor) employer.

(i) To perform case work, where indicated.

(j) To perform individual or group psychotherapy (if properly trained and under supervision) with patient or his relatives or both.

---

*Although orientation is properly the task of specifically-trained staff members, those from all other disciplines must continue to help in orientation from time to time. The social worker, in particular, will be asked to explain and clarify many things. If he doesn't do so with sympathy and understanding, the alcoholic may feel rejected.

(k) To keep pertinent records for periodic review by other staff members, for mutual help.

Social Indices of Change

For further clarification of the alcoholic patient's rather special behavior, before and during treatment, the table below has been prepared. It shows certain prominent characteristics of this kind of patient at intake, then follows him to the period six to eighteen months later, and beyond. The five sections show the alcoholic's behavior, during the three time-periods, toward: (1) himself; (2) family; (3) friends; (4) community; and (5) the Universe. Please keep in mind that changes are sporadic and individual; we are merely indicating *trends* in relation to the time spent in treatment. If these general and easily-observed characteristics change spontaneously, without co-ercion, the changes are probably significant of genuine personality modification.

TABLE II

EXPECTED SOCIAL (BEHAVIORAL) CHANGES IN THE ALCOHOLIC

Intake Behavior	*Behavior, 6-18 months*	*Behavior, 18 mos., plus*
Self		
(1) Appearance:		
Unkempt, unclean, unshaven, untidy.	Moderately clean and tidy.	Clean, presentable, evidence of self-care.
(2) *Sobriety*:		
Evidences of drinking, hangover, & chronic alcoholism.	Reduced drinking; occasional relapses. Little or no drinking in previous 6-12 mos.	Marked reduction in drinking (none in 6-12 months) with very occasional relapse.
(3) *Attendance*:		
Fails or is late for half of appointments.	Cancels or is late for an occasional appointment.	Rarely concels or is late for appointments.
(4) *Motivation and Insight*:		
Almost no awareness (denial) of problems or consequences; no desire to correct them.	Moderate awareness of problems and conse- quences; moderate desire to correct them.	Awareness of problems and consequences; a desire to *continue* to correct them.
Family		
(1) *Commitment*:		
Patient absent for a long time, even if family is available. No contacts.	Infrequent visits to family. Infrequent letters and phone calls.	Frequent visits, attempts at, and successful completion of, reconciliation.

Intake Behavior	Behavior, 6-18 months	Behavior, 18 mos., plus
(2) *Financial Support:* (married male) No financial support to family for a long period.	Minimal financial support.	¾ to total support.
(married female) Avoidance of mother or wife roles; no responsibility or support for a long period.	Acceptance of some responsibility as wife or mother; some support of family.	Moderate to usual support to husband & children, by activity & rededication.
(3) *Participation:* None in family life for a long period.	Very limited. Angry or ineffectual participation in family life.	Partial to relatively normal participation in family life.

Friends

(1) *Number:* None; or occasional drinking companion.	A few non-drinking companions.	Steady friendships; old friends regained; some new ones.
(2) *Duration and Intensity:* Little duration; almost no depth to friendships.	Very minimal duration and depth to friendships.	Trusting friendships of moderate duration; some older friends; some close friends.

Community

(1) *Participation:* Neither membership nor attendance in social, community, or religious groups.	Beginning, spotty membership & attendance in some groups, including A.A.	Moderate & consistent membership and attendance in some groups (incl. A.A.).
(2) *Interest:* No interest in current events, int'l affairs, or local affairs. Does not vote.	Spotty interest, mild concern with current events. Interested in registering & voting.	Moderate & consistent interest in current affairs, local & int'l. Votes.
(3) *Utilization:* No use of community resources. Finds himself taken to hospital. Ignores cultural & athletic advantages.	Minimal, beginning awareness and use of community resources.	Moderate use of community's resources; some avocational interests.

Intake Behavior	*Behavior, 6-18 months*	*Behavior, 18 mos., plus*
(4) *Neighbors:*		
No awareness of neighbors; indifferent to community. Believes both are indifferent or hostile to him.	Beginning awareness; occasional conversing; more rational feelings toward neighborhood & community.	Awareness and some satisfaction from participation in neighborhood & community activities.
Universe		
(1) Life holds no meaning: utter frustration.	Life has some meaning; there is some hope.	Gradual developing of reasonable hope and sense of a meaningful life.
(2) No acceptance of life's inevitabilities, philosophically.	Some philosophical stirring and questioning.	The beginnings of philosophical acceptance.
(3) No beliefs whatsoever.	Some belief in self, in others, and in something beyond the self.	Belief in self, in others, & in an ultimate meaning to life.
(4) Very prejudiced "religious" attitude.	Mildly prejudiced with change in negativity. More certain religious feeling developing.	Reasonably religious beliefs; no longer so disdainful and critical of others; able to help self & others.
(5) Alienation from all cultural values & reliance on idiosyncratic solutions only.	Growing awareness of value in man's culture: "Laws are for my benefit."	Selects some cultural values and finds them helpful to him.

GOALS: GROUP ORIENTATION ABOUT ALCOHOL

Introduction

Unlike most psychiatric patients, the alcoholic—even though his illness is obvious to everyone—is rarely motivated to do anything therapeutically significant. The very first step in rehabilitating the alcoholic, then, must be the awakening of a new self-interest; or the rekindling of an earlier one. In order to accomplish either, the patient must be guided to: (a) take a new look at himself; (b) carefully evaluate his life; and (c) find the means to change. Martha Brunner-Orne, pointing to this basic lack of motivation in the drinker, suggests that psychotherapeutic practices are not sufficiently extensive:

> Our technique of ward discussions can be seen to address itself to a problem which modern psychiatry has avoided. Rather than accepting the concept that a patient must be motivated for treat-

ment, or else be untreatable, we feel that our understanding of dynamics has developed to a point where we may accept the obligation to help a patient develop motivation for treatment (Brunner-Orne, 1956; Brunner-Orne, et al., 1951.) *This means communicating to him that treatment is possible, and helping him accept psychotherapy as a valid form of treatment* (14, p. 223) (italics the author's).

In addition, those people closest to the alcoholic all too often neither support nor understand the potential in long-term, continuous psychotherapy: and, unhappily, will discourage him from continuing or beginning intensive individual or group psychotherapy.

Definition

Orientation, for the alcoholic, is the activation of self-interest. It is a group process, partly didactic and partly interactional, occurring in a structured group composed of patients and members of their families, and supported by the presence of one or more professionals. The group is usually conducted by a physician, or another professional conversant with the characteristics of alcoholism and with the many ways drinking corrodes its victim's life: physically, psychologically, socially, and morally. All facets of the particular problems of alcoholism are discussed, including the roles of culture and society.

Didactic-informative and Interactional-evaluative Aims

The goals of orientation can be conveniently divided into two kinds. The names—Didactic-Informative and Interactional-Evaluative—are descriptive of their techniques.

(a) *Didactic-Informative*
(1) To encourage the patient to continue all activities in his rehabilitation program
    i. Alcoholics Anonymous, Antabuse treatment, medical care, psychotherapy, group psychotherapy, etc.
    ii. To help him accept his particular rehabilitation treatment.
(2) To elicit interest and concern in the following aspects of alcoholism: its definition, cause, epidemiology, differential diagnosis, symptoms, treatment, and prevention.
(3) To confront patients with the physical, psychological, social and moral dangers inherent in alcoholism, in detail.

      i. Social drinking versus alcoholic drinking.

      ii. Specific phases, characteristics, effects, and consequences of alcoholism.

      iii. The compulsive nature and progression of the illness.

      iv. Social, psychological, and—finally—physical dependence on alcohol.

      v. Total sobriety: acceptance of inability to drink again, at all.

(4) To impart the fact that drinking is a sympton of an underlying total, personal malfunctioning.

(5) To give suggestions and support to patients' relatives, if any are present.

(b) *Interactional-evaluative*:

(1) To give the patient a "group process experience," noting his behavior within it: his ability to relate to peers and to the leader.

(2) To give him moral support.

(3) To observe his usual defenses and his potential for treatment.

(4) To keep his anxiety at a level where he will continue to seek help without resorting to drink; or, if he is presently drinking, where he will not increase his consumption.

(5) To establish a beginning transference relationship with prospective group patients (when one person acts both as orientation group leader and group psychotherapist.) Or to encourage a positive relationship between patient and the clinic or agency offering him rehabilitation (when there are separate staff members operating as orientation group leader and group psychotherapist.)

The orientator must be experienced in group dynamics, of course; but, in addition, he must be aware of the particular nature of an alcoholic patient's behavior and inquiries. He should also realize that orientation, important as it is in starting rehabilitation, is not the end-all, but just one part of the total effort toward rehabilitation. One specialist says:

> It is, of course, impossible to achieve any basic changes in a patient's emotional pattern within ten days. We, therefore, con-

centrate on a program designed to awaken interest in further treatment, to make the alcoholic realize that he is a sick person and that his sickness can be treated . . . The goal of these ward groups cannot be a therapeutic one in the strict sense of the word. We want to make the patient realize the need for further treatment after his discharge so that he then willingly joins our regular group therapy clinic. Our approach is neither analytic nor directive (14, p. 220).

Dangers of Extensive Orientation

While adequate orientation is necessary for effective group treatment, care must be taken not to give the patient too much of a good thing. Prolonged, repetitive orientation can help fixate the alcoholic's faulty perception of himself, his condition, and his treatment: a development which can be harmful, as it may strengthen defenses against self-inquiry and increase the tendency to intellectualize and rationalize. Many of the early group treatment hours are apt to be spent in fruitless talk about alcoholism, drinking escapades, and treatment methods, with little (if any) therapeutic change. The aware group psychotherapist, *as much as he understands and sympathizes with the reasons for this kind of discussion,* will not encourage it, once the formal orientation meetings are finished. Later he will actively discourage this line of talk, suggesting that the group members begin to face their past and present experiences more fully, that they reveal their dreams and fantasies, and that they consider the relationships developing in their group (See Chapter X, p. 258).

GOALS: GROUP PSYCHOTHERAPEUTIC INTERVENTION

Introduction

Like his co-workers, the group psychotherapist sees and is affected by the alcoholic's deplorable *mismanagement* of his life. Very early in treatment, he must find a way to respond to this patient's particular type of self-destructive behavior—usually by becoming much more supportive and directive than he would ordinarily be with other patients. To help the alcoholic in his befuddled attempts to establish a more meaningful existence, the therapist will have to make an essential alteration in his usual method: *in the timing.*

In group treatment of alcoholism, where many disciplines contribute to reducing the total problem, the group therapist's specialization makes him *primarily* concerned with the patient's unconscious, his inner conflicts, and his present methods of coping with anxiety. Even so, the therapist cannot afford to overlook the patient's day-to-day faltering attempts to make his way. Empirically, the therapist treating groups of alcoholics, finds that he must at first use his intrepretive abilities sparingly. Instead, he will have to intervene in the patient's social life, give him counsel, direct him and—at times—even demand certain changes. The group psychotherapist working in this setting, with alcoholic patients only, is really supporting the other rehabilitative services by supplementing their efforts and directives. This is in striking contrast to the traditional method of psychoanalysis, which rarely calls for the therapist's involvement with his patients' social realities.

Imperative Pre-therapeutic Aims

There are three essential conditions to the treatment of alcoholism, which are not found in discussions of nonalcoholic patients. Even Spotnitz ignores the tenuous treatment relationship and the absence of motivation found with some patients, notably the alcoholic:

> To effect cures by helping to resolve the emotional difficulties which prevent healthful functioning is therefore our primary concern in administering analytic group psychotherapy. It has the same ultimate goal as individual analytic psychotherapy—the creation of mature well-adjusted human beings (15, p. 384).

Treatment goals with an alcoholic patient, however, must include the gaining of the patient's earliest possible cooperation. At the start and throughout therapy, the alcoholic patient must comply to certain realistic demands which take into account the patho-physical as well as the psychopathological pattern of his existence. He must: (a) abstain from alcohol, (b) use the constructive resources found in his society, and, (c) use all services offered him in the rehabilitation program.

As previously indicated, these are immediate aims of *many* of the different disciplines concerned with rehabilitation. Nevertheless, it behooves the group therapist—who establishes the strongest positive relationship with the patient—to keep his eye on these goals and to work toward them. Consistency within the staff will many times prevent the patient from leaving his treatment group prematurely. And we cannot stress the imperative nature of the above three pretherapeutic aims too strongly. The group member cannot begin to act responsibly unless he attends his group sober and in good physical condition. In addition, as soon as it is practical, he should start trying to fulfill his commitment to society and his family by finding productive employment.

These aims, requiring a measure of patient cooperation, become the early focus of the therapist and—as treatment starts—other group members. This in no way detracts from the therapist's treatment plan, nor does it undermine his purpose which is directed toward the patient's psychological growth. By stressing the importance of *overall* cooperation from the patient, the therapist communicates to him a concern in his welfare, and an understanding and interest in him as a total person. If, by any chance, the therapist should neglect this, the patient is very likely to continue his downhill route and, in most instances, leave his treatment group. Since all the staff members must share in this attempt to keep the patient in his rehabilitation treatment, close communication and cooperation within the staff is absolutely essential. (See Chapter II, pp. 50-54.)

Modification of the Immediate Therapeutic Aim

The alcoholic drinks in order to endure living. This fact alone, as has been indicated, extensively modifies the treatment process and approach. Although this means that the therapist's moment-to-moment aims may also be altered, his endpoint in the treatment may very well be exactly the same as for non-alcoholic patients. In the process of intensive group psychotherapy, not only with alcoholics but with other types of patient as well, three inherent factors alter the therapist's immediate goals:

(a) The patient's fantastic perceptions and conceptions concerning group psychotherapy.

(b) The particular personality, training, experience and values of the therapist himself.

(c) The specific group composition and atmosphere at any given time.

In considering the first point: the patient's own ideas about why he is in the therapy group, the therapist must realize that they will differ markedly from his own. The patient will have quite unrealistic ideas—due in part to his underlying personality and in part to his long addiction to alcohol—and will be characteristically more confused about the nature and process of therapy than another patient. This comes as no surprise; the alcoholic who lives much of his life in his fantasies will have grossly impractical expectations of his treatment. Throughout the weekly therapeutic sessions, it is the continuous task of the therapist and of the more involved group patients to help any new member re-evaluate his unattainable goals. The crucial point is that the patient must give up his fantastic aims in favor of more realistic and practical ones. For example, he may say that he is entering the therapy group "to learn how to handle my drinking so that I can become a poet;" or "to understand how the others get by, so that I can get rich too;" or "to talk about my drinking problem because I want to get a job;" or, "to learn how to live and be successful." The real needs, of course, are that he begin to trust others, begin to relate in constructive interaction. As this happens, the alcoholic develops a feeling of self-worth and belonging. Then, he may say: "I like being here;" or, "I don't know how it helps but I feel better;" or, "I can see now that drinking was one of my problems, but I certainly must change, besides." The disparity between the goals of patient and therapist will gradually lessen as treatment continues.

The importance of the second factor—the therapist himself—is readily seen. After all, he not only brings the group into existence, but he impresses his personality upon it week after week. His basic values concerning the meaning of life and the significance of the process leading to change are his means of moving the group as a whole, or individual members, toward responsibility. Group psychotherapists, in contrast to individual therapists, appear to have a preference for the unstructured group experience, rather than a meeting used for explanation or analysis (16). This kind of behavior on the part of the therapist encourages fuller affective participation and is particularly beneficial to the alcoholic. Isolated and usually overwhelmed by the simplest social task, this patient will begin to look forward to his group sessions, where—in face-to-face group interplay at meeting after meeting—*being together* is emphasized. The therapist with an alcoholic patient will find a preference for group interaction over the learning of facts *about* the members. Patient revelation, *per se* as content, is no longer important; but it *is* significant because of the risk which the patient has taken in telling his "secrets," and the other members' response to them. The group therapist for an alcoholic group focuses upon the members' responsibile activity, not only in treatment, but outside it, too.

And finally, in considering the third point, it has been found that the specific group composition and behavior confronting the therapist will determine to some extent the immediate goals for both the therapist and his patients. In Chapter IX, it is pointed out that the alcoholic group, with its homogeneous symptom, offers resistance to therapeutic intervention. The therapist's aim is to supplant the "cohesive" tendency of a group of alcoholics who focus exclusively on themselves as *alcoholics,* and move them to an awareness and expression of their feelings for one another as persons. Hopefully, this change in "vision" will foster more authentic relationships.

The patients, on their side, would rather maintain a kind of pseudo-closeness than risk the fearsome thought of more genuine interaction. At first, they will use alcoholism as a distraction from long standing internal conflicts; and will talk endlessly about this one problem: alcoholism, its cause, its universal patterns, and "rules of living" that might lead to its cure. The patients hope to deny, through omission, the rest of their unique behavior. The therapist will have to cut across undue verbiage; and, ignoring explanations and generalizations, focus again and again upon his group patients as total, functioning human beings.

The therapist always tries to experience *with* the group. He is concerned with the "here," the "immediate," the "spontaneous," and the "now." Much against their inclinations, patients are encouraged to express fleeting and momentary feelings—however irrational—and to respond *"here* and *now"* by the therapist's full participation. Both intrapsychic and interpersonal conflict is experienced in many possible ways. It is through this kind of interaction that the alcoholic's responsiveness and responsibility—to self, to others, and to the community—is first stimulated. In other words, group psychotherapy with the alcoholic strives to "enhance the patient's *own* potentials so that he can gradually rely more upon himself" (17, p. 31).

Indices of Group Psychotherapeutic Change

Granted that the therapist wants to see changes in basic behavior patterns in his patients: what are the *standards* of change? And what, indeed, is meant in this case by "behavior?" With the term "behavior" including thoughts, feelings, and actions, we consider the major signs of: (a) appropriate, and (b) inappropriate behavior to be as follows:

(a) *Appropriate behavior* is entered upon spontaneously (that is, *actively*) by the patient, for his self-fulfillment. The direction, quantity and quality of this behavior are dictated, in part, by the emerging situation; and in part by the patient's inherent creativity and willingness to risk the new.

(b) *Inappropriate behavior* is entered upon compulsively (that is, *reactively*) by the patient, which denies his self-fulfillment while attempting to maintain an anxiety-free condition. Direction, quality, and quantity of this behavior are dictated by an uncontrollable need to please, appease, or offend others. They have nothing to do with the emerging situation, the individual's inherent creativity, or his willingness to risk being different than he is right now.

More specifically, how does the group psychotherapist rank moment-to-moment, and "beginning of treatment" to "end of treatment" change? On any given night while conducting his group, what are his aims? What does he condier to have positive value and what negative? What kinds of new behavior does he seek, as compared to the patient's activities when he first entered the group?

The group psychotherapists of the recently completed New York Alcoholism Vocational Rehabilitation Project* have itemized their findings on appropriate and inappropriate group behavior patterns. During the three years of demonstration and treatment, it proved helpful to have a measure—however rough and schematic—of the decline in the alcoholic's inappropriate responses along with an in-

---

*The New York Alcoholism Vocational Rehabilitation Project, Project No. 418, was jointly sponsored by the Office of Vocational Rehabilitation, U. S. Department of Health, Education and Welfare, Wash., D. C., and The Nat'l Council on Alcoholism, Inc., New York City.

crease in more appropriate ones. The following figures, under six major headings, list certain patient behavioral characteristics (thoughts, feelings, actions) believed to be significant. The graphic illustrations suggest the expected direction of change in both types of behavior, in a roughly quantitative way. (See pp. 81-87.)

GOALS: VOCATIONAL EVALUATION AND COUNSELING

Introduction

The idea that vocational evaluation and counseling should be an integral part of the alcoholic's total rehabilitation may surprise some, particularly those psychotherapists who see their work as eminently provocative of change. Nonetheless, we feel strongly that the alcoholic should receive vocational counseling along with his group psychotherapy. The New York Alcoholism Vocational Rehabilitation Project's staff concluded that personality changes will pervade all behavior *to a greater extent,* when the alcoholic is offered *both* group psychotherapy and vocational counseling, rather than group therapy alone. We quote in part from this report:

> The major finding of the project, however, was the marked improvement in work performance and attitude of those patients who received vocational counseling . . . (Patients who got both group psychotherapy and vocational counseling) revealed a greater number of positive changes in employment status, earnings, and work relationships and attitudes (21, p. 40).

Vocational counseling, then, is on a par with the other methods of intervention in the overall rehabilitation, because the alcoholic's reality adjustment—particularly his vocational responsibility and activity—must be considered from the moment he enters the clinic. Similar to a "total push" program of treatment, he must be met with a combined approach which not only intervenes *eventually* with his latent and unconscious self, but, much earlier, intervenes in his manifest and current behavior and his conscious self. Failure to consider this second area, one so crucial for the alcoholic, results in early termination of treatment, and the patient's return to self-defeating acting out.

The alcoholic patient is most often an adult who has previously assumed adult responsibilities in a culture that offers him vocational and avocational pursuits. The alcoholic feels defeated, for he can neither undertake his old tasks, nor apply himself to new ones. Much of the time, he is neither productive nor creative, takes no part in any community activity and is isolated from family and friends. He is empty and unfulfilled.

Responsible daily activity would require a sensitivity to reality and would, to some extent, reduce the possibility of the alcoholic's very harmful acting out. The alcoholic who holds down a job also has less time and opportunity to drink. And finally, ignoring his work problem is usually interpreted by him as rejection—very like a child whose parents completely overlook his accomplishments at school.

In general, our complex society requires of its members "regularity, precision, individual responsibility, and integration through self-control and cooperation" (18, p. 91). To state this important consideration another way, when an individual tries to fill a vocational position, however small or simple, he is automatically assuming some of these required characteristics, to some degree. This means that when an alcoholic patient begins to accept the idea of regular work, when he actually takes a job, and actually goes to work day after day, certain desirable characteristics are going to be fostered in him. Bacon indicates the importance of social-level treatment in rehabilitating the alcoholic, when he writes:

> The breakdown of emotionally significant personal relations allows for ridiculous idealism, destructive cynicism, and non-activity to play even greater roles in the individual's life. Ego-centricity can run riot in the isolated person. Ordinary rewards and punishments become less and less meaningful to the individual not belonging to such groups as the parental family, the marital family, the neighborhood or occupational clique or the close reciprocating friendship. Therapy in alcoholism must include reorientation to a real social world along with psychological re-training. If not, the psychological changes are merely intellectual abstractions and will soon wither away. The patient along with psychological changes, must start to practice reciprocating social relations, must start to use socially acceptable (in contrast to selfishly acceptable) ideas, and must start to act in socially acceptable ways (instead of escaping through alcohol) (19).

FIGURE 3. THE PATIENT'S VERBALIZATION DURING SESSIONS

Inappropriate Verbalizations:
The patient speaks:
- about himself as an object
- about his peers as objects
- about authority figures as objects
- only to himself (autistic or detached)
- only to his peers
- only with obvious psychic abnormality
- constantly, monopolizing the group

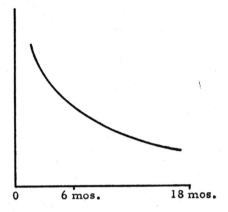

Inappropriate Verbalizations

Appropriate Verbalizations:
The patient speaks:
- about himself as a subject
- about peers as persons
- about those in authority as persons
- spontaneously

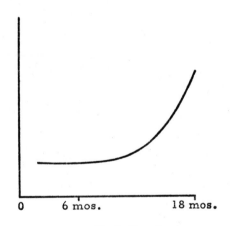

Appropriate Verbalizations

Aims of Vocational Evaluation and Counseling

While it is true that some alcoholics are gainfully employed with some satisfaction, many more are either unemployed or drifting without direction, purpose, or interest from one job to another. And among

FIGURE 4. THE PATIENT'S EFFECTIVE CONTACT DURING SESSIONS

Inappropriate Contact:
The patient:
  • relapses through insobriety
  • exhibits abnormal postural
    positions and movements
  • exhibits other nonverbal cues

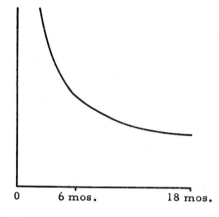

Inappropriate Contact

Appropriate Contact:
The patient:
  • is accessible and outgoing
  • is sober
  • responds relevantly to
    the interpretation of
    the reality situation
  • is alert and attentive in posture
  • responds with directness
    and comprehension

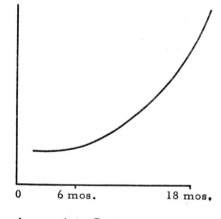

Appropriate Contact

those who are employed, there is usually an intense degree of job dissatisfaction and frustration, lack of responsibility, exceedingly poor employee-employer understanding, inadequate morale and loyalty and so forth. At best, it can be said that the employed alcoholic's work

FIGURE 5. THE NATURE OF FACTS RELATED BY THE PATIENT IN SESSION

Inappropriate Facts:
The patient:
  • blames his past
    (in relating his history)
  • blames external circumstances

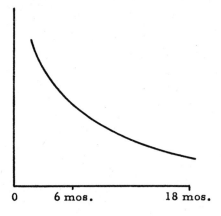

Inappropriate Facts

Appropriate Facts:
The patient:
  • acknowledges his life as
    largely fantasy oriented and
    imaginary
  • identifies the psychological
    problem as being *his*
    primarily
  • identifies that the psychological
    problem is represented in the
    group as between himself and
    another

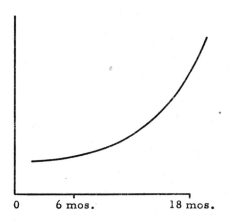

Appropriate Facts

status is tenuous; and it is liable to sudden downward change with loss of position, income, as well as a severe blow to the patient's pride.

The vocational counselor's overall purpose, which is quite different from that of the group psychotherapist, is to present the alcoholic

FIGURE 6. THE NATURE OF IDEATION EXPRESSED BY THE PATIENT IN SESSION.

Inappropriate Ideation:
The patient:
- uses projection as a primary defense
- uses introjection as a primary defense
- uses overintellectualism as a primary defense
- uses rationalization as a primary defense
- uses circuitous thinking as a primary defense

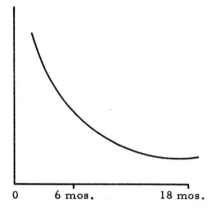

Inappropriate Ideation

Appropriate Ideation
- The patient uses more and still more reality-tested thinking.

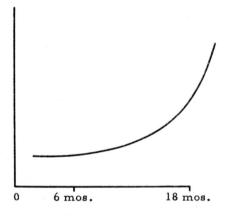

Appropriate Ideation

patient with society's insistent demand that he participate responsibly within his community. Here, the value judgements of the counselor are used to bring about a gradual alteration in the patient's attitudes and thus in his relationship with society. The counselor realizes the dire consequences of nonactivity or of noncreative and nonsatisfying

FIGURE 7. THE NATURE OF THE PATIENT'S EXCUSE FOR POOR ATTENDANCE AT SESSIONS.

Inappropriate Response to Appointments:
The patient obstructs treatment by:
- being late, absent, or leaving early
- saying he has been coerced into coming
- saying that his work requirements prevent him from coming
- saying that social requirements prevent him from coming
- saying that fate prevents him from coming
- saying nothing and ignoring questions concerning his poor attendance

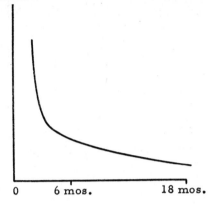

Inappropriate Response to Appointments

Appropriate Response to Appointments:
- The patients forwards his treatment by coming regularly, on time, and sober.

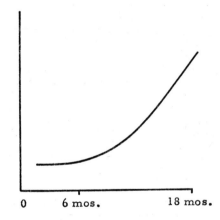

Appropriate Response to Appointments

employment; and assists his patient so that he can be both gainfully and productively employed. An intermediate goal of unlimited value in treatment is keeping the patient in the vocational

FIGURE 8. THE PATIENT'S EXPRESSION OF ANXIETY AND AFFECT IN SESSION.

Inappropriate Expression:
The patient expresses:
- phobic reactions
- free-floating dread
- a general mistrust
- a state of seeming indifference
- undue embarrassment
- irrational anger
- irrational hate
- depression
- suicidal thoughts and feelings

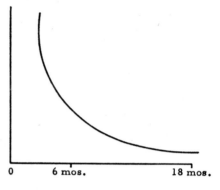

Inappropriate Expression

Appropriate Expression:
The patient expresses:
- a degree of anxiety relevant to *really* dangerous situations
- relevant sadness
- relevant (genuine) caring
- relevant affect—for example, joy or hatred

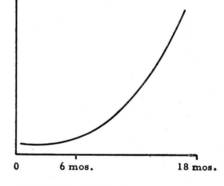

Appropriate Expression

rehabilitative process. As Martensen-Larsen put it: "We believe that the sooner the patient gets back to family and community and resumes some responsibility and work, the better off he is" (17, p. 35).

Vocational counseling aims for the alcoholic patient may be divided into two functions: (1) evaluating the patient's vocational attributes, and (2) establishing and maintaining a counseling relationship.

The activities involved in the evaluative function may be summarized as follows:

(a) To establish a "test" relationship by achieving sufficient rapport.

FIGURE 9. THE NATURE OF A PATIENT'S RELATEDNESS IN SESSION.

Inappropriate Relating to a Member
or the Therapist:
The patient is:
- primarily dependent, questions
  the therapist and demands
  answers
- primarily voyeuristic
- primarily exhibitionistic
- overly aggressive
- overly moralistic
- overly and defensively
  "inspirational"
- contemptuous of others
- hostile
- self-destructively competitive
- unduly submissive
- masochistic
- withdrawn from others
- detached from all others
- alienated from himself

Inappropriate Relating to a
Member or the Therapist

Appropriate Relating to a Member
or the Therapist:
The patient is:
- more or less rationally
  independent
- curious about other members
  wanting to help
- self-revealing, as he gains trust
  in others
- concerned for others in the group
- capable of leading the others
- assertive, not overly aggressive
  or submissive

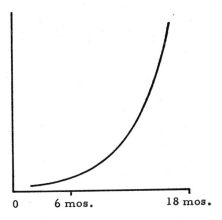

Appropriate Relating to a
Member or the Therapist

(b) To support the rehabilitation efforts of the staff.

(c) To administer the tests either individually or in a group, and
to evaluate results.

(d) To plan a course of action based upon realistic expectations of the patient and his potential employment.

(e) To present this evaluation and the planned course of action to the staff for their information.

(f) To confront the patient with the results of this evaluation; and to offer him a plan of action.

Later on, the goals of vocational counseling will be:

(a) To modify the relationship with the alcoholic from one of tester-testee to one of counselor-patient: and to intensify this relationship gradually.

(b) To induce the patient to investigate his vocational and avocational attitudes and intentions.

(c) To support the patient in his quest for satisfaction, creativity, and material gain.

(d) To encourage the patient to continue with his physician, social worker, group psychotherapist, and other professionals; and to suggest that he bring them those problems relating to their specialty.

Indices of Vocational Change

The signs indicating that the alcoholic's work patterns are beginning to improve are similar to the signs of social change (see p. 68) and therapeutic improvement (see p. 78.) The vocational counselor and his fellow staff members expect growth in the patient beginning about six months after the start of his rehabilitation. At this time, they expect he will be more realistic in appraising his work, that he will assume more responsibility, that he will gain more satisfaction, and that he will start to improve his work relationships.

At the start of counseling many alcoholics, whether employed or not, hold highly fantastic work preferences, which have nothing to do with either potentiality or past experience. As rehabilitation takes hold, including both vocational counseling and group therapy, the patient's ability to evaluate himself more realistically increases. New work preferences are developed which are more in keeping with his experience, ability, and talent. Along with this shift in job preference, the staff expects the patient to stay with a particular task, in the same surroundings, for a longer period. After a few months in the center, it is expected that he will be more stable, with less tendency to shift jobs frequently.

Hand-in-hand with a more even work performance goes a gradual increase in the patient's self-satisfaction. For perhaps the first time, he feels hopeful that one day he might meet the work goals he is now realistically establishing; and these aims now seem more congruent with the other areas of his life. His creativity seems less blocked or misdirected and unrealized talent, both vocational and avocational, gradually comes to the fore.

Typical work relations of an alcoholic are difficult to list; they run the gamut from compulsively distant, to compulsively aggressive, to compulsively submissive. And, in addition, these relationships can be one way with supervisors, another with peers, and still another with subordinates. In any event, as rehabilitation becomes effective, the alcoholic will generally develop work relationships in which there is less tendency for him to either distort or to project. With his peers, he is expected to become less neurotically competitive; and with subordinates, it is hoped that he will develop a rational authority in keeping with his actual supervisory position.

GOALS: CLINICAL PSYCHOLOGY

Introduction

In a multiple-treatment rehabilitation, it is crucial for the staff to know what their alcoholic patients are really like psychodynamically. Giving them this knowledge is the job of the clinical psychologist.

In the group-oriented clinic for alcoholics, the psychologist intervenes the *least* in the patient's destructive process. After careful examination, the psychologist gives the staff an intensive study of the distinctive personality of each patient. This gives staff members a more accurate picture of a particular patient and allows each professional to apply his method of rehabilitation more sensitively.

The psychologist's main concern remains with the single patient although he uses group methods of inquiry and evaluation. (Indeed, when it is indicated, he may phrase his report in group terminology so that staff members will have still another dimension of group behavior to explore and examine.) Tests are offered in a group setting, in the evenings or on Saturdays, a practice that encourages the reluctant alcoholic to attend.

The psychologist's work with an alcoholic, although ultimately much the same as with other patients, differs sharply in timing, support, understanding, and sensitivity. The alcoholic is not tested to determine suitability for treatment, primarily; nor to find the proper time to start. As indicated throughout this text, the alcoholic requires treatment now. Whenever he asks for help, or in any other way shows the slightest inclination to accept help, *that* is the moment to begin rehabilitation. Later on, when he is *in* group treatment, psychological tests will be offered. It is easy to see that it would be poor practice to suggest to such a confused and more or less unmotivated person that he cannot start treatment until he takes a battery of tests to determine his fitness for it. This would be a formidable hurdle—one which few, if any, could surmount; and so it is simply not done with an alcoholic.

Along with the rest of the rehabilitation team, the clinical psychologist will find that his usual procedures, suitable and acceptable in treating other kinds of patients, must be modified if he is to work with alcoholics successfully. When an alcoholic patient appears late for his examination, drunk, he must be allowed to take his tests anyway, if he wants. He should not be excluded from the test program on account of his drinking or even his abusive behavior—unless his behavior invalidates the test for others. Obviously, an inebriated patient ought be given another appointment when hopefully he will be sober and the test results will be more valid for him.

The psychologist, working with the compulsive drinker, must then devise methods to overcome patient resistance and frustrating behavior—methods which are based upon the requirements of the moment and which facilitate a modicum of motivation in the reluctant patient. Only then can he be encouraged to continue his treatment.

Immediate aims, for the clinical psychologist, may be summarized as:

(a) Establishing an atmosphere conducive to test-taking.

(b) Supporting the overtly-resistant, rationalizing patient.

(c) Carefully orienting the patient to the purpose of tests.

(d) Reassuring and encouraging the patient about the tests, their results, and the way these results will be used.

(e) Making sure the patient realizes he must continue all rehabilitative services, regardless of *what* the tests show.

Eventual aims are to:

(a) Administer, score, and interpret the test materials.

(b) Determine the psychological diagnosis of the disturbance.

(c) Evaluate how well the patient will do in group psychotherapy and vocational counseling.

(d) Recommend a course of action to the staff.

(e) Meet with the patients and discuss test results.

There may be some questions as to the therapeutic value in meeting with patients to discuss test results. This function of the psychologist may be filled only at the discretion of the Clinical Director. Whether the psychologist is assigned this duty depends a great deal upon the cohesiveness of the staff and their ability to really communicate with one another. If the clinical psychologist is required to discuss findings with patients, he should keep his remarks as general and nonjudgmental as possible.

It may often be preferable for the group psychotherapist to discuss psychological test results with patients, within the atmosphere of an interacting group session. Here, the therapist, in the framework of evolving relationships and with his special knowledge of the various patients' strengths and weaknesses, can frankly explain test findings without causing untoward therapeutic results for the group members.

REFERENCES

1. *An Introduction to A.A.* Intergroup Association of A.A., 133 E. 39 St., New York, N. Y. 10016.
2. Jackson, J. K.: Alcoholism and the family. In *Society, Culture and Drinking Patterns.* Edited by D. J. Pittman and C. R. Synder. New York, Wiley, 1962, pp. 472-492.
3. Lemert, E. M.: Alcohol, values and social control. In *Society, Culture and Drinking Patterns.* Edited by D. J. Pittman and C. R. Synder. New York, Wiley, 1962, pp. 553-571.
4. McPheeters, H L.: A treatment unit for alcoholics. *Mental Hospitals, 41-*42, March 1960.
5. Fox, Ruth: Treatment of chronic alcoholism. *The Medical Clinics of North America.* New York, Saunders, 1958.
6. Fink, H. K.: To accept the alcoholic patient or not: problems in psychotherapy with alcoholics. *Samiksa, 13*(2)47-74, 1959.
7. Vogel, S.: Some aspects of group psychotherapy with alcoholics. *Int. J. Group Psychother., 7*:302-309, 1957.

8. Mullan, H., and Rosenbaum, M.: Group Psychotherapy: Theory and Practice. New York, The Free Press of Glencoe, 1962.

9. Tiebout, H. M.: The role of psychiatry in the field of alcoholism. *Quart. J. Stud. Alcohol, 12*:52-57, 1951.

10. Moore, R. A.: The problem of abstinence by the patient as a requisite for the psychotherapy of alcoholism: The need for abstinence by the alcoholic patient during treatment. *Quart. J. Stud. Alcohol, 23*:105-123, 1962.

11. Lee, J. P.: Alcoholics Anonymous as a community resource. *Social Work,* 20-26, Oct. 1960.

12. Gliedman, L. H.: Concurrent and combined group treatment of chronic alcoholics and their wives. *Int. J. Group Psyhcother. 7*:414-424, 1957.

13. Mullan, H.: Training of group psychotherapists. *Amer. J. Psychother., 12*: 495-500, 1958.

14. Brunner-Orne, M.: Ward group sessions with hospitalized alcoholics as motivation for psychotherapy. *Int. J. Group Psychother., 9*:220-223, 1959.

15. Spotnitz, H.: The concept of goals in group psychotherapy. *Int. J. Group Psychother., 10*:383-393, 1960.

16. Mullan, H., and Sangiuliano, I.: *The Therapist's Contribution to the Treatment Process: His Person, Transactions, and Treatment Methods.* Springfield, Thomas, 1964.

17. Martensen-Larsen, O.: Group psychotherapy with alcoholics in private practice. *Int. J. Group Psychother., 6*:28-37, 1956.

18. Bacon, S. D.: Alcohol and complex society. In *Society, Culture and Drinking Patterns.* Edited by D. J. Pittman and C. R. Synder. New York, Wiley, 1962, pp. 78-93.

19. Bacon, S. D.: Alcoholism: nature of the problem and alcoholism: its extent, therapy and prevention. *Federal Probation, 2*:1-14, 1947.

PART TWO

EVALUATION, ORIENTATION AND MOTIVATION

CHAPTER IV

CASE WORK WITH THE ALCOHOLIC DIRECTED TOWARD HIS PARTICIPATION IN GROUP PSYCHOTHERAPY

HUGH MULLAN, M.D., AND ESTHER J. GRIFFING, M.S.W.

(The social worker is usually the first professional person the alcoholic patient meets in the clinic. This fact, coupled with the very difficult conditions which exist with this patient at the start of case work, immeasurably increases the social worker's usual tasks and responsibilities. An extended social work approach, with different timing and aims than is customary, is essential in helping this patient enter a psychotherapeutic group and accept the necessary evaluation procedures.

If social evaluation, orientation and referral to the group psychotherapist for treatment are to be successful with a patient as fragile as the alcoholic, the social worker must have a high degree of sensitivity and understanding. He must be aware of the patient's total problem and the physical, psychological, and social manifestations of alcoholism. The social worker's practical methods and personal stability must be adequate to cope with the patient's inordinate demands.

Family understanding and participation in the alcoholic's treatment are essential; therefore, the social worker's meetings with the patient's relatives are very nearly—sometimes, actually—on a therapeutic level. Close liaison with other members of the staff for mutual support is imperative.

Knowledge and understanding of group psychotherapy, preferably through his own experiences in group treatment, will stand the social worker in good stead when the time comes for him to influence the anxious and reluctant patient to begin and continue his treatment. Should an alcoholic prove unsuitable for the treatment group, it is once again the job of the social worker to keep up his support of the patient, by referring him to a community resource which will help in rehabilitation.)

[95]

INTRODUCTION

Definitions

In the preceding chapters, the background of the treatment effort has been examined. In this chapter, we shall begin to discuss systems of intervention between the alcoholic patient and his *outside* world and between the alcoholic patient and his *inner* world. It may be true that the social worker, the orientator, and the vocational counselor focus more upon the patient and his environment, while the group pschotherapist and clinical psychologist are more concerned with the patient and his inner conflicts. Even so, no clear separation of treatments is possible; and, even if it were possible, would not be desirable.

To substantiate this mutual inclusiveness, one has only to turn to a definition of psychotherapy: "Any measure, mental or physical, that favorably influences the mind or psyche. Usually, however, the term is applied to measures that are associated with the amelioration or removal of abnormal constituents of the mind" (1, p. 450). Since *all* procedures used to rehabilitate the alcoholic are there to "favorably influence" him, all of them have an important part to play in the therapeutic scheme.

In view of the extreme social maladjustment of most alcoholics, the social case worker's understanding, experience, and training in social psychiatry is of great significance in the treatment of alcoholics.

> Psychiatric social work is that branch of social work which developed in conjunction with the practice of psychiatry. The psychiatric social worker is a case worker who has achieved, through professional training and experience, a mastery of the subject matter of social psychiatry and mental hygiene and the adaptation and application of this knowledge in case work practice. Psychiatric social workers are usually concerned with the social case study and treatment of children or adults whose personal and social maladjustments are primarly due to mental health problems, including nervous and mental diseases and defects; and emotional, behavior, and habit disorders . . . The term has also been defined as "the branch of social case work that deals with cases of social maladjustment in which a mental factor or a behavior problem is of primary importance" (1, p. 492).

The social worker in an alcoholic treatment center where group psychotherapy is the central intervention not only is *informed* on the subject of alcoholism, but is also aware of the singular value of group treatment because he understands the characteristic behavioral patterns shown by alcoholics, as well as society's usual rejecting responses to them. The social worker will concern himself with the social and cultural realities of his alcoholic patient's situation, of course. But his responsibility does not stop here. When the patient returns to the clinic, the social worker will continue his support, and will attempt to discover the nature of the patient's specific maladjustments with family, friends, employer, and self. At the same time, he will try to guide his patient toward a more total involvement in rehabilitation by influencing him to participate in both group psychotherapy and vocational counseling.

Areas of Special Knowledge and Function

The following outline defines the case worker's activity with the alcoholic more clearly. It emphasizes the case worker's particular knowledge and function which are similar to those of other professionals who intervene in the alcoholic's crippling maladjustments.

The Case Worker with the Alcoholic: Areas of Special Knowledge

I. *Social and Cultural Realities*
   a. Social, particularly family; patterns of behavior favorable to the origin and perpetuation of alcoholism.
   b. Social, particularly family; patterns of behavior favorable to prevention or control of alcoholism.
   c. Cultural factors which tend to induce and support alcoholism.
   d. Cultural factors which tend to prevent and discourage alcoholism.
   e. Group and individual behaviors which encourage and discourage alcoholism.

II. *The Unfortunate Concomitants of Alcoholism & Their Correctives*
   a. Physical disease: treatment and care
   b. Spiritual inadequacy: support and counsel.

    c. Psychological conflict and immaturity: psychological treatment.

    d. Social maladjustment: support and counsel.

III. *The Community Structure as It Supports Rehabilitation*

Knowledge of purpose, function, and operation of:

    a. Medical facilities with liason.

    b. Religious institutions and groups with liason.

    c. Fellowships, especially A.A., with liason.

    d. Psychiatric facilities with liason.

    e. Social agencies with liason.

The Case Worker with the Alcoholic: Areas of Special Function

a. Interprets the Rehabilitation Center to:

    1. The patient.

    2. The patient's family, friends, employer and others—including the referral party.

b. Establishes a relationship between the Center and:

    1. The patient.

    2. The patient's family, friends, employer and others—including the referral party.

c. Establishes continuous contact with the patient.

d. Supports the patient and his family emotionally and even, at times, financially.

e. Describes rehabilitation to the patient and encourages him to take part in it.

f. Motivates the patient to be evaluated for group therapy, to enter the group, and to keep up treatment.

g. Motivates the patient to begin and continue with:

    (1) orientation; (2) vocational counseling and (3) psychological evaluation.

h. Does necessary case work with the patient.

i. Does necessary case work with the patient's family.

j. Refers drop-outs, or those unsuitable for group therapy, to other agencies.

The Social Worker's Unlimited Function

This simplified description of the case worker's job with alcoholic patients is not meant to suggest that his activity is limited to these functions. As a matter of fact, the social worker treating alcoholics is called upon to use much more than his knowledge of social structure; social and cultural forces; and community organization. A competent case worker will turn back the clock, in his work with an alcoholic patient, to previous methods of help; and will offer concrete assistance to the patient while simultaneously maintaining his more modern skills in dynamic case work. In this way, he combines the past function of meeting dire physical need directly, with tangible help: carfare, food, money, medicine, housing and so forth, with the present day case work function of an interactional treatment relationship.

The desperate and conflicted alcoholic tends to turn away from the usual help offered by his community. Hospitals and clinics— to mention only two institutions—often make matters worse by their lack of understanding and their refusal to consider the applications of inebriates. *The New York City Alcoholism Study* makes this point perfectly clear:

> In general, the findings appear to indicate that there is relatively little interest, among relevant individuals or organizations in the community, in either providing direct services for the treatment of alcoholism, or in learning more about this illness. When one considers that the findings quoted immediately above were obtained from that self-selected minority which was sufficiently motivated to respond to the questionnaires, the results become doubly discouraging, for one would expect this to represent the most positively oriented group with regard to the treatment of alcoholism. Thus it is suggested that the general attitude in the community, as regards the alcoholic, is even more discouraging than the above data would indicate (2, pp. 3-4).

The sad plight of the alcoholic, then, is to be divorced from his society and its benefits. His destitution is so complete that it recalls the plight of the nineteenth-century European immigrants: strangers in a strange land, bewildered and unable (at least in the beginning) to communicate. Social workers then realized that, before an immigrant could be helped to help himself, he needed practical help— extensive and unconditional—in order to survive long enough to learn our (to him) alien customs and speech. *Today's social work-*

*er must treat the alcoholic in much the same way: giving uncondi-
tional aid while psychologically stimulating the patient toward those
long-term treatments he needs to alleviate his disorder: the acceptance of group psychotherapy evaluation, the continuance of group
treatment, and the completion of vocational counseling.*

THE ALCOHOLIC AND THE CASE WORKER MEET

Bizarrness of the Encounter

The very first approach of the alcoholic to the rehabilitation clinic
is many times so tenuous, so confused and so indefinite as to be
pathognomic of his difficulty. Intake workers in nonalcoholic treatment agencies expect and appreciate a routine of appointments and
sessions that fill up their day with some regularity. Not so the
worker in the alcoholic treatment center. An appointment made by
the worker at great personal inconvenience and in good faith is as
likely as not to be skipped by the alcoholic with no attempt to
cancel. Indeed, he may never be heard from again.

Although the initial call of inquiry about treatment might be
made by the patient himself, it is frequently others—family member,
friend or acquaintance, physician, employer, pastor, member of A.A.,
and the like—who take the first step. No matter *who* it is asking for
help, the intake worker must capitalize on the inquiry. First of all, he
should consider this call as an indication of emergency. Secondly, he
must set aside time so that he can see the patient immediately; and
for the third step, he must in every possible way nurture this patient's
impulse to seek help.

All those clinic routines suitable for other patients must be abandoned when dealing with an alcoholic. It is useless to make an appointment for some weeks in the future, or to put him on a waiting
list, to be called at some more convenient time. The very nature of
the alcoholic's disturbance will make any delay in giving him help
seem to be a flat rejection. The discouraged and dejected alcoholic,
who sees no immediate aid forthcoming, will generally go back to
the bottle with even more enthusiasm than before.

It is clear, then, that intake practice with alcoholics requires an
immediate meeting of patient and worker. Furthermore, the same
worker who initially talks with the inquiring patient should also es-

tablish the first appointment, and then continue his case work relationship throughout the patient's stay at the clinic.

The Confusion of the Alcoholic

There is no doubt that confusion exists in the aims and methods of treating the alcoholic. This has many bases, but the greatest source by far lies in the alcoholic himself, who visualizes help in his own idiosyncractic fashion. As far as the alcoholic is concerned, help means something concrete and palpable: something *given* to him or *done* for him. This naivete precludes any notion of a *joint effort,* one in which he, too, has a most important part to play. On the contrary, he judges the clinic's worth solely on the basis of the social worker's contribution to his personal welfare.

We emphasize this point because a worker unaware of it may unwittingly alienate his alcoholic patient. In order to establish and maintain any kind of relationship, the worker will have to answer many questions with great patience, demonstrating over and over again a willingness to give. Prompted by the anxious patient, he will find himself making many telephone calls to people who know and are interested in the patient; will deal with the physical needs of the patient; and at times even give the alcoholic money to carry him over a difficult period. These particular efforts, however, do not modify dynamic case work as much as enlarge and extend the usual practice. They are absolutely essential in treating the alcoholic, because many of his complex problems are either caused by, or made worse by, a breakdown in his social functioning.

With alcoholics, the case work process must be kept much more flexible than usual. The worker should be consistent toward the patient, but permissive in regard to broken and late appointments. He must be ready to handle emergency situations in the evenings or over weekends; and to call in others for clinical procedures. He must take a genuine interest in the alcoholic, so that he can meet the unending requests and tests without resentment. The social worker in this kind of work has to extend himself emotionally, countering the alcoholic patient's physical and psychic pain with extraordinary warmth and understanding. He should always keep in mind the great courage necessary for an alcoholic to take that first step toward altering his life. This effort, however faltering it may seem at times, must be supported by a very positive approach.

Patient-clinic Continuity

In group-centered rehabilitation of alcoholics, continuity is vital. Interruptions in treatment, harmful enough in any therapeutic endeavor, prove doubly disastrous here. Left to his own devices by a break in treatment routine—even if only for a day, sometimes—the patient is very likely to turn to drink. Hoff suggests why:

> Alcohol becomes for him a kind of universal therapy—a psychopharmacological substance through which he attempts to keep his life from disintegration. He uses alcohol to give him courage, to escape from intolerable decisions, to tranquilize his nervousness, to give a sense of meaning to life. The abnormal alcoholic use is, in fact, an attempt—usually unrecognized—to handle intrapsychic problems and life situations (3, p. 57).

Those responsible for intake, examination, and case work (and, later, all the other professionals involved in rehabilitation) must encourage the patient to continue his regular appointment hours, regularly. Once successful group placement has occurred and intensive psychotherapy begun, continuity of treatment is less of a problem. And, if a patient is found unsuitable for group psychotherapy, the supportive relationship with his case worker should be continued until he has been appropriately referred to another community resource.

The clinic setting must make the patient feel at home. Both professional and nonprofessional staff will have to learn to accept the patient as he is; and warm informality—particularly at reception—will help him over those first, all-important hurdles. Once the inquiring alcoholic has become the clinic's patient, every effort must be made to keep treatment continuous and consistent. Staff vacations, for one, should be arranged so that there will be no interference with the patient-clinic relationship. Closing the clinic over a summer, or for an extended Christmas vacation, is highly detrimental to rehabilitation; as is a large turnover in staff. No newcomers should be accepted for treatment unless there is enough personnel for consistent work with each patient.

More often than not, the case worker must ask other agencies to assist with the alcoholic and his family, since the alcoholic must feel he can call on his worker at any time to help with any problem— real or imaginary—facing him or his family. The case worker must also get in touch promptly with any patients who cancel appointments, or fail to meet psychiatric, psychological, vocational or medical appointments. At these times the worker must try to repair faltering relationships, or to rekindle motivation: whatever is needed to get the patient to continue his treatment. This close union of patient and case worker is essential to the alcoholic's rehabilitation. For a patient to accept the sometimes frightening suggestion that he have, for example, a physical examination and then come back to the clinic for continuing therapy and counsel, the worker's very close support and overt interest is a prime requisite.

Orientation and vocational counsel, if indicated, should be given just as soon as possible. This participation in other services will further cement the patient's tie to the treatment center (See this chapter, p. 124). The excessively discouraged or upset patient who absents himself from treatment groups, or turns away from the clinic altogether, should be sent—post-haste—letters encouraging continued treatment and offering further help.

The Alcoholic's Family and Friends Are Included

Unlike many other disturbances, alcoholism has severe and far-reaching social repercussions. The family, friends and associates of the chronic drinker are all adversely affected. Characteristically, the alcoholic—especially when he first begins drinking—engages the sympathy of those closely related to him, and manages to maneuver others to act in his behalf. Perhaps this is because reasoning, admonition, pleas and even threats are ineffectual; or perhaps because the alcoholic's piteous condition evokes compassion. And it may be related to the chronic seesaw of behavior the alcoholic rides: good intentions and promises of reform abruptly reversed to insobriety and antisocial behavior. In any event, family and friends find themselves involved in many ways with the patient's destructive progress: and they will want very much to learn about alcoholism—in order to help with the patient's rehabilitation, and for their own reassurance. Few other disturbances have the terrible effect on family structure, morale and health, as alcoholism does. Mary Richmond, in 1930, appropriately included both the patient's family and associates as the case work focus:

> Social case work may be defined as the art of doing different things for different people by cooperating with them to achieve at one and the same time their own and society's betterment (4, p. 374).

The social worker will have to counsel the patient's family, and at times confer with immediate associates, so that the alcoholic will accept the rehabilitation offered and pursue it in spite of its difficulties. In this way the patient, his family, and society all benefit.

Case work with those ancillary to the patient may occur prior to, during, or even after the alcoholic begins to participate in the treatment. Concern may be shown by a husband or wife, or a close associate who notices increased drinking accompanied by strange behavior in the alcoholic. Initial service occurs when the social worker talks to this other person, paving the way for the alcoholic to come to the center and accept aid. Members of the patient's family can give detailed information concerning the form and extent of the drinking problem; and at the same time, the worker has the opportunity to explain the nature of alcoholism and to enlist support in having the patient accept rehabilitation.

In the group-oriented treatment center, the patient, his family, and close friends are offered a series of lectures concerning alcoholism. The intake worker may suggest that interested persons participate with the patients in this orientation group, which teaches the cause, course and consequences of alcoholism by means of lectures and demonstrations (see Chapter V). The first purpose of orientation is eradication of the patient's misconceptions, and replacement with facts. But, even more important, orientation is designed to increase the patient's motivation for rehabilitation and to stimulate him (and his family) to constructive and practical involvement.

Even though this kind of orientation is available in the agency, the social worker is still involved in working with the family of the alcoholic, re-educating them and helping to alleviate their stress. Many times, the worker is called upon to explain the nature of psychoanalytic group psychotherapy. Confusion, fear, and opposition must be overcome: There is often great anxiety that the patient in group treatment will not only reveal himself, but will reveal details about those people he is close to. The social worker's job is to establish confidence, by reassuring the family that, whatever is divulged during the group sessions, it will go no further and will never be a cause of embarrassment. Unduly pessimistic—and, sometimes, even optimistic—ideas concerning the outcome of group psychotherapy must also be countered with more realistic goals.

Frequently, it is found that a nonalcoholic member of the family has deep-seated problems compounding the alcoholic's own difficulties. In such cases, the worker should suggest psychotherapy for this person, either in the center or in another agency. Social case work or group "case work" should be reserved for those nonalcoholic members of the patient's family who have relatively few and not deeply-ingrained conflicts.

KNOWLEDGE, UNDERSTANDING AND CONCERN

Introduction

Evaluation of the alcoholic's personality and behavior followed by case work requires that the social worker use special knowledge and understanding of his condition. The alcoholic's behavior must be accepted without moralizing on the worker's part. Unless these conditions are met, the worker cannot properly use his skills to meet the alcoholic's needs: nor will he be able to stimulate the patient to further self-examination.

The social worker who is interested in working in the field of alcoholism can learn about it by reading texts and clinical papers; attending seminars; or taking special courses. One of the last is given at the Summer Institute, Rutgers University, Center of Alcohol Studies. (See Selected Readings pp. 132).

It is important to know and understand not only the interpersonal and intrapsychic conflicts created by excessive use of alcohol, but also what chronic drinking does to the alcoholic's functioning and behavior. Basic, of course, is the acceptance of the fact that alcoholism is an *illness* with a compulsive drinking component; and that this illness involves social, cultural, emotional, physical, and spiritual areas of its victim's life. The truly aware and understanding worker will look beyond the overdrinking and will see that the alcoholic is a person bent upon destroying his own life. Hoff describes three basic elements in alcoholism:

> First, there is a loss of control of alcohol intake, an essential symptom, signalling the onset of clinically discernible alcoholism. The victim finds himself drinking when he intended not to drink and drinking more than he has planned . . .
>
> Second, there is functional or structural damage. This damage may be psysiological, psychological, domestic, economic, social, or, frequently, a combination of several of these . . .
>
> The third criterion in this definition of alcoholism centers around the clinical fact that an alcoholic uses alcohol to try to satisfy abnormal needs (3, p. 57).

In order to pave the way for the successful introduction of an alcoholic patient into the therapeutic group, his social worker must know his characteristic patterns, his attitudes toward society, and the degree of deterioration in his present interpersonal functioning. Typical of the alcoholic seeking treatment is that he tends to act out, to express intense guilt feelings, and to displace his inner conflict to the outside by persistently rationalizing. Other neurotic and psychotic patients display this sort of behavior; in the alcoholic it is much more pronounced. The worker should keep an eye out for behavior patterns which suggest extreme dependency, insecurity, and generalized tension, accompanied by feelings of despair, remorse, isolation, and rejection. Peltenburg, discovering her own blind spots in case work with alcoholics, pinpoints an important characteristic of the alcoholic's symptomatology:

> I began to see that my difficulty in treating alcoholic patients arose not from any qualitative difference between their emotional problems and those of other patients, but from the peculiar intensity and urgency of these problems in alcoholics, which not only necessitated modifications in therapeutic approach, but which also exposed the therapist to certain pitfalls in the area of his own reaction. Such pitfalls had to be taken into account and dealt with effectively if the therapist was to be helpful to the patient. For instance, the alcoholic patient often feels demoralized and hopeless to such an extent that his demoralization can become

conveyed to the therapist who then feels helpless and easily becomes defensive and critical. The extreme degree of dependency and helplessness displayed by the patient, the degree of demandingness and manipulation, of quiet sabotage and expectance of a magic cure without participation can wear down and exasperate the therapist who is not always sufficiently aware that this patient, overwhelmed with guilt, self-condemnation, expects and "needs" rejection. And since the alcoholic patient is an unsurpassed master at provoking rejection he only too frequently succeeds in doing so (5, pp. 2-3).

The alcoholic is not committed to life and its responsibilities as are —hopefully—most other people. He needs to demand (and receive) special attention; he must manipulate those around him. He tests continuously to see if he is liked and is very sensitive to the least sign of rejection. The alcoholic's low threshold of frustration very often provokes his impulsive and unreliable behavior. He will express inordinate self-esteem at the same moment he is degrading himself. Mainly, he is bent on destruction—of himself and of others, especially those who most care for him.

The Personal Equation of the Social Worker

The social worker dealing with alcoholic patients must become aware of his own attitude toward alcoholism in general and toward the alcoholic problem of any patient in particular. When there are other agencies treating nonalcoholics, why has he chosen to work with this kind of difficult and demanding patient and with all the immensely challenging problems of his illness? Self-examination and self-evaluation is vital—and might well begin with the worker's inventory of his particular attitudes about drinking, its cause, and its immediate and cumulative effects. The questions are simple (although their answers may be far from that): "Why *do* I drink?" ... "What does it do for me?" ... or, perhaps, "Why *don't* I drink?" ... "Am I afraid of it?" ... and so forth. It is also helpful to apply these questions to others: to discover how he feels about drinking done by his family or friends or both. Self-analysis becomes somewhat easier in a group atmosphere, such as a weekly interactional meeting of the entire staff of the clinic (See Chapter II, pp. 50-54). Fink suggests going a step further—from self-help to psychoanalysis.

He refers specifically to psychotherapists about to plunge into the treatment of alcoholics; but his ideas apply equally well to the social worker in the same situation:

> It is obvious that the psychotherapist needs to be well analyzed so that he does not take personally the "insults" and other antagonistic expressions of the patient, particularly during the usually more stormy initial sessions. The doctor's unsuccessful struggle with his counter-transference feelings and realistic antipathies toward his negativistic, "bad boy" patient, may destroy any possibility of improvement of the patient's condition, causing him to bolt from treatment (6, pp. 184).

The case worker will want to achieve an optimum relationship with this very difficult patient, of course. That is why he should do his best to find out if his attitudes about drinking are the same or different from those held by the community; whether or not he passes judgment or moralizes, or is hostile or disgusted by drunkeness. He may discover actions or reactions in himself from overidentification or flat rejection. Whatever is revealed, it is better to know these things before becoming involved in the treatment of alcoholics. As Fink says:

> The personal qualifications of the ideal therapist for the alcoholic patient includes: a sense of ease with alcoholics rather than hostility and strong counter-transference effects, a natural warmth and friendliness, strength and firmness without authoritarianism, and permissive understanding without condescension (6, pp. 183-184).

The Challenge

The social worker who has gained his experience with quite a different kind of patient will find the alcoholic a challenge, both to himself as case worker and to his treatment techniques (which he may find a bit too rigid for success with his alcoholic patient.) This patient's immature behavior, his poor motivation for treatment, his impossible goals in life, and his constant recourse to drink make him extremely difficult to work with, and reduce his chances for a successful outcome to treatment. Merely keeping him in the rehabilitation center (so as to move him into the therapeutic group) demands a great deal of flexibility in technical procedure plus a willingness to risk the different, the unexpected, the radical. It is the different attempt, the unexpected method and the radical approach which very often "reach" the alcoholic and stir him into action.

The ease with which we are able to categorize the patient who drinks compulsively is deceptive. The best of diagnoses cannot indicate how he is apt to behave—at any stage of his treatment and particularly under stress. Some patients, for example, are obviously depressed, anxious, or hostile. Others will cover up and act overly pleasant and ingratiating. Many are defensive, acutely sensitive, suspicious, evasive, or provocative. Many are passive or passively aggressive.

However, there *are* patterns of behavior common to many alcoholics, no matter what the underlying personality structure. One is the inappropriate lack of concern over the chaos he is creating—in his own life as well as in others'. And the alcoholic patient can be depended upon to act out. Of course, the longer he has been drinking, the greater the degree of deterioration; and the greater the deterioration, the more difficult it is to obtain a coherent history or to make the proper evaluation of an experience as the patient describes it.

Bacon, in giving the clinical picture of the alcoholic, emphasizes the patient's pain, immaturity, and extreme ego-centricity—and the inherent difficulties in treating him:

> The pain is not merely or even importantly related to the physical aspects of his condition or the inconveniences occasioned by his type of life. It is centered around his inner feelings of self-depreciation, self-hate, self-pity, guilt, and all-encompassing remorse. Since he cannot explain this, he often attempts to hide it. Pain, however, is the constant comrade of the alcoholic. And a dreadful (in the real meaning of the term) comrade it is.
>
> The immaturity of the alcoholic may be illustrated by his rapid mood swings, superficially sly rationalizations, adolescent self-consciousness, magnificent ideals which are almost inevitably linked with minuscule accomplishments, and juvenile techniques of hiding bottles, lying about drinking, and wheedling pity and free drinks.
>
> The alcoholic generally lacks interest in anything outside of himself and his problems. Such outside interests as he may mani-

fest are usually temporary and directly and immediately related to a desire to show off or achieve some quick benefit. His continual comparison of all things to himself, easy cynicism about anything not connected to himself, self-pity, intense feelings of guilt, and increasingly solitary existance, all bear witness to his egocentricity (7, p. 2).

Even though egocentric, the alcoholic will avoid any consideration of his inner self and particularly any inner striving for healthful change. Self-evaluation is a most remote prospect, as far as he is concerned; yet it is the very goal toward which the case worker must urge him. The worker knows that self-questioning cannot possibly begin until the patient stops his drinking. If, however, the worker bluntly presents the alcoholic with this truth—that he will never be fit for rehabilitation unless he becomes and remains sober—the chances are very good indeed that the treatment center will find itself with one less alcoholic patient. What, then, is the case worker to do?

In the rehabilitation center devoted to group psychotherapy, the social worker is not forced to cope with this dilemma all alone. As soon as possible, even on the first visit, the patient is placed in an orientation group, where he is very likely to learn the facts of his condition and, incidentally, something about himself. (See Chapter V) One of the hoped-for and expected results of orientation is sobriety, or at least an attempt at it on the patient's part, which of course makes the social worker's job that much easier. Orientation has a snowballing effect: as the patient tries harder to fight his problem in a realistic way, he becomes more and more open to suggestions from his case worker that he continue to sober up, continue to attend orientation lectures; and the longer the patient continues, the more amenable he becomes to *further* suggestions for his own rehabilitation.

The center also takes for granted that its alcoholic patients have vocational problems of one kind or another. And many patients are willing to admit that drinking has been a source of job failure, or of lack of interest and low achievement in daily work. It is a wise move at this point for the case worker to show his patient the great value of vocational counseling, and to get him to the vocational counselor as quickly as possible. Once there, the alcoholic will be assured and reassured by the counselor that the clinic is concerned with his difficulties in this practical area of life, too; and will do everything possible to help him overcome them by helping him overcome his compulsive need for drink.

No worker in an alcoholic treatment center should ever feel that he alone is being plagued by his all-too-often recalcitrant patients. Every member of the staff will have to deal with the alcoholic's tardiness, missed appointments, and last-minute cancellations. However annoying, this behavior must be seen for what it is: an indication of the patient's pathological functioning, his lack of responsibility, and his sense of worthlessness. He therefore cannot be handled vindictively. The same holds true of periodic slipping-back into drunkenness. While no staff member would ever show approval of such a lapse, it is well-known—even expected, sometimes—that frustration or extreme anxiety will often cause an alcoholic to relapse.

All in all, the alcoholic patient is quite evasive, and tends to terminate his clinic relationships abruptly. During the beginning stages, especially, the social worker will find that he must chase after reluctant and resistant patients, and encourage them to come back for continued treatment—not an easy task and one that may involve telephone calls, telegrams, letters, conversations with family, friends, business associates and neighbors, and—very often—tedious leg-work. Later on, the problem will be slipping-back, with attendant "disappearances." In *any* stage of treatment, the social worker will find himself facing, every day, patients who are incoherent, or boisterous, or maudlin, or drunk, or hung over, or something else. His best bet is to think of each situation as a special case, and to treat it according to the patient's position in the rehabilitation effort, what is known about him, and his physical condition at the moment. The firm and positive approach will work best in caring for the immediate problem and in persuading the patient that *he* wants to continue (or return) very soon, and in a better state.

The Solid Therapeutic Front

The group-centered agency presents a solid treatment philosophy to the alcoholic, offering him a consistent, constructive environment to make up for and to replace the malignant climate he has been living in up to now.

Any staff aiming for this ideal unity of purpose and plan must work with a high degree of interdisciplinary cooperation (See Chapter II, pp. 50-54). The social worker's role in maintaining this kind of teamwork has been described often. Strayer, for example, says:

> We can readily see that the social worker's role in the treatment of the alcoholic is a rather vital one but that his contribution is part of a tri-interdisciplinary approach to the total treatment experience. He must learn how to relate to and constructively employ the other team members in the same setting as they must also know how to effectively use the social worker's skills in the treatment of the alcoholic. The manner in which all three disciplines are effectively integrated will in part determine the success or failure in reaching the alcoholic and sustaining his motivation in an effective continued use of the clinic's services (8, p. 28).

It is important that the alcoholic patient realize at the outset that this corrective environment has been planned for his *benefit* and will not be used against him. As Price observes: "Some patients, treated by the team approach, may feel themselves 'important' while others may feel 'everybody is against me' " (9, pp. 161-162).

From the very first, it is the social worker who calms the anxious patient by describing and explaining the team approach; and answering the patient's questions with sympathy. He prepares the patient for his eventual meetings with the orientator, group psychotherapist, vocational counselor, and clinical psychologist. By individualizing his approach from case to case, the worker can point out the benefits and pinpoint the usefulness of whichever procedures apply especially well to a particular case.

This preparation does not end, though, with an interpretation of the agency's services. The case worker will also be called on to encourage acceptance of hospitalization, physical examinations, and laboratory tests; and to urge his alcoholic patient to meet immediately with an Alcoholics Anonymous sponsor; or to visit a pastoral counselor of his faith; or to start visits with a marriage counselor. In any and all cases, the social worker's consistent efforts give the alcoholic his first taste of what a therapeutic relationship *really* is like; and, hopefully, gains the patient's trust so that his future participation in a therapeutic group is assured.

Since the case worker deals with his patients from start to finish of treatment—as many of his fellow-workers working within different disciplines do not—it is imperative that he share information with the rest of the staff. And this does not mean objective appraisal *alone;* any proper treatment must also take into account the social worker's own personal feelings about his patients and, of course, any subjective response to them from the patients. This interplay of responses is very meaningful and must become one of the subjects discussed during weekly staff meetings—for information or so that any necessary corrective action can be instituted without delay (See Chapter II, pp. 50-54). From this multidisciplined cooperativeness, the social worker broadens his understanding of alcoholism and also gets support and encouragement in his work from colleagues.

THE SOCIAL WORK EVALUATION
OF THE ALCOHOLIC

Introduction

Case work with alcoholics—and we cannot stress this point too often—is a many-faceted job. The case worker will find himself operating on several different levels at once: a very real and very stimulating challenge.

To begin with, he is responsible for finding the way or ways to keep the alcoholic *with* the agency. Generally, the best method is to accept the patient's concept of help or need—(however unrealistic it may seem to be)—and to assure him that this agency will provide him with what he wants. Actually, this is *not* a deception; the clinic offers such a diversity of approach that, more often than not, even the most unusual demands can be met in one way or another. This built-in eclecticism will stand the social worker in very good stead as he encourages the patient to try first one approach and then another and still another. While the patient is receiving some initial assistance, a strong patient-clinic bond is being established: and it is this bond which will hold the patient in treatment long after he has given up some of his favorite fantasies.

At the same time, the clinic's social worker must convince his patient that the clinic, its workers, its services, philosophy, and methods are all devoted to *him:* his care, treatment, recovery, and betterment. In many cases, tangible evidence of the clinic's good will is called for: mostly in the form of money, freely offered to alleviate immediate and real emergency situations (eviction, starvation or near-starvation, and the like) which might interrupt or halt treatment. And while all this is going on, the social worker is also suggesting—tentatively and cautiously—that the patient begin to try to look at himself and his problems objectively.

One might think this were quite enough for one person to handle at one time. Perhaps in some cases, it is. In the alcoholic's case, though, the social worker is involved in yet *another* level of involvement: It is up to him to evaluate the group-therapy potential of each patient. This examination is judgmental and will determine the immediate disposition of a patient. From the case worker's reports, decisions will be made on whether the patient remains in the clinic or is referred elsewhere; whether or not he is ready for orientation; whether or not he is ready to see the group psychotherapist; and— if not ready for any of these—approximately when he *will* be.

Not infrequently, the worker will decide during the very first interview that physical manifestations of the patient's illness must be tended to before there can be any hope of success through psychological intervention. If this is his evaluation, then he must see to it that immediate medical consulation (or hospitalization) is arranged for; and, if it is called for, must accompany the patient to the appointment to make sure he actually gets there. Or perhaps an initial interview will bring out a serious job crisis in the offing. A visit to the vocational counselor is called for, without delay, so that patient, social worker, and counselor can set about to avert any impending disaster.

Whatever the *particular* problems, all patients should of course be urged to join the clinic's orientation group. Needless to say, this urging comes from the social worker. He is the alcoholic's prime-mover; and, throughout the patient's sojurn in the clinic, will continue to be available, to listen, discuss, or advise.

Evaluation Method

Even though evaluation is distinctly the function of the case worker, it can neither be separated from the overall rehabilitative efforts of the entire staff, nor can it be isolated from preparation for group therapy (See Chapter VIII, p. 210).

As a matter of fact, the social worker should start his evaluation of each patient for possible group therapy participation, from the very first inquiry. Prognosis, of course, will tend to be better if the patient has come to the clinic on his own.

Considering how debilitated, both physically and psychologically, the alcoholic generally is; and how meager his motivation for treatment even in the *best* of circumstances, a feeling of discouragement may color the first meeting. The case worker must not, however, become disheartened if group placement seems impossible right then and there; actually, any dynamic psychiatric intervention would be pointless with a patient in the midst of a severe physical or social crisis. If he is drunk, or suffering a severe hangover, the chances are that the rigors of group therapeutic interaction would be just too much for him to take.

Other kinds of situation also preclude any immediate placement of the alcoholic into a therapeutic group. A real emergency may exist in the patient's life: The family is threatening to leave him; or he has no place to sleep; or he is so depressed as to be actively suicidal. Direct and prompt assistance is called for, and it is the social worker's job to offer and give it. The important result of the worker's efficiency in alleviating the severe reality problem is the confidence his patient feels in him. The quick relief given, helps to pave the way for establishment of a treatment bond; and once this positive relationship exists, the worker can better stimulate the patient to accept the other services offered in the treatment center.

There is, then, a screening-out process inherent in first meetings. Some patients are only temporarily unsuited for the concerted rehabilitative efforts of the staff; and may return for rehabilitation after a prolonged hospital stay. Others will have to be eliminated permanently at intake: those unfortunates who, in the judgment of the social worker, could consider treatment, but adamantly refuse any help whatsoever. Many of these are confused by identifying the treatment center with other, unsuccessful, treatment experiences in the past. As Krimmel and Falkey have observed:

> Alcoholics do not find a ready welcome in most agencies and clinics. There are probably several reasons for this, but prominent among them is the strongly entrenched notion that, without

exception, alcoholics require long months or even years of treatment. If intake is open to many of these applicants, therefore, they will remain interminably, clutter up the case load, and exclude from service other clients and patients whose prognosis is more favorable (10, p. 25).

The best practice is to go along with these resistant patients, referring them elsewhere if need be. The social worker might attempt to persuade them to return at some future time, when an offer of help would more likely be accepted. In any case, and in every instance, *whatever disposition or referral is made, all steps must be taken in a nonrejecting manner. The patient must always feel that only interest and continuing concern for his welfare dictates his being sent elsewhere; and that, furthermore, he is not being sent "away" but only being sent to immediate help.* Implied in this disposition is the possibility of his return when he is in better condition. Take the following case, for example:

> Mr. S. came to the center without an appointment. He was very upset and so was given an emergency appointment. He stated that he had fears of hospitalization and of psychiatric help. He would make plans to receive treatment while sober, but just before the appointment, would start drinking and never show up. The social worker supported him throughout this interview and after evaluating his total condition, decided that Mr. S. should be hospitalized It was suggested that he accept help from Alcoholics Anonymous and then commit himself voluntarily to a state hospital. This he did, staying for a year, after which he returned to the center. This time, he was ready for group psychotherapy and so was offered it.

What of those who *are* in good enough condition to be admitted for treatment? This process of intake is much like that used by other agencies: The social worker records the patient's age, marital status, address, employment, and the source of his referral to the agency; then proceeds to describe what rehabilitative services are available to him. However, the technique used, both for getting and giving information, is a bit different. He must be handled with care and caution. Presentation of the clinic's services must be worded so that the new patient will not see the treatment task as insurmountable.

Social workers should not be discouraged if, despite their best efforts, the new patient appears uncooperative and uncommunicative. This is to be expected because of the alcoholic's special problem; and very often—depending on his degree of insobriety and agitation—the required information, in sufficient detail, will need more than one visit with the social worker to complete the patient-profile. And actually, this seeming difficulty can be turned to the worker's advantage by giving him more time and opportunity for establishing a solid bond with the patient.

Throughout the necessary intake sessions the social worker will also be compiling a social history of his patient. This is not the easiest task in the world, but it can be done; and is an essential part of treatment, since it will be used as an index of the patient's social adjustment. There is no "trick" to obtaining the necessary information; it is a case of asking a series of questions (sometimes over and over again) with unremitting patience, tact, and sympathy; and with relentless, though kind, perseverance. Considerable flexibility in the method used to ask for information is called for, since alcoholics exhibit such variable behavior. It is also wise to be flexible in deciding the relative importance of content: Anyone working with alcoholics must expect his patients to use—in varying degrees—denial, confusion, rationalization, evasion, manipulation, and whatever else may seem useful to avoid giving information of any real value. By staying mentally resilient, the social worker can remain one step ahead of the patient, and *get* the information he needs.

Items of Social History

The typical alcoholic social history emphasizes the patient's drinking habits and bizarre behavior; and so is very unlike the profiles of other kinds of patients. The treatment team must know, for example, the patient's deterioration in social adjustment, his capacity for self-evaluation, and the amount of responsibility he is willing or able to take on. The following items are pertinent to the alcoholic patient's social history:

1) *Identifying Information*: name, present and previous addresses, telephone number, age, marital status, next of kin and *his* address.

2) *Referral*: date and source of referral.

3) *Presenting Situation*: the patient's interpretation of his presenting problem, and the social worker's impression of his appearance and motivation.

4) *Drinking History*: first drink and circumstances; the patient's explanation of when drinking became a problem.

5) *Drinking Pattern*: what does he generally drink; how much; and the character of his drinking: daily, periodic binges, weekends only, sporadic, or whatever.

6) *Information Related to Drinking*: personality changes, violent behavior, blackouts, delirium tremens, psychotic episodes, depression, activity leading to arrest by police, length of periods of sobriety, and any other facts traceable to the patient's drinking.

7) *Remedial efforts*: any experience with A.A; private or clinic psychiatric treatment; medical or psychiatic hospitalization; periods spent in rest homes; recourse to medications (Antabuse, tranquilizers, or others;) social, vocational, pastoral, marital or other counseling.

8) *Physical Health*: present and previous illnesses; frequency of visits with family physician(s); and names and addresses of all physicians.

9) *Personal and Family History*: any drinking in the family (other than the patient); the family's background and various relationships; the current family and marital situation.

10) *Educational Status*: extent of education presently, and any future plans.

11) *Religious Background*: the patient's attitude toward his faith; his participation within the religious group or the church/synogogue.

12) *Recreational Activities*: any volunteer work; membership in any organizations; friendships; hobbies; or particular interests.

13) *Economic Situation*: former and current sources of income.

14) *Vocational History*: employment record, past and present; any vocational problems, past and present.

The Capacity to Relate

After obtaining this information, the case worker, in conjunction with other staff members, determines the patient's capacity to relate. It has been found that this ability has four aspects: (1) relating to self; (2) relating to family; (3) relating to friends; (4) relating to the community. By using very rough quantitative terms, such as "almost absent capacity," "fair capacity," and "some capacity," the effects of drinking in vital areas of the patient's existence can be gauged. While this kind of appraisal is far from exact, it can and does give the staff a good idea of the patient's readiness for a particular rehabilitation service; and, in fact, a clue to his overall prognosis.

(1) Relation to Self

When evaluating the alcoholic's self-relating capacity, the social worker should keep an especially sharp eye out for the following "signals:"

The source of referral which may range from the patient himself to friend or spouse, doctor, agency or A.A., or anyone else who is worried about his drinking and behavior. The patient will generally reflect the nature of his referral which may be a suggestion of a forceful coercion. He may be considered under mild duress if he has been referred to the center for compassionate reasons. However, if he is here because of an irate wife who threatens divorce; an employer who threatens job loss; or has been remanded by the courts to the clinic in lieu of a jail sentence, (in short, has been *forced* to seek therapy) his duress is much greater.

Motivation and insight can be ascertained by seeing whether the patient is aware of his problems or denies them; whether he understands the consequences of his drinking or not; and whether or not—and to what degree—he desires to correct his condition.

Commitment to appointments is one of the easier signals to spot. The amount of responsibility will run the gamut from punctuality and dependability, through frequent and inexcusable cancellations made at the last moment, habitual lateness, to total "disappearance"—with or without excuses.

Appearance speaks for itself, by evidence of care, thought, neatness, and appropriateness of dress; or the converse.

(2) Relation to Family

The patient's social history will show those key factors generally used to determine his relative capacity to relate within the family, to the family.

Family contact, for example, falls into three categories: constant; inconstant (in those cases where the patient keeps in touch infrequently by telephone, letters, or very occasional visits); and nonexistent, in which case there has been a definite separation or the patient has simply absented himself altogether.

Participation in family life can—in the same way as mentioned above—be full, limited, or nonexistent.

Intrafamilial activity and behavior is generally regarded as good, if it is about average for the average family; should be marked as poor, if there is continuous conflict, hostility, and argument; and finally, very bad in the case of frequent explosions of violence.

Responsible support (or the lack of it) is the last signal of the alcoholic's ability to relate to his (or her) family. The male patient is judged by the degree of financial responsibility he takes: total, partial, or none at all. If the patient is a married woman, her history should be examined for the amount of responsibility she assumes for her household duties; and this can be anywhere on the scale from complete responsibility, to some or sporadic neglect, to total neglect.

(3) Relation to Friends

The alcoholic's social adjustment is also determined by the number and kinds of friends he now has and has had in the past. The presence or absence of enduring friendships is significant.

Types of friends: are they men? women? children? drinking or nondrinking? occasional? casual? or has the patient no friends at all?

Degree of friendship will show duration, as well as the relative depth (or superficiality) of the patient's relationships with others.

(4) Relation to Community

The patient's social adjustment to his community can be judged by:

Community awareness and interest, which will depend upon his degree of involvement in the surrounding social environment (block, neighborhood, city, etc.). He may be apathetic, or may respond distortedly to what he considers hostile pressures in his community.

Group activity—membership in and attendance at social, political, or religious organizations—will range from moderate and consistent activity, to no attendance or interest whatsoever.

Use of resources within the community, including cultural, recreational, and medical institutions, varies from a great dependence upon one or more (including hospitals and clinics) to no use of any resource, for any reason, at any time.

Recognition of Integrative and Disintegrative Forces

The social worker at intake will have to be alert to signs—overt and subtle—of both integration and disintegration within the prospective patient's personality. Recognizing those factors operating in the alcoholic's struggle with life—and specifically in his control over drinking—is essential if the patient's initial disposition is to be of the greatest possible benefit to him. Even though the social worker will be assisted in this task by other staff members, he will want to know what major signals to look for.

Personality factors which suggest an integration process in the patient, center about the kind and degree of the patient's adjustments to the realities of his situation: the extent to which he is properly functioning in his family, his job, and in community groups. Adjustment, as such, is not nearly so important a consideration in the treatment of nonalcoholics by psychotherapy or psychoanalysis. For the alcoholic who is to participate in group psychotherapy in an office or treatment center some adjustment is a necessity. The more-adjusted alcoholic, who is able to meet at least some of life's demands, is very apt to accept and cooperate with rehabilitation; and has a better chance of withstanding the pressures of various clinic groups, including the interactional therapy group.

Integrative forces in the personality will show themselves by the alcoholic's recognition of his problems, and by the care he has already taken, on his own, not to let himself disintegrate entirely. If he takes care of himself—pays attention to his physical health, his appearance and dress—he is giving a positive sign. Past attempts to stay sober, or past experiences in psychotherapy also indicate integrative forces at work. He may state and understand that he has both a drinking and a personality difficulty. He may appear to be more or less committed to bettering his life-situation. He may even (not frequently, unfortunately) be clear and realistic about the goals of his group therapy and vocational counseling. If his family life is still intact; if his job is more or less stable; if he has at least a few friends of long standing who care for him; and if he participates, at least to a degree, in some sort of social activities, constructive forces probably balance the destructive ones.

Disintegrative forces are much more obvious and will be easily recognized, probably, the first time the patient comes to the center. For example, he may appear for his interview, drunk and unkempt; may seem undernourished or physically ill. Further indications of severe disintegration are: ambivalence about treatment (especially from a patient so ill and in so much trouble); manipulation tried with everyone; continued and dangerous acting out; and, sometimes, suicidal preoccupation. In the last-mentioned case, there can no longer be any question; this patient's destructive potential has gained almost complete control. More subtle signs of deep-seated problems are marital discord, financial mismanagement, inability to make and keep friends, and no group participation of any kind. The alcoholic's history of help sought (or not sought) will also give meaningful clues to the degree of his self-isolation. Any patient who has repeatedly rejected the assistance of Alcoholics Anonymous, spiritual counsel, and any form of guidance usually proves difficult in group psychotherapy.

THE TREATMENTS OF CHOICE:
GROUP PSYCHOTHERAPY AND VOCATIONAL COUNSELING
Introduction

We cannot reiterate too often how significant a role the case worker plays in guiding the alcoholic patient to acceptance of rehabilitation. If the worker has chosen a rehabilitation center which is group-centered, then he himself must be firmly convinced—in his own mind—that the alcoholic needs group psychotherapy and vocational counseling if he is to overcome his special difficulties. Any social worker who finds himself "hedging," even in the privacy of his own thoughts, will not be able to advocate these treatment measures in a proper, positive and convincing manner. Therefore, it is important to clarify, at this point, the aims and methods of these two disciplines, from the social worker's viewpoint; and also to show what may (and sometimes does) happen when the "positive and convincing" manner is pushed too hard. (For goals and methods, see Chapter III.)

The alcoholic is confused about what he needs, and is generally afraid of therapy—all kinds of therapy. The idea of individual psychotherapy, especially psychoanalysis, which calls for careful, continuous, long-term self-inquiry, with very frequent and regular appointments, is particularly discouraging to this patient who operates in the realm of fantasy and on the principle of immediate gratification. Before sending an alcoholic to see the group psychotherapist, the case worker will have to spend a number of hours helping to alleviate the patient's worries and doubts; and it is during this period that many alcoholics leave the center because of too much pressure to see the evaluating group psychotherapist (which is the necessary first step in group placement.)

The following precis shows a patient during an initial interview, her defensive rationalizations coupled with unawareness of how severe her illness is, plus a fear of personal commitment. This example will also serve to show the effects of a too-precipitous push toward group psychotherapy on the part of the social worker—who might have waited until the patient had established a relationship with the clinic.

> Mrs. C. phoned for an appointment; she had obtained the agency's address from the telephone directory. She was outgoing, made a good appearance, was articulate, but also very defensive. She said it was difficult to talk to a social worker as she was one herself. She wanted psychiatric help for her drinking, which she felt was only a symptom of other problems. She had already had individual psychotherapy the year before, in an alcoholic clinic in a nearby city, but was forced to stop treatment because of her return to New York. Mrs. C. was concerned about financing therapy (a usual complaint and source of diffi-

culty with alcoholic patients); and, in addition, she was reluctant to give time to her rehabilitation, feeling that she would be taking this time away from her family. She said she could not count on her husband's support because he was sick—and would be made worse, should he realize that she needed treatment.

Even though the patient stated a preference for individual therapy, which is unusual for the alcoholic, the social worker suggested that she see the group therapist and then, if possible, immediately enter a therapy group. Mrs. C. felt that she "could never face talking in a group about personal things," a typical objection of patients during preparation for group introduction. Ignoring this clue, however, the social worker set up an appointment for Mrs. C., with the group psychotherapist. Three days later, Mrs. C. called, saying she did not want group therapy at this point: and, even though she was encouraged to return to the center, she stayed away. Nothing further was ever heard from Mrs. C., although the worker attempted to reach her by phone from time to time.

Sometimes a patient will help solve the touchy problem of staff pressure to start rehabilitation, by admitting to a difficulty at work—generally believing that this work problem is not *his* fault, and perhaps not the fault of his drinking, either. In such cases, the patient is very likely to accept an appointment with the vocational counselor—thus starting him into rehabilitation, almost without his realizing it. In all cases, if the intake worker sees that the patient facing him is very uneasy about the idea of psychotherapy, and if the patient has any job difficulty whatsoever he should try the vocational-service tack, telling the patient what it is and how it can help him. Social workers will find that, whether or not a given patient wants vocational counseling during the earlier stages of rehabilitation, in the long run he usually will take advantage of it.

In a recent demonstration and treatment project, jointly sponsored by the National Council on Alcoholism and the Office of Vocational Rehabilitation of The Department of Health, Education and Welfare, investigators early came to the realization that active vocational counseling is a necessary part of any psychological or physical rehabilitation program for the alcoholic (11, 12, 13). They found that almost all patients said that the disruption of vocational and avocational pursuits was one of the most important consequences of their drinking.

Approaching an alcoholic via vocational counseling, however, does not guarantee successful results:

> Miss N. was referred to the agency by a friend, a member of Alcoholics Anonymous. She had been told that she could get vocational help. The social worker carefully outlined all the services available to her in the center—emphasizing group psychological evaluation and vocational counseling as well. Miss N. seemed overwhelmed by this mass of information and said that she only wanted to get a new job. It is very possible that the idea of participating in group psychotherapy was introduced too soon, and that the contemplation of all these services proved too complex and confusing for Miss N. At any rate—even though she admitted that alcoholism had played a part in her job failure—she never showed up for her vocational counseling appointment; and never—insofar as the agency knows—continued in a rehabilitation program.

The Basis of the Social Worker's Conviction about Group Psychotherapy

We have found that group psychotherapy is central to the alcoholic's total rehabilitation. An intensive group-treatment program provides a coherent and pervasive psychological influence which: (1) assures compliance with all the various rehabilitative measures and (2) supports the patient's self-reevaluation and change, by allowing for:

1. Dynamic intrapsychic and interpersonal change, so that sobriety may be achieved and retained.

2. Careful and individualized personality regression followed by reintegration, with a replacement of the tendency to *react* (act out) by a tendency to *act* (self-act) in his own behalf.

3. Access to, and intervention in, unconscious processes; while at the same time offering help, through example and admonition, in impulse control.

4. A constructive and consistent family anologue, different in kind and influence from the faulty biological family, which affirms the

patient's worth through the giving of understanding, acceptance, respect, and love; and assures him that he belongs.

5. A safe testing-ground for reality, where responsibility and commitment to self, family, and society can be sought, encouraged, and found.

The Basis of the Social Worker's Conviction about Vocational Counselling

Social workers in alcoholism centers soon see for themselves just how important vocational counseling is, to these patients. Just because a patient takes part in the therapeutic group for awhile, it does not follow that his work problems will automatically clear up. While this indirect approach to reality problems has been found feasible with other patients, it does not work with the alcoholic. Because the alcoholic is so terribly vulnerable, every setback—in his family or in the community, through job failure or job frustration— delivers such a powerful blow to him that the repercussions usually include discontinuance of rehabilitation.

Briefly, then, the alcoholic patient requires effective vocational counsel because:

1. His job history shows a level of work far below his potential, constant dissatisfaction, and frequent changes.

2. Unemployment or unsatisfactory employment can be disastrous, leading the patient back to insobriety and away from the treatment center.

3. Estrangement from his family, his community, and his rehabilitation, are directly related to his employment status.

4. Self-esteem and self-affirmation are directly related to job interest and creativity.

THE TIMELY USE OF SUPPLEMENTARY RESOURCES

Introduction

A large proportion of alcoholic patients refuse systematic rehabilitation. This unfortunate circumstance, disturbing to all who work with this patient, can sometimes be changed. We have tried to show the ways in which we found that the greatest number of alcoholics could be encouraged to try group psychotherapy and be sufficiently motivated to remain in treatment.

What happens, though, to the patients who continue to refuse help? and to those who are judged to be so acutely ill—psychologically or physically—that they will be unable to cope with group psychotherapy or vocational counsel? What becomes of those alcoholics who, once having started therapy and counsel, leave treatment prematurely? (See Chapter XIII, pp. 305-311.)

This section will attempt to answer these questions and, also, to indicate the use of ancillary methods of treatment which can be useful while the patient is participating in the therapeutic group and accepting vocational counseling.

Vital Community Facilities

It stands to reason that in proper referral of those patients who need immediate emergency care (before or during rehabilitation,) the social worker must know his community's various facilities, and should have a good working relationship with the staffs of these institutions. The case worker in an alcoholic treatment center will often call upon:

a. Fellowship organizations, particularly A.A.

b. Agencies and individuals offering counsel—pastoral, marriage, and vocational.

c. Psychotherapists—psychiatrists, psychologists, and psychoanalysts—known to be interested in, and concerned about alcoholism.

d. Physicians—internists, general practitioners, and certain specialists—known to be interested in and concerned about alcoholism.

e. Out-patient psychiatric institutions, including clinics, agencies, and laboratories, either federal, state, county, city, or private.

f. In-patient psychiatric institutions, including federal, state, county, city, and private hospitals; as well as "half-way" houses and rest homes.

g. Out-patient medical institutions, including federal, state, county, city, and privately-owned clinics, agencies, and laboratories.

h. In-patient medical institutions, i.e., all hospitals.

i. Court rehabilitation and probation systems, and key personnel interested in and concerned with alcoholism.

Existing facilities from community to community will of course differ somewhat, depending upon the awareness of alcoholism as a problem, and the sophistication of those who are giving the help. The process of referral, which in large measure is the responsibility of the social worker, will decide on the appropriate use of these resources, based upon the unique situation presented by each patient, and his motivation for such help.

Cork indicates the significance of the end-purpose of referral, when the patient is an alcoholic; and the amount of effort required of the case worker in this difficult and prolonged process:

> First of all we must recognize that the contact is likely to be a long supportive one, involving endless patience and countless interviews which may have to be maintained whether we refer him to a clinic, a physician, a clergyman or to Alcoholics Anonymous.
>
> Just as in a clinic setting where the patient needs, and is encouraged, to form relationships with a variety of people (in spite of the fact that one particular person may be responsible for his formal treatment) so in the community he needs several different sources of support. We must slowly be able to help him to move out to and make use of these other sources. Unless we know them well and believe in their ability to help him, whether it be clinic, physician or clergyman, we cannot truly help him lose his fears or make the best use of such contacts (14, p. 7).

As far as possible, the alcoholic patient should be involved in the selection of the outside resource to which he is being directed. If, for example, he is to visit an A. A. meeting for the first time, he should be prepared for it and if possible, conducted to the meeting. If he is being sent to a psychiatric hospital, the case worker should make clear to him what he may expect in the way of routines and treatment. The effectiveness of a referral, then, not only depends on the patient's desire for the service, but also upon the worker's familiarity with the institution in question. A referral to Alcoholics Anonymous is much more likely to be successful if the social worker is familiar with the aims, methods, philosophy, and some members of A.A. (See Chapter I, pp. 22-31).

A patient who refuses rehabilitation within the center, when the worker believes he is ready for it, should be encouraged to get help from any other available agency which can best meet his needs — with the assurance, however, that he is not simply being "kicked out," but is being sent for the treatment best for *him* (because he will not accept the center's help) and is welcome to return, if he wishes, at some later date.

The Case Worker and Alcoholics Anonymous

Anyone who has worked with alcoholism knows how fortunate we are to have the support of the fellowship of Alcoholics Anonymous — available in almost all communities. The value of A. A. is enhanced when staff members in a treatment center are aware of its methods, means, and goals (See Chapter I). Lee makes the same point:

> If the social worker who wishes to work with Alcoholics Anonymous will take the time to study the (A. A. Preamble)* carefully, he can avoid many of the difficulties that are encountered in working with A. A. and have a better chance of securing the help of this fellowship for his client (15, p. 20).

When the worker finds himself dealing with the confused, poorly-motivated, more-often-than-not-drunk patient, the use of Alcoholics Anonymous becomes mandatory. The patient will probably say that other approaches to his problem have failed and that even A. A. has been unsuccessful with him.

Nevertheless, this patient is in an emergency situation, and needs a constructive and understanding environment immediately. A. A. has proved itself a most effective means for inducing and maintaining sobriety, and it should be appealed to. Remember that referring an emergency case to A. A. does *not* mean that the worker is unloading his responsibility for the patient's rehabilitation to A. A. (As a matter of fact, many patients in alcoholic treatment centers become members

---

*"Alcoholics Anonymous is a fellowship of men and women who share their experience, strength and hope with each other that they may solve their common problem and help others to recover from alcoholism.

"The only requirement for membership is a desire to stop drinking. There are no dues or fees for A.A. membership; we are self-supporting through our own contributions. A.A. is not allied with any sect, denomination, politics, organization or institution; does not wish to engage in any controversy, neither endorses nor opposes any causes. Our primary purpose is to stay sober and help other alcoholics to achieve sobriety."

—A.A. Preamble

of A. A. *after* they have been in treatment a while.) The social worker is only using another method to get his patient moving toward rehabilitation.

Continuation with A. A. as well as full participation in the alcoholism center's program are not mutually exclusive; they are, rather, complementary, and the social worker making use of the fellowship's many advantages and aids must know and acknowledge its worth. There can be no rivalry, competitiveness, jealousy or antagonisms. It will help the worker immeasurably if he will get to know some of the sponsors personally; by having some idea of the characteristics of certain groups; and by knowing in some detail when and where meetings are held. Familiarity, in this case, breeds allies.

The Case Worker's Aim in Referral

It goes without saying that the social worker should try to know as much as he possibly can about any other agencies available to assist the alcoholic to recovery. Major facts to have on hand are: characteristics of admission, including procedures, fees, treatment methods, and discharge policies. If, by any chance, the worker has not acquainted himself with this information, action is certain to bog down because the alcoholic, like a child, cannot interpret the constructive purpose of an examination, a laboratory procedure, or a stay in the hospital; and, frequently, when a visit to the patient's family physician (or another doctor) is suggested, for nothing more than a simple physical examination and some laboratory tests, the unnerved and anxious alcoholic will be overcome by fear, will resist or refuse to budge. The same anxiety which hounds the alcoholic in evaluating his psychological self is also extended to his physical self. Much careful preparation is required: to alleviate the patient's fear, and to find a physician who will be *sympathetic*.

Social workers will find much of their work greeted with antipathy. They should not be discouraged or disheartened. *All referrals, either temporary or permanent, to services outside the treatment center, even though they have potential to help, will be considered noxious by the patient. This seeming paradox stems from the fact that new anxieties are evoked when any intervention occurs in the fantasized life of the alcoholic* (a thorough discussion of this is found in Chapter X, pp. 263 to 266).

Perhaps more so than when carrying out other tasks, the social worker will have to feel and show great sympathy and flexibility when he is forced to send elsewhere, those alcoholics who are unsuitable for group rehabilitation, or who refuse to participate in a group, or who —once having started—discontinue group psychotherapy and vocational counseling.

Frequently, a social worker will make multiple referrals, to underline to the patient that the social worker as an individual (as well as the center he works for) will continue in his interest and concern for the patient's well-being.

And finally, in these cases, the social worker will never "dispose" of any potential patient, no matter how harsh the prognosis. Supported by other members of the staff, he should continue his relationship with absent patients—by telephone, mail, through family or friends— and will always be trying to have every one of these confused and resistant alcoholics come back to the treatment center for help in the future.

REFERENCES

1. Hinsie, L. E., and Shatzky, J.: *Psychiatric Dictionary*. New York, Oxford University Press, 1949.
2. *New York City Alcoholism Study, A Report*. New York, The National Council on Alcoholism, Inc.
3. Hoff, E. C.: The etiology of alcoholism. *Quart. J. Stud. Alcohol*. Suppl. *1*:57-65, 1961.
4. Richmond, Mary: The social case worker in a changing world. *The Long View*. New York, The Russell Sage Foundation, 1930.
5. Peltenburg, C. M.: Casework with the alcoholic patient. A paper presented at the 82nd Annual Forum of the Nat'l Conf. of Social Wk., May 29, 1955. Pamphlet publ. by Nat'l Coun. on Alcoholism, Inc., New York City, 1-10.
6. Fink, H. K.: Treatment of the alcoholic. *Acta Psychother*. *9*:183-192, 1961.
7. Bacon, S. D.: Alcoholism: nature of the problem and alcoholism: its extent, therapy and prevention. *Fed. Probation, 2*:1-14, 1947. (Reprint Nat'l Counc. on Alcoholism)
8. Strayer, R.: Out-patient clinic social worker. *Conn. Rev. Alcohol., 12*:25-28, 1961.
9. Price, G. M.: Social casework in alcoholism. *Quart. J. Stud. Alcohol 19*: 155-163, 1958.
10. Krimmel, H. E., and Falkey, D. B.: Short term treatment for alcoholics. *Inventory, 12*:1-33, 1963.
11. Mullan, H., and Sangiuliano, I.: Group psychotherapy and the alcoholic:

Early therapeutic moves. Presented in part at the World Cong. of Psychiatry, Montreal, Canada, June 4-10, 1961. Reprint from Nat'l Council on Alcoholism, New York City.

12. Mullan, H., and Sangiuliano, I.: Group psychotherapy and the alcoholic: The phenomenology of early group interaction. Presented in part at the Fifth Int. Congress of Psychotherapy, Wein, Austria, Aug. 21-26, 1961. Reprint from Nat'l Council on Alcoholism, New York City.

13. *The New York Alcoholism Vocational Rehabilitation Project*: Project #418. The Office of Vocational Rehabilitation, U. S. Dept. of Health, Education and Welfare, Washington, D.C.; and The Nat'l Council on Alcoholism, Inc., New York City.

14. Cork, M.: Social workers can help alcoholics. *Canadian Welfare,* Nov. 1954. (Nat'l Council Alcohol. Reprint)

15. Lee, J. P.: Alcoholics Anonymous as a community resource. *Social Work,* 20-26, Oct. 1960.

SELECTED READINGS

1. The Alcoholic and the Social Caseworker. *The Maryland Review on Alcoholism. VII* (5):2-3, May 1961.

2. Cork, Margaret: Social Workers Can Help Alcoholics. The Alcoholism Research Foundation of Ontario. Distributed by National Council on Alcoholism, Inc., New York.

3. Do's and dont's for the wives of alcoholics (and for families and friends), *Inventory,* published by the North Carolina Alcoholic Rehabilitation Program. Distributed by National Council on Alcoholism, Inc., New York.

4. Griffing, Esther J.: Clinic intake procedure with the alcoholic patient. Presented at the 89th Annual Forum of the National Conference on Social Welfare, New York, May 31, 1962.

5. Griffing, Esther J.: Preparing the Alcoholic for Referral. Presented at the New York State Welfare Conference, New York City, November 14, 1960.

6. Institute for Casework Supervisors and Caseworkers. Annual Meeting and Institutes National Council on Alcoholism, Salt Lake City, Utah, 1959.

7. Kant, Fritz, M. D.: *The Treatment of the Alcoholic.* Springfield, Thomas, 1954.

8. Krimmel, Herman, E. and Falky, Bruce, D.: Short-Term Treatment of Alcoholism. *Social Work,* 102-107, July 1962.

9. Lee, John Park: Alcoholics Anonymous As A Community Resource. *Social Work,* 20-26, October 1960.

10. McGenty, Denis: Alcoholic in the Family, Reprinted from *Marriage* (formerly *Grail),* St. Meinrad, Indiana. February 1958. Distributed by the National Council on Alcoholism, Inc.

11. McGenty, Denis: Family Relationships Contributing to Alcoholism. *The American Catholic Sociological Review, XIX* (1): 13-23, March 1958.

12. Peltenburg, Cathrin, M.: Casework with the Alcoholic Patient. Presented at

the 82nd Annual Forum of the National Conference of Social Work, May 29, 1955. Published by National Council on Alcoholism, Inc.

13. Price, Gladys, M.: Social Casework in Alcoholism. *Quart. J. Stud. Alcohol.,* *19, (1)* :155-163, March 1958.

14. Strayer, Robert: Out-Patient Clinic Social Worker. *Connecticut Review on Alcoholism, XII* (7): 25, 27-28, March 1961.

15. Walters, H. J.: A design of suggestions for developing skills in talking with alcoholic patients. Division of Alcoholism, State Department of Hospitals, Baton Rouge, Louisiana, 1960.

CHAPTER V

THE ORIENTATION OF THE ALCOHOLIC
TO HIS ILLNESS

RUTH FOX, M.D.

*(The alcoholic has a limited capacity to form a treatment bond
with the therapist. Yet, a modicum of co-operation is essential if
the destructive effects of alcoholism are to be lessened or reversed.
In this chapter we shall discuss methods of leading the patient to
take an objective interest in himself and his disease. The didactic
orientation to treatment presented herein, which is used quite generally in public health and preventive medicine, achieves this goal
by instructing the alcoholic (and members of his family) about
himself, his illness, its processes, and its end results. Included in this
chapter as well are discussions of other treatment methods applicable to the alcoholic, and supportive measures other than therapy
that are also available in the community.)*

DEFINITION

The Need For Co-operation

Experience has shown that when a doctor takes time to explain in
detail to a patient the nature of his illness, why the symptoms are as
they are, what his plans are for treatment, what the medication is
(if any is given), and what outcome is to be expected, the patient will
not only feel greater confidence in the doctor but will also feel grati-
tude at being treated as an intelligent human being whose cooperation
is being enlisted. This image of the doctor as a competent person who
cares about him and is willing to make his skill, time, and special
know-how available enormously enhances the patient's chance of
recovery. There is no disease imaginable where this point of view is
more sadly lacking or more needed than in the illness of alcoholism.
Age-old prejudices against the alcoholic felt by his family, his doctor,
and society have stood in the way of the alcoholic's treatment and
recovery for centuries. Many still view the alcoholic's bizarre and
destructive behavior as deliberate and perverse and consider that he

should be punished for it, rather than understanding that he has a disease for which he needs treatment. In spite of the educational efforts in the past twenty years of organizations like the National Council on Alcoholism,* the various state programs for the control of alcoholism, the Rutgers (formerly Yale) Center of Alcohol Studies,** and Alcoholics Anonymous, the lack of knowledge about the disease of alcoholism is appalling. The fact that it is a disease, that it is treatable, and that patients can and are recovering by the thousands must be more generally and widely understood. The alcoholic now suffers the same kind of stigma that was associated less than a century ago with tubercular and cancer patients. Education and acceptance of treatment have helped to reduce the incidence of tuberculosis and well-publicized cancer prevention clinics offering early diagnostic examination and treatment, have saved thousands of lives. This same conception of treatment - the idea that an informed patient in a knowledgeable society is more amenable, receptive and motivated - is not only applicable to the alcoholic but basic to proper treatment and recovery.

The Scope Of Orientation

Misconceptions and ignorance about alcoholism abound, and are so much a part of our culture that it is society itself that has to be persuaded that alcoholism is treatable. Few people realize the magnitude of the problem. For every one of the five million alcoholics in the United States there are probably four to five others who suffer drastically as a consequence: wives, husbands, parents, children, employers, employees and friends. In addition to general dissemination of correct ideas about alcoholism, detailed and specific knowledge about this disease must be presented to those persons who treat, supervise, or counsel others - physicians, psychotherapists (psychiatrists, psychoanalysts, psychologists, social workers), counselors (educational, marriage, vocational, pastoral), teachers, administrators

*The National Council on Alcoholism is a voluntary health agency whose goal is the prevention of alcoholism through education, research and community services.

**This is a department of Rutgers University which conducts research in alcoholism as well as a four weeks summer course in alcohol and alcoholism.

and personnel managers and specialists. Finally and importantly the alcoholic must know about himself and his use of alcohol.

Content Of Orientation

The purpose of orientation is to replace false ideas with more expert knowledge about alcohol, its use, the consequences of its misuse, and the methods of obtaining and maintaining sobriety and treatment. The content of orientation lectures therefore can vary widely. Topics discussed most usually deal with the psysiology of alcohol metabolism; nature of alcoholism; symptomatology; surrender and acceptance; therapeutic value of A. A.; planning of recovery program; sedatives and tranquilizers. The chart on page 140 can be of great help in explaining to patients their various symptoms and patterns of drinking, as well as the steps and feelings they can expect in their recovery (see Chapter III).

Willmar State Hospital in Willmar, Minnesota offers a series of twenty-eight lectures which patients are asked to attend. These lectures frequently are illustrated by films; they cover subjects such as the definition, symptoms, and mental mechanisms of alcoholism; learning theories; personality problems; marital problems, and rehabilitation; and the roles that the Church and A. A. can play.

There is some agreement about the content that orientation lectures should have; but the methods of teaching vary widely, depending upon the lecturer, his background, his interests and concerns, his originality and the institutional setting. In the following pages the content and methods of orientation courses are related to clinic, office, and hospital settings.

AVENUES AND MEANS OF PATIENT AND FAMILY ORIENTATION

Introduction

All of our society (which, of course, includes alcoholics themselves, and their families) must understand the facts about alcoholism before this most important public health problem can be brought under control. Few understand the difference between the voluntary excessive social drinking with occasional drunkenness and the disease of uncontrollable and compulsive alcoholism which renders the subject utterly unable to drink any alcohol at all without dire consequences to his whole being. Why some drinkers progress from excessive social drinking into alcoholic drinking is not understood, but a better general understanding that this change can happen, however slowly and insidiously, might prevent alcoholism in many people.

Orientation of the Family

A very small percentage of alcoholics really *wish* to stop drinking, or believe they *can* stop, and for this reason we may have to deal with families before we can see the actual patient. Often, considerable time must be expended laying the ground work for treatment. The spouse is usually at the end of his or her rope, disgusted, angry, hopeless, and afraid, and is apt to believe that *all* of the family problems are due to the alcoholism, and unable or unwilling to see that his or her own actions may be actually perpetuating the drinking.* Studies of wives of alcoholics, for example, have revealed that many are quite normal women who have been inundated by the "crisis" of alcoholism; on the other hand, many were found to be neurotic themselves, some with domineering, punitive attitudes, others with self-sacrificing masochistic traits which militate against recovery of the sick member of the family. Most wives have had to assume full control in order to keep the family together, and too often treat the alcoholic mate as a small recalcitrant child. Some spouses alternate between being overprotective and punitive. Frequently the children are also disturbed and disturbing.

Convincing the family that the alcoholic is ill rather than merely perverse will make them more tolerant and understanding, and can so change their attitude that a frank discussion can take place without the usual recriminations. The point of view of the spouse may be considerably clarified by attending several meetings of the Al-Anon Family Groups, a fellowship for the families of alcoholics which is an offshoot of Alcoholics Anonymous. Teen-age children can be aided by visiting the Alateen groups. This is another fellowship, an offshoot

---

*Though the ratio of women to men alcoholics throughout the country as a whole is 1 to 5, many of us dealing with middle and upper class patients in the Eastern cities and suburbs find it to be 1 to 1. Though the pronoun "he" will be used throughout, what is said applies equally to the female alcoholic.

of Al-Anon, which offers understanding, education, and hope to the children of alcoholics.

Orientation in the Physician's Office or Clinic

When the alcoholic comes to the doctor's office or clinic, he must meet an attitude of complete acceptance of him as an ill person. He may be in the midst of a drinking spree, he may be in the painful state of the withdrawal phase, or he may be in a period of not drinking. It is preferable for the wife to be with him, since she can give a more honest picture of the true situation. I have found it best, however, to see the patient alone first and only to call the spouse in with the patient's permission toward the end of the interview. A judgment must be made almost at once as to whether the patient needs to be put in a hospital for withdrawal or whether he can stop drinking at home with the help of his spouse and a few tranquilizers. Emotions are apt to run high and be quite bitter, so that often a few days in a hospital may have a salutory effect. However, judicious and kindly handling can often overcome the mutual hostility between husband and wife right in the office, so that home treatment may be all that is needed. Remember that the alcoholic, no matter how he acts, is probably angry or frightened or both; a calm, reassuring and objective approach can do much to overcome both feelings.

The first visit with an alcoholic can be most crucial. The tone between patient and doctor is usually set at this meeting. Time must be found to listen patiently while the patient tells his story in his own words. You can expect him to use his most usual defenses of rationalization, denial, and projection, so that the story he presents will usually not be the true one. I try to learn something about the alcoholic's style of life (his marital status, kind of work, state of health, what he feels to be his main worries or problems, where he lives and how) before I ask specific questions about his drinking pattern. This approach helps him feel that I am interested in him as a total person and not as "just another alcoholic." It is important then to go into some detail about his drinking history: when did it first become a problem and under what circumstances? what is his concept of the disease of alcoholism? where, when, how much, and with whom does he drink? what is the effect of alcohol on his personality and his feelings about himself? how does it effect his behavior toward friends, co-workers, and family? what previous efforts has he made to overcome his problem with alcohol? and most important of all, does he wish to stop drinking?

Many alcoholics, especially those who are early cases (although this is also true of some in the late phase), do not know that their drinking pattern is any different from that of the usual excessive social drinker. Most people who have trouble with their drinking find the description *alcoholic* offensive, for it conjures up a picture of the skid row derelict who is rarely sober, though actually only about 3 per cent of the total alcoholic population falls in this class. The fact is that about 80 per cent of alcoholics are employed or employable and are living in a family setting, trying desperately to lead normal lives in spite of their considerable handicap of alcoholism. The alcoholic has to be shown how his drinking does differ from that of the social drinker, and Figure 10, A Chart of Alcohol Addiction and Recovery, can be enormously helpful in giving the alcoholic some perspective on his symptoms, the progressive nature of his illness, and the steps necessary to recovery. Alcoholism must be presented to him as an illness with social, psychological and chemical disturbances. (1) I have found it helpful to refer to it as an addiction with accompanying withdrawal phenomena. This accounts for his lack of control when in a drinking phase.

This first visit must give the alcoholic hope for recovery and make him aware of his need for outside help. The help that Alcoholics Anonymous can give, the use of Antabuse, or Temposil, the possible need for therapy, either group or individual or both, the advantage of a week or two in a hospital or an A. A. rest home, and the possible need for therapy for the family should all be discussed. If the patient is willing, the spouse should be present when the plan of action and therapy is drawn up.

One cannot force an alcoholic to stop drinking but one can help to create a climate more favorable to his recovery. One may fail at first—and indeed, one *often* fails—but usually the alcoholic stores away somewhere in his mind what has been said and will return in a few weeks or months to undertake treatment. The therapist dealing with alcoholics needs to be level-headed and objective and realize that he is not omnipotent. He must often be satisfied to make small gains at first. He must keep in mind that he is dealing with a serious, chron-

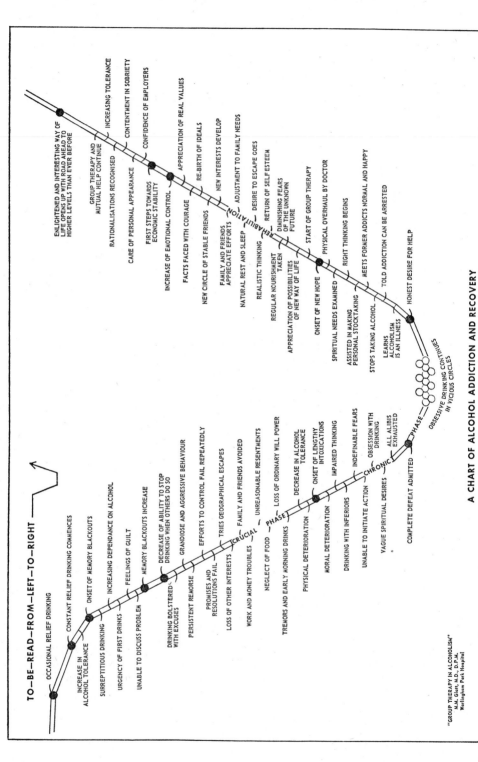

TO—BE—READ—FROM—LEFT—TO—RIGHT →

A CHART OF ALCOHOL ADDICTION AND RECOVERY

"GROUP THERAPY IN ALCOHOLISM"
M.M. Glatt, M.D., D.P.M.
Warlingham Park Hospital

OCCASIONAL RELIEF DRINKING
CONSTANT RELIEF DRINKING COMMENCES
INCREASE IN ALCOHOL TOLERANCE
ONSET OF MEMORY BLACKOUTS
SURREPTITIOUS DRINKING
INCREASING DEPENDENCE ON ALCOHOL
URGENCY OF FIRST DRINKS
FEELINGS OF GUILT
UNABLE TO DISCUSS PROBLEM
MEMORY BLACKOUTS INCREASE
DECREASE OF ABILITY TO STOP DRINKING WHEN OTHERS DO SO
DRINKING BOLSTERED WITH EXCUSES
GRANDIOSE AND AGGRESSIVE BEHAVIOUR
PERSISTENT REMORSE
PROMISES AND RESOLUTIONS FAIL
EFFORTS TO CONTROL FAIL REPEATEDLY
LOSS OF OTHER INTERESTS
TRIES GEOGRAPHICAL ESCAPES
FAMILY AND FRIENDS AVOIDED
WORK AND MONEY TROUBLES
UNREASONABLE RESENTMENTS
NEGLECT OF FOOD
LOSS OF ORDINARY WILL POWER
TREMORS AND EARLY MORNING DRINKS
DECREASE IN ALCOHOL TOLERANCE
PHYSICAL DETERIORATION
ONSET OF LENGTHY INTOXICATIONS
MORAL DETERIORATION
IMPAIRED THINKING
DRINKING WITH INFERIORS
INDEFINABLE FEARS
UNABLE TO INITIATE ACTION
OBSESSION WITH DRINKING
VAGUE SPIRITUAL DESIRES
ALL ALIBIS EXHAUSTED
COMPLETE DEFEAT ADMITTED

CRUCIAL PHASE
CHRONIC PHASE

Obsessive drinking continues in vicious circles

LEARNS ALCOHOLISM IS AN ILLNESS
HONEST DESIRE FOR HELP
STOPS TAKING ALCOHOL
TOLD ADDICTION CAN BE ARRESTED
MEETS FORMER ADDICTS NORMAL AND HAPPY
ASSISTED IN MAKING PERSONAL STOCKTAKING
RIGHT THINKING BEGINS
SPIRITUAL NEEDS EXAMINED
PHYSICAL OVERHAUL BY DOCTOR
ONSET OF NEW HOPE
START OF GROUP THERAPY
APPRECIATION OF POSSIBILITIES OF NEW WAY OF LIFE
DIMINISHING FEARS OF THE UNKNOWN FUTURE
REGULAR NOURISHMENT TAKEN
REALISTIC THINKING
NATURAL REST AND SLEEP
RETURN OF SELF ESTEEM
FAMILY AND FRIENDS APPRECIATE EFFORTS
DESIRE TO ESCAPE GOES
NEW CIRCLE OF STABLE FRIENDS
ADJUSTMENT TO FAMILY NEEDS
FACTS FACED WITH COURAGE
NEW INTERESTS DEVELOP
INCREASE OF EMOTIONAL CONTROL
RE-BIRTH OF IDEALS
FIRST STEPS TOWARDS ECONOMIC STABILITY
APPRECIATION OF REAL VALUES
CARE OF PERSONAL APPEARANCE
CONFIDENCE OF EMPLOYERS
RATIONALISATIONS RECOGNISED
CONTENTMENT IN SOBRIETY
GROUP THERAPY AND MUTUAL HELP CONTINUE
INCREASING TOLERANCE
ENLIGHTENED AND INTERESTING WAY OF LIFE OPENS UP WITH ROAD AHEAD TO HIGHER LEVELS THAN EVER BEFORE

REHABILITATION

ic disease in which relapse is very apt to occur, and far from being discouraged by a relapse, a doctor should take the time to discuss what preceded the slip to see what he can learn.

Any procedure mapped out on the first visit should be quite specific; all directions should be put in writing and subsequent appointments should be made for ensuing days. The alcoholic is too sick to be kept waiting. He needs to feel a genuine interest in his welfare and needs to be seen almost daily at first. Most doctors working alone find this schedule arduous, but it is necessary to obtain a good result. The first visit will necessarily be a long one, but the next few subsequent ones can be shorter. The doctor who is working in a clinic has an easier time of it for he has his team to help him — the receptionist, the social worker, the psychologist, the internist, the public health nurse. One doctor practicing in a rural area in Kansas has used a team made up of a minister, the alcoholic's employer, and A. A. members. (2)

Orientation in a Special Hospital for Alcoholics

There are now a number of excellent hospitals for alcoholics in the United States and in Canada but I will describe here only one of the best of such facilities, the hospital at Avon Park run by the Alcoholic Rehabilitation Program of the State of Florida (3). This is an inpatient facility consisting of sixty beds, about ten of which are used for "drying out" purposes. Withdrawal symptoms are treated by internists in one section of the hospital, where medical care is also given for any physical complications. Attention is paid to electrolyte balance, to nutritional disturbances, and to the need for sedation; routine care is available for intercurrent infections, gastritis, liver disturbances, and so forth. After a variable number of days in the medical department, patients are transferred to the residence section, where all patients are ambulatory, and where an intensive educational and rehabilitation program is undertaken during the remaining days of the total four weeks stay. The patients are housed in attractive four-bed wards. There is a high level of patient government, two chairmen being elected by the patients themselves, one for the women and one for the men. These chairmen help the hospital staff orient new patients and plan entertainment; they also help settle disputes which are not serious enough to be taken to the staff itself.

Five days a week there is a meeting of the entire patient body with one member of the staff as a leader. After a little discussion a film is shown, sometimes about alcohol but often it is a mental health film which serves as a focus for discussion about feelings and attitudes. Feelings of hostility, immaturity, inadequacy, self-punitive tendencies, depression, loneliness, self-pity, anxiety, and despair are talked about. The various defenses and mental mechanisms that people use to deal with their impulses are discussed in practical terms, and are related, when pertinent, to the events of the film shown.   Patients discuss their own problems at home or at work, share their troubles, and often give helpful suggestions to each other. During one of the five meetings each week a film is shown on the medical facts of alcoholism; the moderator of this session is an internist who answers any medical questions that are brought up.

After lunch, which is eaten cafeteria-style with the staff, the group of all patients breaks up into smaller groups of ten for a more intimate type of group therapy. These smaller groups meet twice a week for sessions of one-and-one-half hours. The patients also attend occupational therapy meetings and various sports groups — fishing, rowing, croquet, handball, cards. Some form of entertainment is planned for the evenings, usually dances, movies, or parties.

The staff of psychiatrists, internists, and social workers are always on hand for individual counseling, and whenever possible, interviews with family members are arranged.

On leaving this in-patient facility, each patient is referred back to the out-patient clinic for alcoholics nearest to him; if he does not live near one, he is referred back to his family physician. Each patient pays his own fees at the hospital if he can. If he cannot, the cost is paid through state funds. Close liaison with A. A. is encouraged.

Orientation Through an Information Center

These centers are not for actual treatment of alcoholism, but serve as centers for information and referral. Most of them are the products of local committees formed with the help of the National Council on Alcoholism with which they later may become affiliated. Very often it is a member of the family who comes first for information about resources. Usually a social worker or a qualified recovered alcoholic undertakes this initial interview, giving guidance, help, and information about getting the patient under treatment. When the patient comes, advice is given as to where he can get the most effective help. An information center must have listed all the available resources, including hospitals and doctors to whom the patient can be referred. A general air of acceptance of the patient as ill and worthy of help and sympathy is most important. The closest kind of co-operation with A. A. is imperative. Recovered alcoholics can be invaluable workers in these information centers.

Orientation in an Out-patient Clinic

Orientation meetings have real value in a busy out-patient clinic. If a patient comes in drunk, he is most often seen first by the admitting nurse, though the internist may be needed. The services of the clinic are explained to the patient by the nurse or social worker and practical matters, such as whether or not a hospital will be needed for sobering up, are discussed and arrangements made for this. If the patient has been drinking heavily for a long time hospitalization is imperative to prevent or mitigate delirium tremens or withdrawal convulsions. Help is given by the clinic personnel in getting the patient into a city or a private hospital, depending upon the means of the patient and the expected severity of the withdrawal symptoms. It may be necessary to consider a month or two in a private or state mental hospital if there is no medical hospital in the state geared for long-term care of the alcoholic. If the drinking has not been too long or too severe, one or two weeks in an A. A. rest home may be best. Many patients can, of course, sober up on their own. Others may need only three to five days of "drying out" in a general voluntary hospital.

The Adult Guidance Center in San Francisco gives six orientation meetings to all patients and families. (4) These are given in the evening three times a week. Lectures and discussion groups are arranged so that a patient may enter at any time. The meetings are quite informal and deal with the general disease nature of alcoholism and practical methods of handling it. The topics discussed are as follows:

1st Meeting—"How the Clinic May Help You"—Psychiatric Social Worker
2nd Meeting—"Eating, Sleeping and Good Health"—Nurse
3rd Meeting—"Feeling, Thinking and Acting"—Psychologist
4th Meeting—"Ways to Stay Sober"—A.A. Member
5th Meeting—"Medicine and Alcohol"—Physician
6th Meeting—"Discussion, Questions & Answers"—Psychologist

During the patient's initial contact with the clinic, interviews are arranged with the internist, the psychiatrist, sometimes the psychologist, and the social worker. Members of the family are seen and their co-operation is elicited. Contacts are made with A. A. and Al-Anon (see Chapter IV).

One important function of orientation lectures is to screen out the patients who really do not wish to undertake a program of recovery. If they fail to show up after one or two appointments, it probably means they are not yet ready to give up alcohol. The door should be left open for them for the future when they may be more sincerely receptive. Follow-up calls by phone or visit should always be made after missed appointments.

Orientation Lectures for Doctors and Professionals

Courses on alcoholism for medical students, county medical societies, and hospital staffs should deal not only with theoretical matters but practical matters as well: how to guide the alcoholic to other resources, especially A. A. and group therapy; when to use Antabuse or Temposil; when to refer to a psychiatrist for counseling or deeper therapy; when hospitalization is needed for either a short sobering up or a prolonged rehabilitative stay. The task will often be too great for one doctor alone and he will need the resources of a team of workers. Lectures should be given by internists, psychiatrists, social workers and A. A. members.

SUMMARY

For a given alcoholic we do not know which is the most valuable form of orientation. Certainly he must learn the facts of his illness; but whether he can do this best in a one-to-one relationship with his doctor, in a small therapeutic group, in the more didactic orientation sessions that are outlined here, through reading and study, or through A. A., has yet to be decided. The one necessary ingredient of any method of working with the alcoholic is an honest attempt to understand him and to reach him on an intellectual as well as an emotional level.

I have tried to point out here that the alcoholic needs to understand that he is suffering from a disease process and that he ought to have help in understanding his illness. The medical profession and society as a whole must also become aware of the facts. This educative process may be carried on in a doctor's office, in special hospitals for alcoholics, in information centers, and in out-patient clinics.

The Catalogue of Publications of the National Council on Alcoholism can be of inestimable value to any student of this problem. This can be obtained by writing to the National Council on Alcoholism, 2 East 103rd Street, New York, New York 10029.

REFERENCES

1. Reprinted from Group therapy in alcoholism by Glatt, M. M., M. D., *The British Journal of Addiction, 54*:133-148, 1958.
2. Voldeng, Karl: *Recovery from Alcoholism,* Chicago, Henry Regnery Company, 1962.
3. Henderson, C. Brooks: From a talk given at the Annual Meeting of the American Group Psychotherapy Association, January 27, 1962, New York City.
4. Personal communication from Cathrin M. Peltenburg, M. S., Chief Psychiatric Social Worker, Adult Guidance Center, California Department of Public Health, San Francisco.

FILM BIBLIOGRAPHY

Films on Alcoholism, which are currently available for rental or purchase can be obtained from the sources indicated on this selected list. Further information on other films on the subject can be secured by writing directly to each of the various agencies listed. Many of the State Programs on Alcoholism and on Mental Health also offer film services.

Alcohol and the Human Body

Designed for public school use to show the psysiological effects of alcohol. A good film for basic information. (16 mm. Black and White, Sound, 14 Minutes.)

Rental:	Encyclopedia Britannica Films, Inc.
	202 East 44th Street
	New York 17, New York
Rate:	$4.00 1 to 3 days
	.50 for each additional day
Purchase:	Encyclopedia Britannica Films, Inc.
	1150 Wilmette Avenue
	Wilmette, Illinois
Price:	$75.00

Alcoholism

Delineates various treatment approaches and gives special details concerning alcoholic clinics. A good film for general use. (16 mm. Black and White, Sound, 22 Minutes.)

Rental:	Encyclopedia Britannica Films, Inc.
	202 East 44th Street
	New York 17, New York
Rate:	$5.50 1 to 3 days
	1.00 each additional day
Purchase:	Encyclopedia Britannica Films, Inc.
	1150 Wilmette Avenue
	Wilmette, Illinois
Price:	$120.00
	Film No. 548 BW

Alcoholism: The Hidden Disease

Portrays in detail the broad services which can be rendered in a general hospital and how services developed as a result of community action. (16 mm. Black and White, Sound, 28 Minutes.)

Rental:	Ideal Pictures Corporation
	321 West 44th Street
	New York 36, New York
Rate:	Free Rental
Purchase:	Mr. T. E. Trouton
	CIBA Pharmaceutical Co.
	556 Morris Avenue
	Summit, New Jersey
Price:	$65.00 - Waiting Time: 4 weeks

Alcoholism: The Revolving Door

Portrays activities of Blue Hills Clinic, Connecticut, and includes interview with Dr. Marvin A. Block, Chairman, American Medical Association Committee on Alcoholism. High School to Adult Groups (16 mm. Black and White, Sound, 28 Minutes.)

Rental:	Smith, Kline & French Laboratories
	Medical Film Center
	1500 Spring Garden Street
	Philadelphia 1, Pennsylvania
Rate:	Free Rental from Medical Film Center
Purchase:	Not available for purchase

David   The Profile of a Problem Drinker*

This story of David Spear, a young architect, dramatically portrays the signposts and behavior symptoms which indicate the insidious progression of the disease of alcoholism and some of the forces which lead to recovery. (16 mm. Black and White, Sound, 27 Minutes.)

Rental:	Yeshiva University Film Library
	526 West 187th Street
	New York 33, New York
Rate:	$6.50 1st day - Client billed for postage
	3.25 each additional day
Purchase:	McGraw-Hill Book Company
	Text-Film Department
	330 West 42nd Street
	New York 36, New York
Price:	$135.00

For Those Who Drink*

This extensive lecture film features R. Gordon Bell, M.D., member of the Medical Advisory Board of the Alcoholism Research Foundation for Ontario. Using effective blackboard diagrams, Dr. Bell deals with: the physical, psychological and social aspects of alcohol addiction. The film is especially effective for professional workers, doctors, etc., and to accompany lectures to alcoholics under treatment in a group setting. Total time: 40 minutes. Available in two segments (20 minutes each). There is also a 29-minute version.

Rental:	The film can be obtained on a free loan basis or for a nominal rental in most states from the

	State Department of Health, a city department of Health (also County) and from many libraries.
Purchase:	L. L. Cromien and Company, Inc.
	652 Book Building
	Detroit 26, Michigan
Price:	40 min. version - $195
	29 min. version - $165

How Long The Night

This film, accompanied by a leader's guide, *should only be used with adult discussion groups*. Excellent for this purpose. Story of an alcoholic husband who suffers from a deep sense of unworthiness and inadequacy stemming from early parental attitudes. The minister's role in counseling the wife, guiding her study of the disease and referring her to other resources for help indicate a broadly based approach. (16 mm. Black and White, Sound, 30 Minutes.)

Rental:	For nearest source of rental contact address listed below.
Rate:	$8.00 per day
Purchase:	General Board of Christian Social Concerns of the Methodist Church
	Communications Department
	The Methodist Building
	100 Maryland Avenue, N.E.
	Washington 2, D. C.
Price:	$160.00

It's Best To Know

This film features Steve Allen and a professional Hollywood cast, and was designed to help high school teachers get the most out of classroom discussion with young people who are interested in questions about the use of alcoholic beverages. It has also proved effective in establishing rapport between adult discussion leaders and teen-age groups. (16 mm. Black and White, Sound, 8 Minutes.)

Rental:	No Rental
	Free Loan, *within the Province of Ontario*
Purchase:	Education Department

Alcoholism & Addiction Research Foundation
of Ontario
24 Harbord Street
Toronto 5, Ontario, Canada

Price: $50.00
Contact Education Department for
Preview Arrangements

Out of Orbit

This presents a story about an alcoholic and the conflicts, feelings, and attitudes of his wife and son, as the whole family attempts to get help. It is geared for viewing by the general public and is designed to show how the community and various forces within the community can aid in solving the costly problem of alcoholism. (16 mm. Color, Sound, 14 Minutes.)

Rental: Michigan State University
Audio-Visual Center
East Lansing, Michigan
Rate: $1.00 plus postage
Purchase: The Jam Handy Organization
2821 East Grand Boulevard
Detroit 11, Michigan
Price: $100.00

Teaching Teenagers About Alcohol

Intended specifically for showing to teachers, several scenes illustrate techniques of alcohol education successfully applied in the classroom. The setting is a summer course in Health Education, and the topic for discussion is the place of alcohol education in the classroom. The film demonstrates that it is possible to do a constructive teaching job without jeopardizing the role of the teacher, and potential changes in popular attitudes toward drinking are reflected. (16 mm. Black and White, Sound, 15 Minutes.)

Rental: The Pennsylvania State University
Audio-Visual Aids Library
University Park, Pennsylvania
Rate: $3.50
Purchase: McGraw-Hill Book Company

Text-Film Department
330 West 42nd Street
New York 36, New York
Price: $95.00

To Your Health*

Against an outline of the history of drinking uses and customs, this film illuminates the problem of alcoholism in a novel and effective way. Cartoon style has strong impact for all groups. Excellent as a preface to lectures and talks before almost any kind of group. (16 mm. Color, Sound, 11 Minutes.)

Rental: Yeshiva University Film Library
                 526 West 187th Street
                 New York 33, New York
Rate: $5.00 for first day
                   2.50 (half) for each additional day
                 Plus Postage
Purchase: Columbia University
                 Center for Mass Communication
                 1125 Amsterdam Avenue
                 New York, New York
Price: $100.00

What About Drinking?

A "leader" with the purpose of stimulating the discussion with youth groups which should follow the showing of this film. Presents various objective points of view regarding drinking. For both youth and adult groups. (16 mm. Black and White, Sound, 14 Minutes.)

Rental: Yeshiva University Film Library
                 526 West 187th Street
                 New York 33, New York
Rate: $3.00 first day
                   1.50 each additional day, plus postage
Purchase: McGraw-Hill Book Company
                 Text-Film Department
                 330 West 42nd Street
                 New York 36, New York
Price: $100.00

What About Alcoholism?

Same as *What About Drinking?* but goes deeper into discussion of alcoholism as a problem with youth groups. (16 mm. Black and White, Sound, 12 Minutes.)

Rental:	Yeshiva University Film Library
	526 West 187th Street
	New York 33, New York
Rate:	$3.00 first day
	1.50 each additional day, plus postage
Purchase:	McGraw-Hill Book Company
	Text-Film Department
	330 West 42nd Street
	New York 36, New York
Price:	$60.00

* We have found these films to be particularly good

CHAPTER VI

PSYCHOLOGICAL TESTING OF THE ALCOHOLIC IN A GROUP CENTERED REHABILITATION SERVICE

ROSE WOLFSON, Ph.D.

(The function of the clinical psychologist in an alcoholic treatment center is to administer psychological tests to alcoholics, then to evaluate them and present the findings in a relevant form to the staff. The successful completion of this task requires unusual skill, a keen sense of timing, and a sensitive and tactful method of examination.

The anxious and easily frustrated alcoholic views the test as a threat to his already vulnerable and fragile self-image. He therefore may resist taking the examination by absenting himself, by lateness, by acting out, and sometimes by coming in drunk. To cope with these situations the psychologist must meet and test the patients in small groups, reassure them in various ways, and continue the support offered by the rehabilitation center.

In this chapter, Dr. Rose Wolfson describes the tests which when completed, offer the most practical knowledge about the patients, the use of the test situation and material, and certain indications of personality change in follow-up studies.)

INTRODUCTION

Flexibility of Method

In the team approach to the alcoholic's problem each discipline must sacrifice some of its traditional methodology. This is particularly true as far as psychological evaluation of the alcoholic patient described herein is concerned, since the treatment milieu (a rehabilitation center), the testing setting (a small group), the timing of the test (after the commencement of group treatment), and the homogeneity of test subjects all tend to modify the administration of the examination.

The psychologist is apt to be identified by the confused alcoholic as a harsh and demanding authority figure with uncanny mental powers, and must therefore exhibit great flexibility, improvization, and generosity in this particular test situation. Most alcoholic groups will labor under extreme misconceptions about the nature of the tests and their use; they will also be flagrantly unco-operative, and tremendously anxious. Some subjects will show up inebriated.

The psychologist must realize that the proposed test is viewed by the alcoholic as an imposition upon his inner fantasy existence, a means of discovering who he actually *is*. His resentment, coupled with his tenuous tie with the group psychotherapist and other staff members, means that if the psychologist is at all brusque or the least bit insensitive, the patient may leave the center fortified in his rationalization about terminating therapy.

The Purpose of Psychological Testing of the Alcoholic

The traditional use of psychological testing is to shed light on one or more aspects of an individual's personality which he cannot or will not communicate readily even under skilled and considerable interviewing. It follows, therefore, that it is necessary to select tests appropriate to the objectives of each testing program so that the purpose of the testing may be particularized. In different settings, as for instance, industry or education, the kinds of information sought through psychological examination vary, and so must the tests employed.

In a venture with multiple disciplines for treating patients who drink uncontrollably, the purpose of testing is most often defined and established through staff discussion. Generally this purpose is thought to be threefold: (a) to learn about each patient as an individual, not as a part of a group thought to be homogeneous by society; (b) to determine how each patient will fare in group therapy; and (c) to study how habitual attitudes and expectations affect vocational destiny (see Chapter VII).

Under the first goal of testing come such questions as: How does the patient view himself? How does he view the world? What are his characteristic concerns, and how does he cope with them? What is the nature of his relationship to people? What are his resources for altering his way of life? And finally, why does he drink?

Under the second come such questions as: Can he participate in intensive group psychotherapy? If not, will he be disruptive to the group, or will the rigors of group interaction tend to disorganize him? Can he benefit from a different therapeutic approach, or another group, more appropriate to his needs?

Under the third come questions like: What are the attitudes, outlook, and expectations that help or hinder vocational development and accomplishment?

Psychological Tests Used

Good sense dictates that for testing results to be clinically trustworthy, it is advisable and expedient to choose from among many possible tests those which have proved their value in diverse professional situations and fields. This should be the minimal standard for the examiner's selection of tests. The following tests have been found most useful in the group examination of alcoholic patients:

The Rotter Incomplete Sentence Test (1) indicates conscious preoccupations (economic, physical, and social), ready self-awareness, self-concept, conscious conflict and helpful or obstructive humor, and matter-of-factness.

The Machover Figure Drawing Test (2) evaluates self-organization, self-concept, social and sexual identification, attitudes based on sex differences, and interaction with the environment, real and fancied.

The Rorschach (3, 4) helps determine the patient's characteristic ways of perceiving, adjusting, and defending himself, and the relative strength and resilience of these characteristic ways.

The Thematic Apperception Test (TAT) (5), in ordinary clinical practice, reveals much about the patient's characteristic attitudes, strivings, hopes, and goals. When used with alcoholic patients, the test tends to reflect also how the patient copes with the tangible world in which he must perforce live. In many instances, the drinking patient's stories are almost a liberal account of actual experiences, and thus a reflection of how the patient views and/or copes with hard reality.

Group Versus Individual Testing with the Alcoholic

Testing alcoholic patients in groups is preferable to testing the individual by himself. This preference has mostly to do with the patients' fears and reluctance, and little with the psychologist's predilection. An alcoholic appears to be much more at ease in a group testing situation than he is alone with the examiner. In a small group of five to six patients, the examiner and the tests themselves are considered less threatening.

METHODS

Practical Considerations

Logically, two questions arise the moment the decision is made to test the alcoholic patients in groups: (a) how to assure their arrival for the examination appointment, and (b) how to treat the patient who arrives inebriated for the examination. In regard to the first question, discussion with the patients concerning convenient and alternative examination dates usually results in agreement on a particular date. To be sure, there are always one or two patients who continue to complain, but generally, if they are consulted, the patients try to work out adjustments of time among themselves, and select the most convenient date given; if that is unsatisfactory, they will suggest another. The point to be remembered here is that scheduling of group appointments for these patients requires greater flexibility and consideration than for many other patients.

Concerning the second point, how to deal with the inebriated patient, it is best to allow him to proceed with the examination if he is relatively quiet and non-obstructive. To exclude him may antagonize other members of the group who will identify with him and resent the examiner's decision though they may not show their feelings directly. There is a good clinical reason for including a drunken patient if his behavior is within bounds: his record will offer a clinical opportunity to study the differences and similarities in this patient in his drunken and sober states. It goes without saying that another appointment must be arranged to examine him when he is sober. Patients who come to the examination intrusively drunk must be persuaded to leave. In this instance the reason for exclusion is apparent, and more acceptable to the group. One or two members may even lend a hand in convincing the inebriated patient to leave.

Over-coming Resistance

Testing alcoholic patients in groups presents problems of procedure for which the traditional friendly yet non-committal attitude of the examiner is insufficient. If it is used it is instantly attacked, while on the surface the patients appear attentive and polite. They nod and seemingly obey, but at the same time, they quip, often very cleverly, or point out their responses to one another. During their interchanges, they ignore the examiner as a person. Very obviously, the patients are trying to dilute the results of the examination by treating it as a lark. Occasionally a patient becomes openly hostile to the examiner, accusing him of doubtful motives. Interestingly enough, at such times, as though apprehensive of a breakdown of their own genial pose, the rest of the group good-naturedly take the antagonistic member in hand so that the examination can proceed.

The Examiner Extends Himself

The behavior of these patients during the testing session is often like that of young children. The alcoholic adults will digress, using any item or none as a jumping-off point. A patient may suddenly ask an irrelevant question, and the others wait for the answer, postponing their work or interrupting the examination. In short, the examiner who attempts to use traditional ways of coping with resistances to examination when testing alcoholic patients in groups is under fire from the start. Three procedures, however, have been found to reduce these resistances substantially if not completely.

First, the examiner has to be ready to reveal something of himself prior to the examination. This means that he must do more than formally introduce himself. It means he must be ready to explain his function on the staff, the helpfulness of the tests to the patients as well as the staff members, and the necessity of confidential participation by each patient; he must also encourage the patient to ask questions at indicated, suitable times. Usually a simple statement suffices for this last: "Are there any questions? Please ask them now because once the testing begins, I may not have the chance to answer without interfering with the tests." This procedure, however, has its hazards. Personal questions may be asked, like, "Do you drink?" meaning, "Are you one of us in spirit?" Or, "Why do *you* think you can tell about us?" which implies, "Are you good enough to judge us?" Once the invitation to ask is extended, though, the examiner must answer each question openly and honestly. He cannot prepare himself for what may happen except to achieve a sustained awareness that questions of varying nature can be asked and must be answered with candor if testing is to proceed. For an alert examining psychologist, the questioning may pay dividends, by making him aware of edgy and/or rebellious patients who will require additional watching or reassurance during the session.

Secondly, the examiner has to keep his sense of humor, for these patients know how to use a genuinely funny remark to the detriment of a test. For example, once during the Machover Figure Drawing Test, after the patients had been asked "to draw a person" (6) and had complied, the psychologist said, "Now draw the opposite sex." Solemnly staring down at her drawing, one of the women patients said, "I'm stuck." The examiner glanced at the spindly drawing and said, "All right, you've drawn a woman. Now draw the opposite." "Oh," replied the patient, "so *that's* what it is. What d'you know?" The examiner, aware of having made the procedural error of naming the sex of the drawing for the patient, laughed nonetheless. "It looks like it to me," she said, "but if you think not, then draw the opposite sex anyway." The group laughed in turn, and went ahead with the assigned task.

Last, the examiner would do well to keep the number to be tested in a group to five or six rather than more. This allows the examiner to circulate among the patients while they work, giving whatever help or additional direction is needed. This limitation on the size of groups has been found to be not only beneficial to the patients but also economical by way of time for the examiner. With smaller groups and closer supervision of the patients, he is likely to eliminate at once many ambiguous and uncertain responses which in ordinary group testing usually require the return of the patient for questioning at another time (7); besides, any procedure that obviates additional appointments without sacrificing test data is all to the good when coping with patients as habitually elusive and resistant as alcoholics. Generalizing, one may say that the psychologist who modifies the traditional methods of administering tests to include greater self-involvement and flexibility of role when examining drinking patients in groups is likely to meet with more genuine cooperation from them.

The Examiner Supports the Staff's Rehabilitation Efforts

The contacts and interaction between patients and examining psychologists cannot be confined to the testing room, as is usually preferred in examining patients. On the contrary, the sooner alcoholic patients can identify the psychologist with the total treatment setting, the sooner they tend to accept the examination itself as part of the total treatment effort. Thus, prior to the examination, while the patients gather together as a group, and/or drink coffee provided in the waiting room, the examining psychologist joins them. His self-introduction is direct and plain: "I'm Doctor ————. I'll be giving the tests tonight. May I know your names?" He chats with them, giving them a chance to look him over and, hopefully, find him less threatening than the *idea* of the tests themselves. Likewise, patients often linger at the end of the examination session, directly or indirectly divulging their concern about what they have revealed through the tests. At such time, the examiner has another opportunity to relate the tests and his function to the total treatment. He should recognize the reality of the patient's fears and doubts and comment on the helpfulness of *all* the test material to the other staff members in contact with the patient. Even if the examiner does not always succeed in allaying the alcoholic patient's fears, he may give the patient a feeling that the effort he has put forth has value for the staff.

One side effect of the involvement of examining psychologist with the alcoholic patient is exceptionally important. Experience shows that the way the patient remembers the examining psychologist tends to influence his attitudes toward the interpretations of the material, although these interpretations are communicated by the therapist at his discretion. Remembrances may be pleasant or unpleasant, with corresponding willingness or resistance to taking the interpretations seriously. Needless to say, any treatment program that envisions follow-up psychological examinations may be greatly facilitated or hampered by what happens in the initial encounter between examining psychologist and the patients. This development tends to be true whether the examiner tests a group or an individual inebriate.

As far as testing a single alcoholic is concerned, the examiner often finds himself even more involved than with a group. The single drinking patient may feel inordinately exposed and endangered in his solitary meeting with the examiner. To control himself, he may talk compulsively throughout the examination, requiring constant reassurance and direction. Anxiety may take the form of numerous questions and self-derogatory complaints: "Should I continue?", "Should I think about it or say something fast?", "This is stupid, isn't it? I know I'm not smart." No attempt is made to answer all the questions and comments. In contrast, however, the examiner does respond to the patient's needs: "You remember, I can't answer anything until the end. Do it the way you can and if I need more, I'll ask." A shake of the examiner's head after this explanation is enough of a reminder that he is listening but may not answer.

At the close of the examination, the single patient, like the patients in the group, wants to know what he has revealed, but may be more insistent and persuasive. Thus, "I was afraid of the tests because I know my mind is no good,"; or "Can you tell if someone's nuts?"; or "I had tests like this before but I didn't answer the same." Once more, the examiner responds to the patient's implied need rather than to the question or statement: "I have to study the material carefully to know what it shows, then I'll give the report to Dr. ———— (the therapist). He knows best how to help you understand what I've found. In any case, it is quite important that you did whatever you could with the tests I gave you. What is happening *now* is what matters most."

TEST RESULTS

Heterogeneous or Homogeneous Personality Structure

The literature on the personalities of drinking patients indicates that no one structure characterizes them (8, 9). Clinical experience confirms this finding; one patient is found to have a serious character disorder, another, to be neurotically involved, while yet another is psychotic, and so on. Systematic theorizing, psychoanalytic or otherwise, comes to terms with this variegated personality picture by implicitly acknowledging that all personality structures may fall victim to early predisposing types of experiences or sensitivities. Thus

Knight (10) believes that the source of the alcoholic's weakness is an excessively indulgent mother; Rado speaks of "a special type of emotional alteration . . ." (8). Throughout all this discussion, one fact is abundantly clear: the so-called "homogeneity" of the inebriate refers more to his drinking habit than to his personality. The differences among these patients are often great, as any experienced psychologist knows. Inaccuracies in interpreting the psychological tests are likely to occur more readily when psychologists study the data to verify preconceived versions of the presumable alcoholic personality. For instance, among some schools of thought (10) homosexuality, not necessarily overt, plays a major role in alcoholism. Once an examining psychologist accept this premise, his interpretation of the test material must be influenced *a priori*. There is danger, in other words, that a biased view may be imposed on the independent record.

Is the Alcoholic Homosexual?

After examining over one hundred patients with long drinking histories, this author, aware of the theoretical correlation between homosexuality and alcoholism, questions the applicability of the theory. It would seem, at least to this author, that if homosexuality is critical for alcoholism, many other kinds of patients showing strong homosexual indicators in their psychological material (11, 12) should have a high drinking incidence. This is not borne out by a study of unadjusted missionaries of both sexes whose Rorschach records and drawing characteristics contained many similarities to those of alcoholics (12). The results of the comparison of the two groups are interesting, especially in respect to homosexual indications in the test material; the records of the missionary men, like those of the alcoholic patients, showed feminine and/or interchangeable sexual identification. Nor could one argue from the data that the missionaries were less dependent, though they were more aggressive than the alcoholic men, but not more so than the women of the alcoholic group, who, in aggression, led all the other patients.

These were missionary men and women recalled from the field for a variety of reasons, one of which was incipient homosexuality, descriptive of one man out of a total of twenty men. None drank.

These patients' ego control as reflected on the Rorschach (by F+%) did not exceed that of the alcoholics nor did they show greater ideational activity to balance their impulsivity (M:C). In the drawings, line differences (steady, tremulous, faint, and so on), placement and size, all clinically important in showing control, are as good in a little less than half of the alcoholic drawings as in those by the missionaries.

It is beyond the scope of this chapter to detail the methods used to systemize and analyze the data for the mentioned comparison. It is, however, worthwhile pointing out that all tallying, and categorizing were done by two independent judges after agreement on criteria. The point to be noted in this comparative study is that although latent homosexuality, at least as measured by the clinical tests, existed in the missionary group, they were not impelled to drink as a way of escape. This fact is not refuted, of course, by the observation that they have other kinds of escape. What is pertinent for the examining psychologist is that the dynamics of homosexuality do not invariably or even usually compel drinking. So this preconception may not be safely applied to alcoholic records indiscriminately. Each is an instance in itself, and should be treated as such, with attention focused on the usual clinical concerns like ego adaptability, characteristic defenses, self-concepts, and unconscious conflicts. When he does this, the examining psychologist is more likely to arrive at an unbiased, individualized description of each drinking patient.

Pervasive Personality Characteristics of the Alcoholic

To be sure, it is possible, after much clinical experience and research to describe the alcoholic patient more or less accurately; yet this must always be done with the knowledge that the description may not fit any one actual patient. The alcoholic is thus described psychologically as immature; unrealistically involved in fantasy in place of coping with actual problems, generally to avoid recognizing weaknesses and limitations in himself; overly concerned with people's reactions to him, usually to prove rejection; strongly passive, yet capable of considerable indirect aggression to resist recognizing responsibilities and limitation (8); schizoid and depressively inclined (9).

Without gainsaying this description, or contradicting the findings against homogeneity, this author would like to suggest that the psychological records of inveterate drinkers show three similar basic conditions: (a) a strongly entrenched depressiveness; (b) unusual vulnerability to stress and challenge; and (c) noticeable absence of a well-defined, esteemed self-concept. These findings agree with those discovered independently through similar and different tests in the New York State University Study of alcoholic patients (6, 9, 11).*

Depression

In respect to the first point, frequently all, but certainly at least three tests, not always the same ones, will reflect a pervasive, persistent depression that characterizes the alcoholic patient's functioning. To illustrate, the Sentence Completion Test will evoke such responses as: AT BEDTIME *I am lonely and afraid;* THE FUTURE *is nothing;* I SECRETLY *want to die.* Likewise, stories on the Thematic Apperception Test (TAT) tend to dwell on the loneliness, defeat, and/ or pessimism of the main figures: "A young man is sitting on his window ledge, looking out into the dark night. There are no stars and he is very lonely and blue. He wonders what kind of a day it will be," "This child is absolutely exhausted and sick and tired of all the constant practicing . . . but he . . . can't think of any way out . . . and his father will punish him . . ." Klebenoff's study of alcoholic patients with the TAT also stressed the pessimism and defeat reflected in their stories (8).

Patients' drawings show characteristics indicative of depression in their size (usually large with few well-articulated details), line quality (usually fuzzy, erratic and/or black and continuous), placement (usually toward the left, upper, lower, or center), and facial expressions. In connection with the drawings, it is important to note that very often the alcoholic patient's associations to his products express feelings contrary to the impressions given by the drawings themselves, thus emphasizing a wishful element connected with the depression. For example: "The woman drawn, to my thought, is

---

*The New York State University Study included only male patients, and technically the findings should apply only to the same sex. Experience and tentative research, however, suggest that with the exception of aggression, which is greater in alcoholic women, these findings apply to both sexes.

a most interesting nurse, whose cheerful, well-balanced, understanding . . . personality is dedicated to the helping of others"; but the woman drawn looks frightened, bleak, and inactive.

Both in objective scoring and content the Rorschach elicits striking evidence of depression: an inordinately high number of responses which refer specifically to the blackness or greyness of the blot (C'), low regulating control (F-%), and markedly low energy reserve (F%). Examples of content are: "symbolic of a life or death struggle—in the end death takes his due"; "a black shoe leaning on a dirty post."

Alcoholic patients, more frequently than nondrinking, nonpsychotic ones, tend to free associate to the Rorschach, often naming feelings or moods rather than percepts; some patients even relate a story stimulated by the blot. Discreet questioning by the examiner during the formal inquiry period helps clarify what the patient actually perceived.

Vulnerability to Stress and Challenge

Vulnerability, takes the form of a generalized hypersensitivity and/or intolerance, reflected in ways characteristic of each test. Thus in the Sentence Completion Test, responses are: I CAN'T *seem to find a milieu;* THIS PLACE *is beginning to bore me;* WHAT ANNOYS ME *is not always very annoying.* The Sentence Completion Test is especially enlightening about the alcoholic patient's tendency to externalize his problems through great sensitivity to other people's supposed weaknesses. So he often states: WHAT ANNOYS ME *are people who are phony;* or, . . . *people who claim to know everything.*

Drawings indicate vulnerability through sketchy, erratic, pale, and/or actually omitted lines on figures that are often wobbly, poorly placed (particularly in view of the structural sensitivity), and/or dimly detailed facially.

The main indicator of vulnerability in the Rorschach is the traditional one, c, added to the noticeable depressive element, C', the low F/%, signifying degree of ego control, and the low F%, reflective of limited reserves for high ego functioning.

Stories on the TAT make abundantly clear the hero's inability to contend with external obstacles and internal conflicts. "This man's wife has just died in childbirth. There had been a horrible snow storm that day and all the telephone wires were down. The birth was premature and it was impossible to contact the doctor. In panic first, and then despair, the frantic husband tried to get a neighbor. The woman . . . came and sat the rest of the night . . . The baby was born dead. As soon as the blizzard stops, the husband will walk to the nearest town to contact the undertaker."

Chaotic Self-concept

Evidence of the third basic condition of alcoholism, the noticeable absence of a well-defined, esteemed self-concept, is accumulative throughout all the tests. The Sentence Completion Test will contain frequent indications that the patient is riddled by many contradictory feelings and ideas about himself, without possessing a dependable guiding image. For instance, I WANT TO KNOW *what?* followed by I FEEL *lousy,* and I SUFFER *pain,* and I *don't know.*

The drawings, often vague, crudely-drawn figures, show graphically the patient's unclear *identity.* The patient's tendency to draw first a figure of the opposite sex and/or figures with opposite sex attributes in an integral aspect of his grossly inadequate self-identification—*without* homosexual implications. The problem is one of identity, with all its inherent social and sexual implications. The contradictions between drawings and associations, mentioned earlier, follow similar lines. The drawings suggest that the alcoholic's image of himself is vague, diffuse, and confused; his association reveals what he wishes he were. Interestingly enough, despite the drinking patient's oft expressed protests that he dislikes regulation, conventionality, and conformity, his associations frequently describe ordinary people living simple lives, spent in discharging everyday responsibilities. In the back of his mind, the patient seems to have an ideal image of what he *ought* to be; yet, significantly, even this image is undistinguished and generalized. So even here the question of identity continues.

The Rorschach, a projective test that taps the patient's perceptual characteristics, will show his general confusion, conflict, and indecision. Though sexual role and identification are often confused, more often the confusion and conflict are more general, involving clashes between infantile passivity and brutal aggressiveness. What he wants to do at the moment may establish for the alcoholic what he is, without any conscious knowledge of the image.

More than any other test that depends on verbal expression, the TAT reflects the drinking patient's lack of meaningful identity and identification. Whether male or female, the patient frequently confuses the sexes of the hero figures and/or involves them in relationships or situations undermining to adult identification. This undermining is most often indicated by a passively expectant attitude that the way will be paved for the hero figure, or that problems are solved for him: " . . . the doctor finds the childhood trouble and she is cured . . . " Even the patient's image of himself as a drinker shifts and changes noticeably, at one time eliciting sympathy, at another, provoking rejection. Though the tone of the stories suggests much self-pity, there is also much self-hatred to confuse the image. McCarthy's penetrating observations regarding this country's lack of a pleasant, acceptable national image of the drinker are very relevant here (13).

In all, to repeat, clinical analysis of the tests free of preconceived ideas about the alcoholic patient soon turns up a crucial problem of identity that transcends the related question of sexual identification and role.

STAFF'S USE OF THE PSYCHOLOGICAL·FINDINGS

General Application of Test Results

Clinically, in a multi-disciplinary setting, just as the entire staff participates in establishing what information realistically they may demand of the psychological tests, the staff determines the most effective ways of utilizing the test reports. Practice suggests that the greatest benefit to patient and staff is derived from a policy that makes the examination results available to all members of the staff closely involved in the treatment program. In this way the tests inform not only the patient's therapist but the social worker, the vocational counsellor and any other staff member who has questions about the patient. Each member of the staff uses the report in ways most relevant to his field and the patient's needs. Each report is different because each patient is studied as an individual. Nevertheless, in the report, the examining psychologist tries to answer the three questions originally set by the staff: What is the patient like? How will he fare in group therapy? How do habitual attitudes and expectations affect vocational destiny?

Particular Application of Test Results

Though in matters of interpretation the examining psychologist is concerned chiefly with answering predetermined questions, he is not confined solely to this function. Individual therapists often raise additional questions relative to certain patients, and request diagnosis and prognosis, in addition to individual dynamics from his psychologist to help refine a patient problem. Moreover, different therapists use different testing programs. Some require examination prior to inclusion in a group, without considering the examination as a screening device; others require examination immediately upon the patient's admission into a group, using the report as a guide. At other times, a therapist may ask that a prospective patient be examined individually rather than be asked to wait for the next group testing. In these cases, the therapist has in mind a diagnostic as well as the prescribed interpretation.

Communication of Test Results to Patients

Communication of test results to the patient rests with the therapist, who is in a better position than others on the staff to weigh such considerations as timing, current group involvement, and the individual patient's readiness for interpretation. There are occasions, however, when therapists request that the examining psychologist interpret to the patient. At such times, the psychologist must be careful to touch on only the issues indicated by the therapist. It is always easy, during an interested discussion, particularly when the psychologist knows a lot about the patient, to introduce additional interpretations; and extra caution is necessary with patients as persuasive and seductive as alcoholics are. The psychologist should be prepared for the fact that telephone calls and chance encounters will be exploited by patients to wheedle psychological opinions.

It follows from all this that just as the clinical psychologist must be flexible about scheduling examinations and modifying test procedures, he must adjust his views concerning post-examination contacts with the patients and the dual functions he may be called upon to perform as a member of the staff. One might say that within this context, flexibility is the *sine quo non*.

COMPARISON OF INITIAL EXAMINATION MATERIAL WITH FOLLOW-UP DATA

General Impression

What changes occur in the follow-up records of patients whose behavior shows altered social, vocational, and attitudinal patterns? Machover and Puzzo, reporting on patients who had had two to three years of group therapy, suggest that the greatest difference refers to ego factors, with related increase in reaction-formation, conscious striving, and overcontrol (6). Simultaneously, the "greater mobilization of ego energies" brings its own brand of tension and fear; that is, the drinking patient is haunted by the fear of breakdown. Characteristic ambivalences remain but are under better control than they were prior to treatment. These results are based on a comparison of records of remitted patients with those of unremitted ones, rather than on a comparison of test results of the same patients preceding and following therapy. Nevertheless the conclusions concerning persistent strain in remitted drinkers have bearing for the treated patients also, especially if the treatment period covers only a little less or a little more than a year. At such time, the follow-up records of apparently improved patients show a *tendency* toward a more rational outlook, toward greater tolerance of social contact and toward a diminishment of depression. This tendency is often very delicately balanced, with many continuing ambivalences and conflicts.

To illustrate: A woman patient saw, before treatment, on Card III of the Rorschach (commonly perceived as two people engaged in some kind of action) "Two men bowing to each other, they wear tux and top hat; two acrobats falling from space [side red figures]; two men with high heels like Spanish dancers — with penis protruding [same figures as in the first response]." Her post-treatment responses to this same card were: "Two top-hatted dancers taking a bow with trapeze artists spinning in the background; bull fighters in cowboy boots in an arena with bulls." The patient's omission of the sexual perception is obvious, suggesting increased rational control and social judgment. Further, in place of a morbid defeatism reflected by the falling acrobats, she seems to be working actively to keep her balance, but she is still spinning, with sharp conflicts involving brutish aggressiveness. Likewise, this patient's post-treatment drawings reflect greater effort at realistic action and increased identification with her own sex. She discards her original, aestheticized figures with mixed sexual features for easily recognized female and male ones, but extremities on both the female and male figures are nebulous and incomplete, and the concepts generally are very adolescent. The patient apparently is in transit—in a promising direction.

Evidence of Minimal Change

At times, after treatment, tests show changes which if studied separately for each test, appear negligible, but which, in the aggregate, reflect a constructive internal difference. For instance, before treatment, a patient drew a profile figure of a woman draped in a long cape, carrying a muff. Placement was at the extreme left of the page, with the figure turned left as well. Noteworthy in the Rorschach were fairy-tale references, overemotional responses ("dismaying sight"), and detached responses ("unrelated to anything"). The Sentence Completion Test reflected a mixture of self-pity, pseudo-sophistication, and evasion. Her TAT stories showed covered aggressive attitudes, unrealistic adoration of women by men, and wishful thinking in respect to success. The post-treatment record still showed a profile drawing of a woman in a long gown, facing left. Placement, however, was now in the center of the page, and cape and muff were omitted. Instead she drew hands with long, sharp fingers. Her drawing line was thin and light, however, suggesting timidity and uncertainty in regard to social contacts, edged with hostility. The post-treatment Rorschach record showed a tendency to omit fairy-tale responses and overemotionalized associations, although there was still much conflict. The patient, though, is more disposed to see the conflicts more realistically. Thus, for example, "a Scottish castle" is later seen as "a small penis." The greatest changes occurred in the TAT and Sentence Completion Test. In the TAT, interpersonal relationships were more normalized and feelings expressed more openly; in the Sentence Completion, there was less evasion though humor came into greater play. To repeat: separately, no one test may point convincingly to positive change; yet, together, the evidence may be cumulative that the patient's chronic, pervasive depression is thinning and his rational sense and control have increased.

Machover's and Puzzo's study suggests that the continuance of characteristic conflicts and sensitivities does not necessarily halt constructive adaptation; indeed, as part of a premorbid structural weakness, these may be expected to torment the patient even after noticeable readjustment (6). However, these researchers are hypothesizing. Future research may well address itself to the obvious question concerning recorded personality changes in alcoholic patients five and ten years after constructive adaptation. Are the records significantly the same as earlier, or are they now indistinguishable, say, from familiar neurotic records? Concentrated longitudinal clinical studies would provide valuable data in this connection.

It follows from all this that the length of the treatment period is significant in the matter of changes in the patient, but a period of gradual reorganization and integration may follow treatment with durable changes recorded only many months after treatment. So, the examining psychologist should be aware of the possible relevancy between the stage at which follow-up examination occurs and the obtained results.

SUMMARY

In all psychological examinations, the kind of information sought should determine the specific tests used. This rule holds in examination of groups as well as single individuals. In a multiple discipline venture of treatment of alcoholic patients, questions to be answered by the psychological material pertain to the patient's individuality, his fitness for group therapy, and the relationship between his customary attitudes and vocational outcome.

In selecting tests best-suited for the purposes of a given program, the examining psychologist is better advised to use clinically established ones rather than recent innovations. Further, using a number of tests that elaborate and support one another is more reliable than using only one. In the light of these two considerations, the following tests have proved unusually helpful in answering specific questions of identity, self-awareness, perception, and strivings: The Rotter Sentence Completion Test, the Machover Figure Drawing Test, the Rorschach, and the Thematic Apperception Test. In addition to their traditional insights, these tests provide information specific to drinking patients.

The examination of alcoholics does present difficulties in scheduling of appointments, and in maintaining control of the examination sessions. These patients characteristically avoid committing and/or revealing themselves, so that ostensibly they may seem to comply, but actually they are eluding and resisting serious involvement with the test situation. Consultations with the patients as a group about convenient appointment dates will eliminate most scheduling difficulties. In the examination room itself, though, patients may be flippant, pseudo-social, indirectly subversive, and demoralizing to others. Their maneuvers are often clever, humorous, and challenging.

In general, the examiner must drop his traditional attitudes of detachment and matter-of-factness when working with drinking patients. If anything, he needs to develop greater involvement, although of course without endangering the validity of test results. By confining groups to five or six, offering introductory explanations of purpose and procedure of examination, and showing an appreciative sense of humor, the examiner can steady the group. Further, he can reassure the more frightened and unstable among them by circulating from patient to patient during the examination. Again in contrast to traditional methods, the examining psychologist who will mix with the patients informally before the examination will find them more receptive and amenable during the actual testing.

The results from the psychological material of the alcoholic patients tend to conform with research findings, especially in regard to heterogeneity of personality structures and homosexuality. There is no inevitable tie between homosexuality and drinking. Patients differ more from each other than the literature at times reflects; nevertheless, test results show similarities, in three respects particularly: (a) a deeply entrenched depression; (b) extreme vulnerability to stress; and (c) a noteworthy lack of an esteemed self-concept. Individual tests readily reflect one or all of these features. In interpreting test results, however, the examining psychologist should be free of preconceived notions about the so-called alcoholic personality.

Comparison of ante- and post-treatment records raises important questions of durability and extensiveness of changes in adjustment and personality, and the relevancy of recorded changes to length of treatment and stages of readjustment. The question of whether the record of a remitted alcoholic tends to remain relatively constant over the years (barring expected changes due to chronological age) or increasingly resembles those of nondrinking neurotics may be answered in the future through longitudinal studies of drinking patients. Such studies are sorely needed.

REFERENCES

1. Rotter, J. B., and Rafferty, J. E.: Manual: Rotter incomplete sentences blank; college form. New York, Psychological Corp., 1950.
2. Machover, K.: *Personality Projection in the Drawing of the Human Figure.* Springfleld, Thomas, 1949.
3. Piotrowski, S.: *Perceptanalysis.* New York, Macmillan 1957.
4. Rorschach, H.: *Psychodiagnostics.* Bern, Switzerland, Hans Huber; New York, Grune & Stratton, 1942.
5. Rapaport, D., Schafer, R., and Gill, M.: *Diagnostic Psychological Testing, Vol. II.* Chicago, Year Book Publishers, 1946.
6. Machover, S., and Puzzo, F. S.: Clinical study of personality correlates of remission from active alcoholism. *Quart. J. Stud. Alcohol,* 20(3):520-527, 1959.
7. Piotrowski, S.: *The Movement Score: Rorschach Psychology.* New York, Wiley, 1960.
8. Zwerling, I., and Rosenbaum, M.: Alcoholic addiction and personality *Amer. Handbook Psychiat.,* 1:623-644. New York, Basic Books, 1959.
9. Machover, S., and Puzzo, F. S.: Clinical investigation of the "alcoholic personality." *Quart. J. Stud. Alcohol,* 20(3):505-519, 1959.
10. Knight, R. P.: Psychodynamics of chronic alcoholism. *J. Nerv. Ment. Dis.,* 86:538, 1937.
11. Machover, S., Puzzo, F. S., Machover, K., and Plumeau, F.: An objective study of homosexuality in alcoholism. *Quart. J. Stud. Alcohol,* 20(3):528-542, 1959.
12. Wolfson, Rose: Some results from the psychological examination of alcoholic patients. Presented at the Annual Meeting of the New York Medical Chapter of the National Committee on Alcoholism, 1962. Unpublished.
13. McCarthy, R. G.: Social and cultural factors in control of alcoholism. *Alumni News, Yale Summer School of Alcohol Studies,* 17(1):5-8, 1961.

PART THREE

VOCATIONAL COUNSELING AND
GROUP PSYCHOTHERAPY

CHAPTER VII

VOCATIONAL COUNSELING
WITH THE ALCOHOLIC

HUGH MULLAN, M.D.

(All areas of the life of the alcoholic are adversely affected by his drinking; in addition, his irresponsibility affects society and particularly his family. This patient (client) is handicapped vocationally and avocationally. He is often unemployed; he is disinterested if he is employed, and irritated and frustrated with his lot in life. His inconsistent work pattern causes him to suffer loss of self esteem, the daily stresses of life become too much for him; and as he slips more and more into alcoholic reveries he eventually alienates both family and friends.

Vocational counseling in the treatment center for the alcoholic is a difficult and precarious operation. Vocational aspirations of this patient, a part of his distorted fantasy life, are apt to be unrealistic and many times impossible. His imagined and highly impractical goals are supported neither by careful and consistent planning nor by day-to-day effort. At first the alcoholic pays scant attention to the counselor and yet he demands an instantaneous and miraculous cure for his occupational difficulties without offering any effort of his own. He misses appointments, or comes late or sometimes shows up drunk. The alcoholic's erratic and difficult behavior requires that the counselor modify his usual methods and goals. Vocational counseling for the alcoholic should be a part of the adaptive process whereby the patient comes to cooperate with the counselor and the other staff members so that his interests, aptitudes, and resources may de discovered and/or strengthened. When counselor and patient together can begin to make realistic and successful decisions, and when the patient is able to gain and maintain sobriety, there is strong likelihood that the patient will return to his family and to his community and once again be employed.

A close relationship between the vocational counselor and the other staff members, particularly the group psychotherapist, is essential. Ideally group psychotherapy and vocational counseling

[175]

should occur simultaneously during the rehabilitation period; the usual procedure, however, is to place the patient in the treatment group first and then institute vocational counseling. Many alcoholics resist vocational counseling; for these patients group sessions conducted by the group therapist, at which the vocational counselor is present and professionally participating, have been found effective.)

INTRODUCTION

General Statement

One of the significant currents in the mainstream of the alcoholic's rehabilitation is vocational counseling. Directly focusing upon the patient's responsibility to society, this service aims to return the patient to productive activity or, if the patient is already employed, increase his job satisfaction and productivity.

The authors, in suggesting vocational support and guidance for the alcoholic by a trained and experienced vocational counselor, in conjunction with the other rehabilitative services, indicate the considerable importance they feel this discipline has in the center which treats alcoholics exclusively. The two main reasons for which vocational help is offered to the alcoholic patient are: (1) the alcoholic disability itself is lessened when the patient is gainfully employed, and (2) the disastrous effects that a disabled alcoholic has upon society are lessened if his poor work habits are corrected. As far as the first point is concerned, the *working* patient usually has less access to alcohol during his working time and therefore tends to go for longer periods without alcohol. As far as the second point is concerned society benefits when the patient is able to put his energies to constructive use in work. Untold harm is done to society by inebriates who fail to show up or who are inept in their jobs.

Social conditions, the easy availability of alcohol, its social acceptance, and its quite general use, encourage the alcoholic to use alcohol as a way of coping with anxieties intrinsic in his condition. The tendency to drink, however, will be somewhat lessened if the patient is gainfully and satisfactorily employed, busy with interesting activities, or in close contact with sympathetic and understanding persons. Holiday periods, especially Christmas and New Years, and weekends present special difficulties for the alcoholic. When planned activity or usual routines are interrupted the patient becomes anxious, dejected, and feels incomplete and disoriented. Left to his own devices, free from the requirement to be somewhere doing something, he often finds life unendurable and starts to drink. Slips from sobriety and alcoholic escapades are so common at these times that the professional worker must expect them and further extend himself by being available for consultation. The guidance counselor working with the alcoholic client* must redouble his efforts during these periods when the client is relatively inactive and temporarily away from his job.

The symptoms expressed by the sober or nondrinking alcoholic as he *prepares* to drink vary with each individual. However, for each alcoholic, the hoped-for and the expected results of his drinking are somewhat the same. He drinks to cure himself of his malaise in living, to ready himself for companionship, to allow him to feel at ease and to make him generally more effective. In short, the alcohol is supposed to make him more human and to help him perform his duties and engagements. Thus one person may drink to perfect his social competence, another to fulfill his job requirements more exactly and a third to enlarge his sexual prowess. Many of these demands made by the alcoholic on himself are so extreme and fantastic that they are impossible to attain. It is especially important for the vocational counselor to discover with the patient *his* reason for relying on alcohol, since, in the final analysis, the patient and counselor must find other more appropriate ways for the patient to handle his stresses, ways that will allow his work pattern to be altered in a positive manner without recourse to drink. A rather obvious difference between the vocational counselor's aims and those of the group psychotherapist is observed. The counselor is interested in a reality adjustment that will put the patient under less stress while the therapist is concerned with the constructive alteration of the entire personality. As part of the therapeutic result the anxiety level of the patient should be permanently decreased and the nature of this anxiety changed so that the patient may live with the anxiety but without drinking.

*In this chapter and as well in other sections of this book the terms patient, client and counselee are used interchangeably to mean the alcoholic in rehabilitation and treatment.

Many uncounseled alcoholics tend to equate each new and different job situation with similar earlier experiences at home and during early maturation. For example, an alcoholic may be sensitive to minor discriminatory practices of his employer because he reacts to them with the same keen hurt that he felt when his mother preferred a sibling to him. As the alcoholic proceeds to make his present job situation reflect these earlier circumstances, he suffers anxieties equivalent to those earlier ones when he was first humiliated by his parents. Many times to offset the rejection and the discrimination that he feels at the hands of his employer he has recourse to alcohol. The alcoholic who wants to remain on his job must face the fact that he has to learn to control his anger with employers and fellow employees but without recourse to "self-treatment" with alcohol. The alcoholic must realize that he exaggerates out of all proportion the negative feelings that others on the job have for him.

Fields of Endeavor

In Chapter II, we discussed the aims of the various disciplines, including vocational counseling, in the treatment center for alcoholics. The counselor, in contrast to the group therapist, works with primarily conscious content which has to do with the real world and the insistent demands that this world makes upon the client. The counselor, at least to some extent, represents society's demand that adults work and improve their work patterns. The counselor conveys society's needs for the efforts of the alcoholic, by his insistence that even though the alcoholic is a patient in treatment, he must nonetheless be gainfully and successfully employed.

The group psychotherapist is primarily involved in the intra-psychic forces and conflicts within the patient's unconscious and the patient's interpersonal and emotional behavior in the psychotherapeutic group. Working closely with the other disciplines, the group therapist mostly is able to focus upon the patient's inner life and his changing relationship to himself and to the others. But this does not mean that the therapist so engaged ignores the realities of the alcoholic's maladjustments to life and specifically to his job. Quite the opposite is true: the therapist will soon discover that in order for group psychotherapy to continue with a chance for successful outcome, it is essential that the alcoholic patient be employed and also be reasonably satisfied with his job.

The vocational counselor who works with alcoholics — like every other worker in the field of alcoholism discussed in this text — must be experienced in working with alcoholics. The reason, once again, has to do with the patient's inner distress felt whenever he has to try to deal with commonplace demands. Not infrequently, a patient who seems by vocational evaluation to be well suited for a certain position, and, in addition, when it appears that the prospective employer is keenly interested in him, will for some unexplained reason fail to show up for the pre-employment interview. This need to frustrate others as well as himself may sometimes be connected with some petty grievance against the counselor or other staff member. The seriousness of this situation is compounded when the alcoholic fails to continue his rehabilitation efforts and does not return to the center.

Definitions

It is important to define what we mean by vocational counseling with the alcoholic in a treatment center where the other mental health professions are present and where only alcoholics are being treated. The vocational counselor plays the key role in helping the patient regain his social responsibility through getting him to accept the reality of having to work in order to live.

Vocational assistance, also called vocational guidance, or vocational counsel, is seen to be quite different from other kinds of help (therapy) which do not specifically relate to the client's vocation or avocation.

> Vocational guidance is perhaps the newest addition to the professions whose clinical purpose is to help people with their problems ... I believe that any formal definition of vocational guidance, no matter how carefully expressed cannot be equated with guidance itself (1, p. 3).

In general terms, vocational counseling then may be defined as both the evaluative and supportive activity, conducted by a trained professional, with a definite methodology and particular aims.

> Vocational rehabilitation counseling may be defined as a process in which the counselor thinks and works in a face-to-face situation with a disabled person in order to help him understand

both his problems and his potentialities, and to carry through a program of adjustment and self-improvement to the end that he will make the best obtainable vocational, personal and social adjustment. *The job of the vocational counselor is to help the handicapped person maximize his vocational potentialities* (2, p. 6).

Vocational counseling with alcoholics, therefore, is this kind of activity specifically related to a client disabled because of drinking, who must become advantageously employed. The counselor and client (alcoholic) enter upon a process involving evaluation, guidance, and counseling by turns; after a period of time, that differs for each client, the two people reach an agreement about employment aims, values, and procedures. This interchange produces some modification in both the counselor's and the patient's points of view; nevertheless the counselor's value system as an extension of society's concern over gainful employment for everyone, is the guiding principle. Pepinsky emphasizes this agreement — or, as he calls it, a coalition, and defines its importance and its dynamics.

> The coalition itself comes, over a period of time, to act as if it were a single strategist or entrepeneur. The idea is that if a number of persons form an alliance to do something together and if the resulting coalition continues to exist, then, as time goes on, the coalition will begin to act more and more like a single decision-maker (3, p. 70).

This coalition of which Pepinsky speaks, however, cannot come about if the counselor uses the usual client-centered approach that he ordinarily uses with nonalcoholics, to the exclusion of a more positive and directive method. To accept the *drinking* alcoholic totally, to be permissive in the conduct of the counseling sessions, or to believe wholeheartedly in the alcoholic's capacity for self-direction, all fundamental characteristics of the counseling climate with non-alcoholics, would only serve to further disorganize the already confused and unstable patient. The alcoholic patient who is both struggling to regain and to maintain sobriety and at the same time seeking to modify his work patterns requires a *structured* counseling system. At first, especially, the counselor must supply attitudes that characteristically the patient will lack: the counselor must offer direction to offset the client's lack of direction, motivation for its almost complete absence, and responsibility for irresponsible behavior, including acting out.

The Economic Problem of Alcoholism

From society's point of view, alcoholism has to be a major concern of both management and labor, because its results erode the effectiveness of both institutions. Any organization that considers it does not have a problem with alcoholism is simply ignoring the facts. For example, one authority estimates that at least three per cent of industrial workers are alcoholic and that two-million Americans are problem drinkers (4); the potential economic impact of alcoholism is therefore considerable.

> Excessive drinking causes a loss of about a half billion dollars a year in industry through lack of efficiency, reduction in productivity and carelessness. More than 20-million dollars is spent by private agencies in the care of families of problem drinkers; a like amount is spent by public agencies for the same purpose. Preventable accidents account for about 125-million dollars a year. About 30-million dollars a year is spent for taking care of alcoholics in mental hospitals. Another twenty-five-million dollars goes to jails throughout the country for the care of alcoholic prisoners. The millions of dollars that are lost indirectly through the relationship of the alcoholic and his fellow workers is too great to evaluate (5, pp. 53 and 54).

Medical and personnel workers in industry have come to realize that to fire the problem drinker, as a matter of policy, neither helps him nor the company he works for, since the time and money devoted to his training can never be recovered. Furthermore, since about a billion dollars a year is paid in wages to problem drinkers who either work ineffectually or are absent from their jobs, it seems reasonable for industry to try to rehabilitate alcoholic workers so that their productivity will be increased. What seems to be required, therefore, is industry's use of the alcoholic treatment center. A worker might then while he is still employed and employable be referred to the center for vocational counseling. Once motivated to do something about his vocational problem the alcoholic worker would be stimulated to enter a therapy group and participate in a more total rehabilitation effort.

The advantages of giving the alcoholic vocational counseling while he is still working are many. Evaluation sessions can establish and clarify the alcoholic worker's problem, identify the faulty work situation and help the alcoholic see the stumbling blocks in his interpersonal relations. The counselor should attempt to influence the client to achieve and maintain sobriety by shifting and increasing his work motivation and by guiding the patient toward group psychotherapy. It may be necessary, as a part of the counseling process, to eliminate unwarranted or perhaps unfair practices that may be causing friction between the employee and his supervisor. If the worker is contemplating changing his job the counselor, in close liason with the personnel department, can help him make the choice and prepare him for the new responsibility. Then after this placement the counselor continues his guidance during the follow-up period. Throughout all of these activities the vocational counselor of the alcoholic treatment center should be in very close touch with the worker's employer, the worker's group psychotherapist and the other agencies which support the worker's sobriety such as Alcoholics Anonymous.

Through its control over the alcoholic employee, an industrial firm can sometimes help bring about sobriety in the patient and thereby assist in his rehabilitation. When the worker realizes that if he continues to drink he may lose his job he is more likely to cooperate with the treatment center's staff and attend his various appointments with great regularity. Less stringent means are also very effective without recourse to firing the worker. For example, an industry's medical or personnel department may be empowered to put a problem drinker on probation; or pay based upon longevity can be withheld pending the employee's accepting the rehabilitation program and sobering up. Stricter measures might be to deny the recalcitrant drinker his advancement, his promotional pay, or even his pension rights. When they are imposed fairly and with sufficient warning and when the patient is in the treatment center, these measures may move the alcoholic to forego his drinking to save his career, and to save his family life. Therapy and counsel are required at these times to prevent the patient from acting destructively upon the resentment which is usually present and to allow him to capitalize on his sober moments, by gaining some self-awareness.

The vocational counselor working in the treatment center does not have these kinds of reprisals available to him except in conjunction with certain employees of certain companies. Yet he must understand these devices which put pressure on the employee to gain sobriety, and, as well, the aims and methods of personnel departments which use them. To misunderstand the goals of industry in regard to this problem of drinking or to side with the angry and resentful patient against his employer would prove fatal to the patient's successful rehabilitation and to his career. The situation is analogous to one in which the alcoholic patient is sent to the clinic by his wife who threatens separation if the patient does not accept treatment. Its gross dynamics are also identical to those court cases where the judge initiates treatment by imposing *it* instead of a jail sentence.

VOCATIONAL EVALUATION OF THE ALCOHOLIC

Introduction

The alcoholic's drinking adversely affects all areas of his life; it therefore seems realistic to suggest rehabilitation which includes both an appraisal of the patient's vocational status and also the means for enhancing it. It must be emphasized again here that although group psychotherapy is helpful to this kind of patient, it is more effective when combined with other supportive and treatment measures, including vocational counsel (6). A total treatment effort should be simultaneously directed at: (1) reducing the compulsion to drink (social work, orientation, group psychotherapy and vocational counseling); (2) determining and reducing the preoedipal and oedipal conflicts (psychological evaluation and group psychotherapy); and (3) enhancing the patient's vocational and avocational effectiveness (vocational counseling.)

Vocational development is an integral part of physical and psychological growth; it is a dynamic process that begins early in life. The factors that determine the course and shape of an evolving career are psychological, social (especially familial) and economic. Children observe adults and begin at an early age to experiment with jobs, courses of study, and various occupations that are related to these early experiences. Teenagers often rely upon fantasies to make their initial vocational choices; but then with greater age as they come to feel more aware of responsibility, they change to more realistic although still tentative selections. As the young adult matures, more and more he tends to choose careers that reflect his changing social status, his family's expectations and the opportunities afforded by his culture. Gradually the fantasy factors which characterize his career choice are modified putting his expectations in closer line with his capabilities. In adulthood, the reality of the employment situation becomes more pressing and the individual finally becomes more or less set upon his life's work.

If the adult, however, uses reality considerations *entirely* so as to block all imagination and risk taking he may be denying his creative potential. With maturity, vocational activity must represent a balance between factors which insure security and satisfaction and those factors which make for inner questioning, growth and increasing awareness of self. There must be a balance between job responsibility to satisfy oneself and job responsibility to satisfy the community.

The vocational development of the alcoholic, as is also true of his psychological integration, is characterized by unevenness and incompleteness. The nonproductive fantasy about himself and his world that marks his general adaptation to life prevails in this area of his life also. The alcoholic who has been drinking for a considerable length of time thus has an extremely low tolerance for frustration, unrealistic and impossible aspirations, and occupational values at variance with both his training and experiences.

Vocational evaluation of the alcoholic is a primarily diagnostic process, since before a counseling program can be inaugurated the counselor must first obtain a profile of the patient's ability to endure the stress and the tension of the everyday working world. The counselor must do this without reference to the specific vocation the patient says that he wants. Once the counselor finds out what the employment problem *is,* then through individual, group guidance and combined group therapy and counseling sessions he will be able to guide and direct the patient toward a work activity commensurate with his ability and his evolving self-awareness. The counselor who is working with alcoholics, particularly in a treatment center which emphasizes group psychotherapy must maintain a direct approach toward his clients.

> The counselor knows best... The counselor analyses and interprets the accumulated data and subtly, or otherwise, suggests the appropriate plan of action as well as the most feasible objective (1, p. 15).

Timing and Method of Evaluation

The case worker in the treatment center for alcoholics will have a knowledge of vocational counseling, understand its importance for the alcoholic patient, and realize the significance of this discipline in the center's teamwork (see Chapter IV, page 126). The social worker will therefore refer the new patient to the vocational counselor, if his needs and problems warrant this referral. If, for example, the patient suggests that his malfunctioning is mainly in the employment area — "My drinking is responsible for my losing my job" — the social worker will refer the patient to the vocational counselor. It must be stressed, however, that this appointment is made primarily to keep the uncertain patient motivated. Elsewhere we have pointed out that in his first sessions with the alcoholic the social worker must be primarily concerned with the patient's acceptance of a total treatment plan; therefore both the social worker and the vocational counselor during this early period act so as to influence the patient to continue in the center and to begin group psychotherapy.

In the usual case, immediate referral of the alcoholic to the vocational counselor is not indicated. Most incoming patients find the strain of their social work appointments and the preparation sessions for group psychotherapy as much as they can stand. After a patient has been placed in a group where he is being actively supported by the older group members and after he has become somewhat more stable, then more intensive vocational counseling can be instituted.

> Evelyn told the social worker that her only difficulty was a vocational problem since her alcoholism had been under control for the last five years because of her participation in A. A. Even though she only wanted vocational counseling, the worker thought that she should be evaluated for group psychotherapy

and she was given an appointment with the group psychotherapist.

Evelyn reported during her first appointment with the group
therapist that she had had previous group psychotherapy for six
weeks, but that she had been disappointed with it because people
kept coming and going. She then began to talk about her mother
and her mother's attitude toward women. The mother believed
that a single woman was lucky to be able to get any kind of a job.
Evelyn was thereupon questioned about her own sense of worth
as a woman. She burst into angry tears. She muttered that she
was always being bugged by psychiatrists. "And then right away
you bring up my homosexuality." Evelyn, over a period of ten
group sessions, identified herself first as a "drunk" then as a "homosexual" and lastly as a "human being." During the sessions of
preparation it was pointed out that although she felt labeled,
she was also quick to label the therapist as a detached scientist
and to anticipate a definite sort of response from her (the therapist.)

The therapist experienced Evelyn as very rigid and overly
intellectualized, but nevertheless able to form quick and intense
involvements. The therapist was moved by Evelyn's openness and
affective intensity. Her brittle and rather sophisticated manner
appeared to be a facade covering a deep-seated feeling of self-
contempt. Evelyn's vocational problems were certainly present
but these were not her focus or the group therapist's during the
preparatory and early group sessions. By the tenth group session,
however, it had become clear that Evelyn's vocational difficulty
centered around her feelings of inadequacy about being a woman.
Once she was launched in therapy, therefore, it became possible
for efforts to be made for her to begin vocational counseling.

The meeting between a patient who is very hesitant and indeed
resistant about accepting group treatment, and the vocational counselor will often be most valuable since the counselor is able to start
an evaluation by focusing on an external and realistic set of work
problems. During these early interviews as the counselor establishes
a positive relationship with the client he will then be able to use it to
urge the alcoholic to remain in the center and eventually accept group
psychotherapy. This approach is an important avenue for reaching

the patient who denies that he has a psychological problem and who rationalizes his drinking difficulties by stating that they merely interfere with his work, not with any other part of his life. The counselor, at this early period, should *only* evaluate and support the patient and refrain from a more intense counseling relationship, for in this way he will be instrumental in fulfilling the center's initial goal — that of offering the alcoholic continuous contact with a professional *regardless of discipline* (see Chapter II, p. 45).

In the center devoted to the group treatment of alcoholics most referrals to the vocational counselor are made from the treatment group. As we have already suggested, it is *after* the patient has been placed and started treatment in the interacting group that vocational counsel is likely to be most effective and also most likely to be accepted by the patient. During the group sessions the details about each patient's job difficulties are quite naturally aired, discussed and interpreted. The duties of the group therapist lie, however, primarily with the unconscious conflicts of the patients; furthermore, therapists are untrained in handling specific realities of the vocational problems. For these reasons, group therapists should not attempt to play the role of counselor. The therapist encourages the patient to avail himself of the service of the vocational counselor. Appointments may either be set up by the group therapist or the counselor himself during the group sessions (see this Chapter, pp. 198 to 201).

Depending upon his own predeliction, the vocational counselor can evaluate clients in groups of five to ten. The patients may come from one or more treatment groups. They may know each other from their therapy group, or they may be acquainted from either clinic contact or A. A. association. The meetings with the vocational counselor must necessarily take place in the evenings or on Saturdays so as not to disrupt the alcoholic's attendance at work any more than necessary.

Tests to be Used in Vocational Evaluation

The tests used in working with alcoholics should permit a ready appraisal of the patient's previous work history, responsibility, and ability and present occupational interest, activity, and satisfactions. Among the possible tests that might be used, the following battery has been found useful:* (1) The Otis Employment Test; (2) The Hoppock Job Satisfaction Blank; (3) The Kuder Preference Test; (4) The Alcadd Test, and (5) The California Psychological Inventory. The general findings of the Vocational Counseling Department of the New York Alcoholism Vocational Rehabilitation Project are pertinent here.

The work histories are spotty, show frequent job changes and, in general, downward mobility of career pattern. Most clients are working below levels appropriate to their training and potential and at lowest levels of income for their occupational classifications which range from unskilled to professional. A majority are engaged in clerical and sales activities. Predominantly they have had some college education and the scores from the *Otis Employment Test* indicate good, average intelligence. At intake, 72 per cent of the men and 45 per cent of the women were employed. Twelve per cent of the women were home-makers. Assuming a full year's employment, the median annual earnings would be $4,774.00 for the men and $3,785.00 for the women.

Scores were obtained from the *Hoppock Job Satisfaction Blank* and other scales designed to rate career satisfaction, self and family expectations, and attitude toward work performance. A relatively low degree of job satisfaction is indicated, although satisfaction with past employment is slightly higher than that with recent employment. Predominantly they perceive themselves as about as successful as other members of their family and as meeting family expectations. They report they are not doing nearly as well as they themselves expected but they feel they do as good a job as others doing their kind of work.

Work values scores were obtained from the patient's ranking of ten statements which were designed to represent values people commonly associate with work. Self expression (of talents and ideas) was ranked first, good interpersonal relations second, and independence third, followed by financial reward, working conditions, prestige, service to others, variety, structured work situation and security. The emphasis appears to be on individuality and acceptance more than on tangible rewards and more specific aspects of work.

---

*Our appreciation is given to Mr. Robert L. Jacobson, Vocational Counselor, The New York Alcoholism Vocational Rehabilitation Project, for making this material available.

Vocational preference profiles from the *Kuder Preference Record* reveal a tendency to emphasize unrealistic preferences rather than practical performance. Literary preferences are first choice and Music and/or Art are second choices. Clerical preferences are quite low although a large percentage of patients are engaged in clerical activities when they work. There appears to be a reversal of usual findings for Outdoors, Mechanical, and Persuasive scores in which the women in the project show a greater preference than the men for these activities which are usually accepted as masculine activities. On the other hand, the men score slightly higher than the women for Music and Art activities.

Scores on the *Alcadd Test,* a 60-item test designed to measure alcohol addiction, indicate that the project patients closely resemble the alcoholic population with whom the test was standardized. Critical scores are exceeded in the total score and in areas purporting to measure specific maladjustments in alcoholics. Pertinent aspects of the *California Psychological Inventory* profile point toward a marked preference for achieving by way of independence, relatively low intellectual efficiency, and a tendency to become disorganized under stress of pressure to conform. They are pessimistic about their vocational futures.

In general, these are people who are working below their potential but who harbor unrealistic vocational goals, work attitudes and preferences. They appear to expect acceptance and success without realistic effort. They neither experience nor expect much satisfaction from work and they have been unable to conform or adapt to the everyday problems and pressures of work. The results of their alcoholism has been a scattering of efforts, downward mobility and very unstable career patterns (7, pp. 7-8).

VOCATIONAL COUNSELING WITH THE ALCOHOLIC

Introduction

Therapeutic interventions are defined as systematic clinical approaches brought to bear on a patient by trained professionals so that he may achieve his potential for self-realization. Both intensive group psychotherapy and continuous vocational counseling are by this definition therapeutic interventions. The difference between the two lies in the fact that group therapy is concerned with the inner dynamics of the patient's personality while vocational counseling is concerned with the effective reality adaptation of the patient's personality in the areas of employment and occupation. The vocational counselor, working with an alcoholic, does not simply solve whatever occupational problems may exist. Rather, he attempts to stimulate the patient's self-directive abilities, new adjustments to an ever-changing world and to increase the client's work responsibility.

> Counseling, therefore, may be defined as an attempt by a counselor to create a permissive situation in which the client may reevaluate his experiences and so to bring the self into closer harmony with experience. It is characterized by a change from negative or disapproving feelings (feelings of insecurity, inadequacy and worthlessness) to positive feelings toward the self (feelings of security, adequacy and worth) (8, pp. 13-14).

When the therapist and counselor work with the same patient some overlap in the assistance they offer to the patient is inevitable. Depending upon the personalities and methods of therapist and counselor, there may also be an overlap in method, as well as in patient response. A patient may remark, "They're both alike. They both tell me what I have to do, but neither one shows me how to do it." In a center whose staff meets weekly in joint consultation, common points of view, common principles of action, and common methods of handling emergencies are bound to develop. Despite these outward similarities in the activities of the therapist and the counselor, a real distinction between the two exists which must be maintained for effective rehabilitation.

Generally speaking, the group psychotherapist foregoes authoritarianism toward the group patients. Instead, he relies upon the formation and intensification of relationships, and the resolution through analysis of the distortions expressed in these ties. The bonds which hold the group together, especially at the start, are believed to be extensions of earlier relationships that the patients had with parents, siblings and other significant figures. The inappropriate quality and untimeliness of these attachments as they are exhibited in the treatment group in a way that is pathological for adults can be maintained only in fantasy and only when supported through drink. The therapist thus facilitates and focuses upon the nonrational aspects of these early patterns of relatedness. He attempts to control harmful acting out while at the same time encouraging group confidences, so that discussion of intimate behavior and the accompanying feelings can be elicited. Much of the group therapist's activity is devoted to the spontaneous reporting of dreams, encouraging a response to these dreams, and intrepreting them (see Chapter XII). These are some of the principle duties of the therapist with alcoholics; but, as we have pointed out before, his task does not stop here. He must also carefully support the over-all plan for rehabilitating the patient, and he must back up each staff member's individual approach—*especially the vocational counselor's.*

Vocational counseling is different from group psychotherapy in many ways. It is practiced in a more or less fixed and relatively authoritarian format; and the counselor, after carefully evaluating the patient, tells him he "knows what is best for him." In other words, the atmosphere of the situation—although sympathetic to the troubled alcoholic—is at the same time, directive, purposeful, supportive, goal-oriented and, indeed, compelling. The vocational counselor must administer a concrete and tangible service while the group therapist does not.

> The psychiatrist (psychotherapist) rarely takes it upon himself to change the patient's environment by, let us say, finding him a job. When he does so, by referring him to an employment agency, the job itself is not the ultimate objective, but merely an intermediate step toward a broader goal (1, pp. 25-26) (parentheses the author's).

Although the vocational counselor, to be effective, must establish a good relationship with the patient, their interaction is distinct from the psychotherapeutic one. The counselor sees the alcoholic client far less frequently than the therapist; he should confine his guidance to specific topics refusing to discuss matters that are too personally exposing for the patient. Thus, the possibility of establishing an intense transference is small. Limiting the conversations in this fashion is particularly important in the vocational counseling of an alcoholic who simultaneously is receiving group psychotherapy. For, if he is encouraged by the vocational counselor to go into, for example, intimate details of his sexual life, he may never be committed to his treatment group nor to his therapist, evading group therapy and relying instead upon the one-to-one relationship with the counselor. Not only does vocational counseling differ from therapy, it also differs from the other disciplines offered the alcoholic patient in the treatment center. The social worker, for instance, is equipped to focus upon all phases of the patient's malfunctioning within his family and society; the vocational counselor's expertise should be confined to lessening or eliminating occupational problems. Sanderson points out that, although the vocational counselor's ultimate goal is established, his methods for attaining that goal must encompass the total person:

> Although the emphasis is on occupational adjustment, vocational guidance also embraces the educational aspects of growth and certainly the attitudes, feelings, and anxieties that revolve around the all-important problems of work, occupational status, job satisfaction, security and many other facets of earning a livelihood on which our society places such a premium ... Although the content of vocational guidance is the manner in which one earns a livelihood, the *focus* is the helping process, which enables the person to effect appropriate changes within himself and the environment about him (1, p. 7).

Because the alcoholic patient at the start of his counseling experience, and for a long time thereafter, is unable and unwilling to make constructive decisions about his occupational responsibility, the vocational counselor must support the patient by offering him consistency through fairly-well structured sessions which are fundamentally didactic. The alcoholic must be helped to make the best possible use of his potentialities; consequently, we do not agree with the schools of vocational counseling whose methods are more or less nondirective, because these will not offer this particular patient the optimum degree of help. For example, the following point of view is not effective with the alcoholic.

> The activity (vocational counseling) is not guided by the diagnostic findings nor is it initiated by the counselor (1, p. 12).

Even the client-centered approaches to vocational counseling seem to lack sufficient structure to make the resulting experience beneficial to the alcoholic. The counselor with the alcoholic patient may not accept as true either the client's perception of his abilities or his rationalizations concerning the vicissitudes of his life. To accept either would be to ignore the alcoholic's destructive behavior; it cannot be stressed too strongly that his motivations are dissimilar from those of the usual vocational counseling client. We therefore do not espouse, for the alcoholic patient, the use of the "help-centered" or "client-centered" approaches defined by Dreyfus.

> During the course of therapy the counselor does not guide or lead the patient. Rather, the client moves at his own pace, discussing what he wants to discuss when he wants to discuss it, without coercion on the part of the counselor (9, p. 29).

The Formats of Counseling

Depending upon the interest, ability, and experience of the counselor, three possible configurations of guidance are open to him in a treatment center: (1) individual; (2) group, and (3) group psychotherapy and vocational counseling acting together.

(1) Individual

Individual counseling, like other treatment methods that rely upon a one-to-one relationship, emphasizes the uniqueness of the client and his individualized vocational problem. The counselor in a series of face-to-face meetings establishes a reciprocal relationship with the client, the purpose of which is to change the alcoholic's vocational attitudes and behavior.

The counselor knows the patient has reached an *impasse* in his occupation, and that his block is due to alcohol or at least complicated by recent or current drinking. The alcoholic patient who lacks both motivation and responsibility for his work is confronted by a responsible and highly-motivated nonalcoholic vocational counselor, who is willing and able to help.

What seems to work best with the alcoholic, who sorely needs direction, is a structured meeting where a trained professional with knowledge, experience, and concern expects and obtains a degree of cooperation. The counselor, after carefully evaluating the client, begins to see him as often as practical. The counselor must take care not to confuse his function with that of the group psychotherapist, and must clarify his position by describing his role as often as necessary.

"In these sessions we are concerned with your occupation and how we can better it." From time to time the counselor finds that he must bring the content of the discussion back to the general area of employment or avocation. "I *am* interested in you. But perhaps what you're now telling me might better be taken up tomorrow night in your therapy group." Over and over again, the counselor must keep the client on the track, by suggesting that he discuss at length his vocational problems, his present and future interests, his past and present satisfactions in employment, his opportunities for advancement, his feelings and actions with superiors, peers, supervisors, and so forth.

In a word then, the counselor must form a *counseling* relationship with his client, in which the feelings and thoughts that the alcoholic has about his counselor are not focused upon. Unlike the group psychotherapist, the vocational counselor must stay away from the truly *personal*. His meetings are directed toward stable and better employment for his client. This fact gives the sessions their content, as well as their form and ultimate purpose. Granted, this point of view is perhaps a limited one in terms of the entire discipline of vocational counseling; but we believe it is essential in a center set up to offer both group therapy and vocational counseling for alcoholics. If the vocational counselor as a team member in a treatment center embarks upon a more therapeutic course, he will only succeed in confusing further, the already confused alcoholic. What is even more disrupting, he will give the alcoholic the opportunity to play one staff member off against another, to the detriment of his rehabilitation.

The vocational counseling relationship, unlike the psychotherapeutic one, does not include any recounting of present or past sexual material. The sexual thoughts, feelings, and behavior of the patient must be reserved for the group therapy sessions where maximum use of this material, with certain safeguards, can be made. Childhood experiences, dreams, and fantasies also belong in the weekly group treatment sessions, for ruminations on these topics encourage the patient to establish a strong transference relationship. If the patient discusses this kind of material with the counselor, the transference relationships in the group, with both the group therapist and group members, would be diluted. This would be detrimental to treatment.

The alcoholic, in most instances, has substituted fantastic ruminations and imagination for actual accomplishment. His abilities for self-direction and self-determination are faulty. Realizing this, the counselor must sympathetically investigate the client's current and past interests, abilities, satisfactions and dissatisfactions, in both real and fantasized work and avocational pursuits. At the start, there is usually a great discrepancy between what the client states he is interested in, and what he is doing now, or what he did in the past. The counselor allows the client to discuss this material spontaneously; then, he begins to point out that this manner of relating to self and others can lead only to frustration, increased anxiety, and perhaps unbearable tension. The counselor supports the patient's gradual attempts to test reality, and to re-evaluate his talents, his experiences, and his abilities. Taking a second look at his actual accomplishments allows the patient to accept goals which are more in keeping with his actual potential.

The alcoholic makes many demands upon his counselor. He may, for example, ask or expect the counselor to call a prospective employer, to write an excuse for lateness to a supervisor, or to supply a recommendation for admission to school or college. All such requests must be responded to individually. The counselor must keep in mind the maturity of the client, the client's need for backing in new ventures, and how necessary it is to preserve and strengthen the client's concept of self. With these demands then of patients, the counselor responds quite differently: With some, he may comply immediately; with others he may delay for a while; and with still others, he may attempt to have them initiate changes in their occupations themselves. In this regard, however, the vocational counselor must bear in mind his dual responsibility; that is, to his client the alcoholic patient, and also to the industrial community. If he is to properly fulfill the latter responsibility, he can only suggest employment for the alcoholic who is sober and who is ready to assume his vocational responsibility.

The vocational counselor must be prepared for a prolonged period of guidance with the alcoholic, with breaks in the relationship, and with misunderstandings and confusion on the part of the patient. The counselor must accept the fact that the alcoholic's primary work problem is one of motivation. The following excerpts from a recent symposium indicate the difficulties which one might expect in the vocational counseling of the alcoholic.

> Recovery from alcoholism is a long-range problem. Initial sobriety is only a first step. Relapses are common and the counselor should be prepared for them. The compulsion to drink is not completely dissolved by acceptance of the problem and willingness to do something about it. One must allow time for recovery. Initially, the dry alcoholic is frequently in a confused state and it may be many months before he can use his powers realistically and constructively. He may experience severe depressions and anxiety which he formerly alleviated by the use of alcohol. The dry alcoholic may have to face sobriety against a background of closed doors. His family may be lost to him, his friends replaced by drinking acquaintances, he may be debt-ridden, and often he is in poor physical health. In the early stages of recovery, he may need, more or less, continuous and many-sided support.
>
> There was considerable resistance to regular appointments. Many tended to cancel regular appointments but expected the counselor to be immediately available when they were troubled. Most especially this was so when they were experiencing negative feelings toward their group therapist or were suffering a relapse. Basically, they tried to avoid a confrontation with reality, that is they attempted to avoid facing their actual vocational dilemma (10, pp. 2-3).

(2) Group Vocational Counseling

Group vocational counseling with the alcoholic most conveniently grows out of the group evaluation period. Seven to twelve clients who have been tested together can subsequently continue together to discuss test results and implications, and to make and hear job recommendations.

Advantages to group counseling with alcoholics, although outweighed by disadvantages, are two in number: It is easy to establish the beginning sessions; and there is an early cohesion.

In general, all patients are keenly interested in test results; this is especially true of alcoholics. Unlike psychological testing, where there may be some question about divulging the results or implications of certain examinations to the patient, vocational evaluations, when they are made known to the alcoholics offer a baseline for active counseling. It is undoubtedly true that care must be shown in specific cases when reporting scores, but the sensitive professional counselor is able to manage this situation without causing any untoward effects.

The second advantage—early cohesion—is related to the fact that all the patients have been brought together for evaluation and since they all know that they are alcoholics with work problems, they expect to be handled as a group. Elsewhere we have discussed the tendencies of alcoholics to group together; and, in this instance, the cohesion may prove beneficial to the counselor who wishes not only to discuss the test findings, but who also wants to conduct group vocational counseling.

In these group guidance sessions, readiness for individual counseling may be established. The following items can be covered which will implement client cooperation in the individual guidance sessions which are to follow: (1) Describe the vocational counseling service, its differences from the other disciplines in the center and its over-all purposes; (2) Suggest the reasonable results to be expected from continuous attendance at vocational sessions; (3) Both generally and selectively give the results of the group's tests together with recommendations; (4) Attempt to allay the patients' fears and anxieties both about the testing and about employment; (5) Suggest the duties that clients must accept in their rehabilitation, especially in vocational counseling; (6) Attempt to establish and cement a counseling relationship, and (7) Provide information for common work indecisions, problems and needs.

Disadvantages to the group method, if more than a preliminary step to individual counseling, however, are many. For one thing, the patients grouped in a random fashion present different psychological problems, and have different racial, ethnic, social, and educational backgrounds. They are homogeneous in their alcoholism, but diverse in all other respects. It seems impractical, therefore, except perhaps at the very start of vocational counseling, to attempt to generalize advice and support in a situation where each person requires individual attention and help. For example, to counsel a physician-patient recently discharged from a state hospital, jointly with a nonskilled laborer who has been unemployed for ten years, is a difficult task at best, and may well prove to be impossible. Prolonged vocational counseling of groups of alcoholics only seems possible, when it is offered by the medical or the personnel departments of a large organization. In this situation, persons from similar circumstances who work in comparable positions might conceivably benefit from the inherent homogeneity of their institutional backgrounds, training, job experiences, and over-all aims.

> Group vocational guidance is concerned primarily with dissemination of occupational information, broadening of occupational horizons and stimulation of interest in vocational self-help among the individual members of a particular group (1, p. 4).

The foregoing statements do not imply that the vocational evaluating sessions and those sessions in which test results are revealed to patients, cannot be conducted in group settings. If, however, the patients are from all walks of life and possess completely different work interests, skills, and accomplishments, it is far better to resort to individual counseling than to continue to see such a variegated group for common guidance.

(3) Combined Vocational Counseling and Group Psychotherapy

The third form of vocational counseling is one that offers promise for the alcoholic. It combines the skills of the counselor with those of the therapist in the same treatment group. This method originated as a supplement to individual counseling in the N. Y. Alcoholism Vocational Rehabilitation project. In response to the way that the alcoholic's emotional and vocational problems overlap, and in reaction to the alcoholic's frequent reluctance to continue to attend individual counseling sessions on a regular basis the counselor enters the therapy group. Abstracting from this experience.

> For most of our patients, emotional and vocational problems were inseparable. The patient's alcoholism, his fears of success or failure, his faulty interpersonal relationships, his low frustration tolerance, anxiety, and his unrealistic goals, were all factors

operating detrimentally in his vocational life as well as in other life endeavors (10, p. 3).

This method calls for the vocational counselor to visit the treatment group, usually at least once a month. At these sessions, the counselor follows up on his previous suggestions, gives additional help and support, and attempts to overcome the vocational impasses which some of the group members face. In these endeavors, the guidance specialist is supported by both the group therapist and the group members. For example, the counselor asks the patients who may have refused to keep their vocational counseling appointments why they haven't appeared and the group therapist and members attempt to interpret their reluctance. In short, during these monthly sessions, the patients are faced with their responsibilities to society, and the dynamics involved are discussed in terms of each person's personality structure, his relationship to others and to the therapist, vocational counselor and other staff members. The patient benefits from this method of vocational counseling in many ways. For one thing, the patient's motivation or lack of motivation becomes more clearly understood. The dynamics of each patient are individualized. Both the counselor and the client and as well, the therapist and other group members, experience themselves more fully. And finally, the aims and purposes of vocational counsel are maintained even though the patient is unwilling or too threatened to make the effort to see the vocational counselor alone for regular individual sessions.

> Our approach to the problem was to bring the vocational aspects directly into the dynamic processes of group interaction. This was accomplished by having the vocational counselor attend the group sessions approximately once a month at which time he participated with the group therapist in the airing of vocational problems. In this manner, a number of patients were reached who were not accepting regular individual counseling appointments either because they were trying to avoid facing their vocational dilemma or were not ready for vocational counseling. This brings up an important and as yet unresolved point—that of timing. Just when should vocational counseling be instituted? To be most effective, vocational counseling should begin when the patient is able to make some realistic decisions and to take action on these decisions. However, most of our

patients had to have some means of livelihood immediately and therefore the problem became one of emphasizing short range and long range goals at the same time. The timing of patient readiness to act, therefore, became a matter for staff decision.

Typically the nature of the problems broached in the group were those of day to day frustrations in working or seeking work. It was possible to point out the distortions in their perceptions of their colleagues, superiors, and the working world generally and at times to relate them dynamically to historical roots; as for instance where the difficulty was in working harmoniously with others of the opposite sex, or for that matter of the same sex; or where the person unrealistically sought a paternal relationship with the employer or perhaps egocentrically demanded independence. Sometimes, in the case of a compulsive, self-demanding type of person, it was necessary to point out what one does *not* have to do (10, p. 4).

The patient is prone to see the counselor and the therapist as parental figures. When this does occur, the alcoholic may prefer to be with one or the other, often siding with the one he believes is the "stronger." If the counselor and the therapist are of different sex, a further complication, in the patient's preference, arises. From the vantage point of dynamic understanding, the group therapist must interpret reluctance on the patient's part to continue individual counseling sessions. Parental preference and hidden sexual feelings must be brought out in the open and explained to the patient so that he will be able to return to individual counseling sessions.

It is apparent that, for this joint method to be effective, close team work must exist between the counselor and the therapist. This goal cannot be reached immediately but with the weekly staff meetings (see Chapter II, pp. 50 - 54) and with a careful analysis of the dynamics occurring in the joint therapy and counsel sessions, the two professionals become more united in their understandings and purposes.

This technique [joint therapy and counseling sessions] brought about a closer working relationship between the therapist and counselor than would have been possible by staff meetings alone. It was of considerable help also in handling the manipulative aspects of the patients' behavior and minimized their opportunities to play one staff member against the other. This multi-level approach to patients' problems, wherein reality factors could be related to underlying behavior mechanisms, afforded the patient a chance to reevaluate his goals in light of his abilities and to see the self-defeating aspects of his behavior in more than one life area (10, p. 4).

TIMING AND TERMINATION OF VOCATIONAL COUNSELING

Timing

The timing of intensive individual vocational counseling must be based first upon the patient's readiness to participate in the relationship and, second, his readiness to accept guidance in his vocational life. No such prerequisites are necessary for either group counseling or combined group psychotherapy and counseling; primarily because these last two methods are less threatening and require less intention on the part of the alcoholic. The patient generally is less resistant to these two procedures; he takes them as a matter of course because they occur in group settings.

Timing of vocational counseling, then, is significant only in individual guidance. In working with alcoholics, the question is never one of offering or not offering counseling; but rather one of identifying the best time to establish the guidance relationship. The patient is told by the intake worker that vocational counseling is available (see Chapter IV, pp. 122 - 126). From this point on, the availability of this service must be made apparent to the patient who is being considered or prepared for group psychotherapy; or for one who has already entered the treatment group. Many times the group therapist must use his support to encourage the patient to take up his work difficulties with the "expert," and this pressure is usually sufficient stimulus for the patient to enter counseling, particularly if he has been given his vocational evaluation tests earlier.

Some patients reach out for vocational assistance too early; this must be viewed as a denial of emotional and drinking problems. "I don't need group therapy, all I need is the right kind of job." A patient may come to the center and immediately request aptitude tests, claiming thereby that he has a serious desire to better himself. However, if he is still drinking, or if he is suffering from withdrawal symptoms, it is not likely that he is ready either for an evaluation or for a realistic appraisal of his past job experiences and his current abilities.

It is common in these cases to find that the alcoholic is actually merely looking for support for his fantacized career in which therefore, he only becomes creative in fantasy. Other patients make an early demand for vocational guidance in terms of a request for the counselor to find them much better jobs, ones for which they are not suited and better than any that they have held previously. A patient who does this is actually trying to circumvent both vocational counseling and psychotherapy; he will be successful in this if he is not urged to reconsider, to remain in the center, and to accept therapeutic evaluation, group therapy and continuous vocational counsel. The vocational counselor must be sensitive to this maneuver and carefully suggest to the patient that he reconsider and enter rehabilitation more earnestly. These patients must be supported through this early period of evasiveness and denial; otherwise, they are apt to leave the treatment center.

The vocational counselor should be aware that, when a group patient is frustrated and negative about his treatment group, he is prone to use the vocational sessions to form a neutralizing relationship with the counselor. This may represent an attempt on the patient's part to replace his therapist; or to play one member of the treatment team off against another; or to find an outlet for the hostility which he is not able to express in his group. The counselor must use this kind of opportunity to establish a good working relationship with the patient so as to further the aims of guidance but at the same time the counselor must try to make the patient return to his group and re-engage in the interaction.

Generally speaking, counseling for alcoholic patients is most likely to be effective only after some progress in group therapy. This fact means that coordination must exist between the vocational counselor and the group therapist. It requires communication and the sharing of knowledge relevant to the patient's current behavior, his strengths, and his readiness to face the realities of his work situation. Vocational planning with the patient must, therefore, represent at least to a degree, a staff group concensus and include all aspects of the patient's adjustment to life.

Termination

Termination of vocational counseling with the alcoholic is based upon the achievement of certain individualized goals which in general agree with the vocational counselor's and staff's over-all plan for the patient. These goals have been jointly discovered by the counselor and the patient over a period of time. The attainment of a worthwhile position, the completion of enrollment in college or school, increased interest, creativity, and satisfaction in work, the betterment of work relationships, the lessening of distorted perceptions of employees, supervisors, peers, and subordinates—all are indications that the counseling sessions should either be terminated or their number reduced. If the patient wishes to continue—if, for any reason he gains an unusual gratification from the counselor and their sessions together—separation should be very gradually concluded. Here, once again, however, the counselor must attempt to have the patient relate more fully to his fellows in the therapy group, rather than to himself and the counseling situation.

REFERENCES

1. Sanderson, H.: *Basic Concepts in Vocational Guidance*. New York, McGraw-Hill, 1954.
2. McGowan, John F. (Editor): *An Introduction to the Vocational Rehabilitation Process*. U.S. Dept. of Health, Education and Welfare, Nov. 1960.
3. Pepinsky, H.: Counseling and psychotherapy as an instance of coalition. Eds., Jacobs-Jordaan-DiMichael: *Counseling in the Rehabilitation Process*. Bureau of Publications, Teachers College, Ohio State University. New York, Columbia University Press, 1961.
4. Hirsh, J.: Public health and social aspects of alcoholism. Editor, Thompson: *Alcoholism*. Springfield, Thomas, 1956.
5. Block, M.: Alcoholism: the physician's duty. *GP, 6*(3):53-54, 1952.
6. Bailey, M.: Final Report, *New York Alcoholism Vocational Rehabilitation Project,* Project #418. The Office of Vocational Rehabilitation, U.S. Dept. of Health, Education and Welfare, Washington, D.C.; and The Nat'l Council on Alcoholism, Inc., New York City, January, 1963.
7. Project Progress Report, *New York Alcoholism Vocational Rehabilitation Project,* Project #418. The Office of Vocational Rehabilitation, U.S. Dept. of Health, Education and Welfare, Washington, D.C.; and The Nat'l Council on Alcoholism, Inc., New York City. July 25, 1961.
8. Sostrom, E. L., and Brammer, L. M.: *The Dynamics of the Counseling Process*. New York, McGraw-Hill, 1952.

9. Dreyfus, E. A.: Couseling and existentialism. *J. Counsult. Psychol., 9*(2): 128-132, 1962.

10. Jacobson, R. L.: Vocational counseling in group-centered rehabilitation of the alcoholic. Group treatment and vocational rehabilitation of the alcoholic. Symposium presented at the Annual Conference of the Nat'l Council on Alcoholism, New York City, the Waldorf-Astoria Hotel, April 11, 1962.

CHAPTER VIII

PATIENT SELECTION, PREPARATION
AND GROUP PLACEMENT

HUGH MULLAN, M. D.

(The alcoholic, like the usual group patient, requires private preparation before his placement in a group. Unlike the non-alcoholic patient, however, he usually resists any private interview with the therapist, and requests or even demands immediate group placement. This is considered to be resistance and therefore the therapist should continue to try to prepare this patient by means of a series of private sessions during which feelings are elicited. These preparation sessions differ from orientation meetings because their content has mostly to do with the emerging relationship between therapist and alcoholic patient.

In selecting each patient for a particular group, the group therapist keeps in mind the current dynamics of the group, the needs and the abilities of the incoming patient, and his own changing subjective responses to the patient. The purpose and result of the preliminary private sessions where the therapist and patient get to know one another and where they develop a therapeutic tie are thus to arrange integrated preparation, selection, and placement. The bond developed during the sessions stands the patient and therapist in good stead at the time of placement; later it allows the patient to participate, gives him a true sense of belonging, and many times forestalls his too early and unwise departure from the group.)

INTRODUCTION

Early Gross Selection

When the clinic staff member, especially the group psychotherapist, considers a patient population consisting only of alcoholic patients, he is beset with many problems, not a few of which center about the proper selection of patients, their preparations for, and finally their introduction into the treatment group. The uniqueness of these problems stems from the fact that the alcoholic is not only a *patient*

[205]

—he is also an "alcoholic." It is only very superficially that the alcoholic who seeks group psychotherapy resembles other patients. He differs remarkably from most neurotic and psychotic patients who choose or are referred for group treatment; for, regardless of how his condition is conceptualized, he suffers from a specific pathophysiological burden, addiction, which complicates all treatment and all clinical procedures. It is essential that all staff members sympathetically get across to the alcoholic patient the point that the patient's malady precludes his drinking alcohol for the rest of his life.

> One clinical fact supports the conclusion that alcoholism is a symptom which has become a disease. Experience repeatedly proves that no amount of probing and unraveling allows a return to normal drinking. Once the state of alcoholism has supervened, it seems to remove any later possibility of controlled drinking. This new element survives as if it were a sensitized phenomenon, sure to be touched off sooner or later if drinking is attempted. The alcoholic always harbors the disease potential once that potential has come into being. He is forever susceptible (1, p. 54-55).

Ideal selection criteria for patients for group psychotherapy, methods of preparation, and the timing of patient's introduction into the group have all been established for nonalcoholics (2). Practically, however, even these fairly stable procedures depend somewhat upon the clinic population, administrative necessity, and professional aim. In the group treatment of alcoholics the criteria of major importance considered by the therapist in determining the acceptability of the patient for the rigors of this method are the factors of: (1) age; (2) mental capacity; (3) the extent of affective defect; (4) the degree of patient's motivation, and (5) the therapist's subjective response to the patient during the private sessions of preparation.

Naturally, the determination and weight given each of these five factors will considerably depend upon the methods and the values of the particular group psychotherapist. Generally speaking, alcoholic patients who are under twenty, and in addition either undeveloped or inexperienced sexually, or, at the other extreme, elderly patients who are deteriorated should be excluded from the very active form of intensive group psychotherapy suggested in these pages. Patients should also be excluded from group participation if they possess only limited mental endowment, and present affective disorder of the magnitude of overt psychosis or severe psychopathic personality.

The Significance of Selection, Preparation, and Placement

Continuous group psychotherapeutic treatment of the alcoholic patient over an indefinite time is the goal of the entire staff. In fact, it is the ultimate purpose of the treatment center. In a broad sense, then, every activity from the case worker's thoughtful response to the hesitant call of inquiry, through the confused and hostile patient's first visits to the various departments, up to the point of the alcoholic's introduction to the group, should tend to prepare the patient to participate in intensive group psychotherapy. This present discussion, however, will focus on the specific treatment methods, preparatory in nature, which are the responsibility of the group psychotherapist. These procedures insure: (1) the proper selection of patients for particular groups; (2) the readiness of these patients to be able to participate and withstand the impact of the involved and cohesive group, and (3) the proper timing of patient placement in a group suitable for him.

Most group therapists working with nonalcoholic patients carefully select them for group psychotherapy, offer them a period of individual preparation, and at the proper time introduce them to the group. Even though it has been established empirically that these procedures are sound, most therapists who treat alcoholic patients because they feel pressured almost entirely omit them. This oversight alone—that is, conducting groups made up of unprepared and unselected patients —may account for the general lack of consistency with which the alcoholic patients attend group sessions, as well as the high percentage of early drop-outs and the later premature terminations. Consider the handicaps that the unprepared alcoholic patient is under. He has not been chosen for a particular group because of his own underlying personality and behavior; he has not had a chance to develop a close and trusting relationship with his therapist; and he does not enter the group at the most propitious time either for himself or for the group. Small wonder that the alcoholic many times fails to form an enduring relationship after group placement with either the therapist or any member. All too frequently, since he has not been properly prepared for what may happen, he finds the rough give-and-take in the group too much to cope with, and hastily departs.

The therapist, however, is not necessarily to blame for failures in the proper selection of patients who will benefit from group psychotherapy and will fit constructively into a particular continuous group. The hard-pressed therapist sometimes bypasses the preparatory period because the antisocial behavior of the frustrating alcoholic seems to require the treatment group's control, restrictions, and example. In addition, group placement seems mandatory when there are staff shortages and inadequacies and when the community requires that "something be done immediately" for the disturbed and disturbing patient.

However, the therapist's forced acceptance of the nonselected alcoholic patient for group psychotherapy and this patient's attendance and fruitful participation are two different things. Many times, once nonprepared and nonselected alcoholics are placed in a group, they immediately leave. It is usually only the relatively few patients who have developed a small amount of motivation either through private individual sessions or through some counseling or guidance experienced in the past, who tend to remain in the treatment group.

On the other hand, the therapist is negligent when he omits preparation and selection because he believes that the alcoholic patient by reason of his *alcoholic identification alone* is entitled to membership in a treatment group. Sometimes the failure of the group therapist to prepare the patient emotionally in a series of private sessions is based upon two misconceptions: (1) that patient orientation and knowledge of his symptom of alcoholism is identical with dynamic interactional preparation for psychotherapy, and (2) that preparation can be offered after placement in the psychotherapeutic group.

In the first instance, it should be remembered that orientation has a limited function which is didactic in nature and not actually psychotherapeutic. In addition, whenever possible orientation should be completed early in the patient's rehabilitation and preferably performed by someone other than the group therapist. To continue the orientation program so that it becomes a continuing part of the content of group therapy retards treatment.

In the second instance, the therapist mistakenly relies upon the group's homogeneous character, which however mostly allows patients to relate to one another *only* as alcoholics. This kind of "preparation," in which one patient focuses only upon his and the others' alcoholism, does not truly ready him for the unique and exacting total emotional involvement of group interaction.

Failure to introduce the selected and prepared patient into the proper continuous group at the *correct time* also mitigates against his successful group participation and a good therapeutic outcome. Naturally, it is important for the alcoholic, who needs so woefully to lessen his extreme isolation, to be in immediate treatment. But even though this is so desirable, the careful and considered introduction of the patient into a group is significant and should not be overlooked. Untimely placement usually is interpreted by the patient as a double rejection. On the one hand, it seems to him that the evaluating therapist who sees him a single time and who is perhaps a symbolic parent, no longer wants to be with him alone. On the other hand, the group into which he has been placed at the wrong time fails to acknowledge him as a total person and considers that he is "just another alcoholic." A paradoxical situation thus arises. Although he is in the group and among others, the patient who is conditioned only to discuss "alcoholism" is still isolated. He is cut off from himself, from most of his past life, and from his constructive possibilities.

For these reasons, preparation, selection, and timed introduction, even though they prolong the period before the actual start of the group therapy, must become an integral part of the total treatment scheme of rehabilitation. The patient must be readied for the group by an individualized period of private sessions that provide a supportive, and dynamic milieu.

The Responsibility for Selection, Preparation, and Placement

The responsibility for selection, preparation, and the timing of introduction rests directly upon the therapist who is conducting the alcohol treatment group. He is assisted in these decisions by the many evaluations, suggestions, and cues which come from the other staff members who are also involved in the patient's welfare and in his rehabilitation; but the final decision as to who comes into the group and when, is the group psychotherapist's. These functions of the group therapist should not be set aside by administrative policy or need, nor should they be delegated to another staff member, not even a staff psychiatrist.

The reason for this is that group psychotherapy is the central method of intervening in the alcoholic's pathological functioning, and therefore, primary consideration must be given to making the therapeutic group as efficient and effective as possible. In dealing with the alcoholic, with whom a transference relationship is extremely difficult to achieve, the therapist must work doubly hard to insure the activation of a positive transference and then to enlarge and deepen it while the patient is becoming a constructive member in his therapy group. If at the outset, before the group therapy experience, the staff psychiatrist offers preliminary diagnostic sessions to the confused alcoholic before turning him over to the group therapist, the group therapist-patient relationship is either diluted or even undermined. This is particularly true when the group therapist is not a psychiatrist. It is most unfortunate when this happens, for then the patient, after admission to his group, will continue to look to the psychiatrist for help, advice, assistance and even love; he will fail to use the members of his group and his therapist for maximum therapeusis.

PREPARATION AND SELECTION

Preparation

It is not easy to systematically prepare alcoholic patients for group psychotherapy. One reason is that in most instances, an alcoholic will either express a desire to enter a therapeutic group immediately; or he will refuse psychotherapy altogether.

In the first case, where the patient only wants to come into the group, it is an error to believe that he needs no individual preparatory sessions, because he is well-motivated. It is also wrong to think that this decision to enter the group is a good prognostic sign. Actually, this patient in all likelihood is escaping from intimate self-evaluation in private meetings into the group. He hopes in this way to continue his defensive pattern of not admitting or avoiding experiencing the fact that he is much more than only an alcoholic. In private sessions he finds feelings about himself and his therapist which he is required to muster both noxious and upsetting. If this kind of patient is admitted to a treatment group at the group's inception, when the subject of alcoholism is the main focus, he may stay in treatment; however, if he should be placed in a more intensive group where patients are expressing their varied experiences, their unusual backgrounds, and their unique behaviors and feelings toward one another, the ill-prepared newcomer will probably not be able to remain.

When a patient refuses either private or group therapy altogether, the group therapist must rely upon the other phases of rehabilitation. For example, he may suggest to such a patient that he continue in the orientation group or perhaps continue case work for a longer period of time. Hopefully, by offering him something that is not so threatening, later on he may perhaps again be brought to the point of individual sessions and accept preparation and finally introduction into the treatment group.

The alcoholic's difficulties about preparatory sessions, during which the group therapist relates to and intimately interacts with him, may be due to any of a number of reasons. The patient may be confused about the goals and methods of group treatment, for instance. Other sources of difficulty are the realities of the patient's aberrant behavior and his ill-considered preferences. If the group therapist does not see the ultimate aim of treatment to be a lasting personality change in the patient, he will avoid the formation of an intimate tie with the patient. And again, a therapist who needs to establish his authority in the patient's life interferes with the proper preparation of the alcoholic for the group. Such a therapist will neglect the significance of the patient's inner relationship to himself, as well as the patient's relationship to the therapist and the other members in the group, and be apt to mistakenly focus on the evils of alcohol; this educative approach establishes simultaneously, the patient as powerless and sets up the therapist as an authority. This kind of therapist will also view the patient's compliance with social work, vocational counseling, and psychological test appointments as indicative of preparation whereas they actually indicate a kind of motivation exhibited *only* in highly structured situations. These experiences do not necessarily help in achieving readiness for the involved, affective group interplay. Only in an interactional, private session in which the therapist and patient dare to be open and responsive, one with another, can real preparation occur.

It is understandable that the staff of the treatment center is, at times, impelled to find and to use every sober moment the patient has. However, at these crucial moments, there must be a clear distinction in the staff member's mind between the use of a psychotherapy group and Alcoholics Anonymous. It is desirable to use A. A. as a method to control and continuously support a patient who is sobering up; however, to use the treatment group primarily for these purposes is detrimental both to the other patients and to the new member who is thus foisted upon them. Any group so used becomes a repository for a stream of inebriates who keep the group in a constant state of emergency, and prevent its members from establishing relationships and working these through to constructive conclusions.

One reason underlying many current therapists' avoidance of individual sessions of preparation may be that the alcoholic patient does present them with great problems in one-to-one meetings.

> Individual treatment of alcoholics takes a lot of time, and asks for more patience than most people can afford. The therapist has to be very liberal at the outset and have courage to carry on in spite of many failures. The alcoholic is seldom a grateful patient during therapy, although he may turn into one after successful treatment ... The patient will take what is given but usually not give anything. It turns out that the relationship is a dependency of the patient on the therapist ... He will only accept treatment so far as it gives him immediate relief; he does not want to work through painful sessions where he must provide the material for discussion. If the therapist cannot give the patient ready-made solutions and advice about his difficulties, the patient will regard the therapist as a quack and find his own "solutions" (3, pp. 7 & 8).

Often, patients, in their confusion about psychotherapy, do not encourage the therapist to use individual sessions of preparation.

Many alcoholics, for example, mistakenly believe that Alcoholics Anonymous and group psychotherapy are identical. Therefore, when these persons are offered individual sessions in any of the rehabilitative services, and especially in psychotherapy, their only demand is "to meet with the others." Or, they become upset and dejected because they believe that each conference in the center is offered merely as a test situation prior to being found either acceptable or unacceptable for the group therapy experience. Claiming that they know how to conduct themselves in groups, they refuse to consider the importance of private hours. And because they are reluctant to focus upon the nonalcoholic aspects of their lives, they resist attending regularly spaced, individual hours prior to group placement.

Function of Preparation

It is true that gaining the alcoholic's confidence and his cooperation is done by other staff members before he comes to the group therapist to be evaluated for group psychotherapy. However, as we have indicated, the therapist must have the sole responsibility for the objective and subjective sizing up of the patient, his selection, and the timing of his entrance into the group.

The group therapist, therefore, should determine the number and the frequency of preparatory hours, the use of ancillary services in the center and outside, the content of the preparatory sessions, and the methods of interaction to be used. He must realize that the greatest part of the preliminary private hours must go toward identifying the patient as much more than alcoholic and carefully confronting him with this fact (See Chapter IX).

The therapist keeps in mind the following five goals as he begins to prepare and select the alcoholic patient for introduction into and responsible participation in the group meetings.

1. He must establish a psychiatric diagnosis besides that of alcoholism, and determine whether this patient in the future will be able to enter a particular treatment group.
2. He must establish a treatment relationship with the patient.
3. He must confront the patient either with the fact that he is to go into a therapy group after preparatory hours, or with the fact that he is not yet ready (even) for group preparation and is to be referred elsewhere.

4. He must establish with the patient the fact that he is much more than alcoholic. This is facilitated by the patient's revealing himself to the therapist in an emotionally charged atmosphere.

5. He must establish an understanding with the patient about what the patient's responsibility will be in the group, and what the patient may expect in the early group sessions. Even though these things are hard to predict, the discussion can be reassuring to the anxious patient (2).

Self-selection

Establishing and operating a treatment center solely for the rehabilitation of the alcoholic means, by definition, that the patient population will consist of a fairly similar group of patients, whose resemblances are even more emphasized through their own election to come and to remain in rehabilitation. Persons suffering from alcoholism who have some motivation for treatment voluntarily choose —and those with little motivation are forced—to come to the center. Those who arrive and who stay are thus doubly chosen: first, they are selected because they are alcoholic; and second, they are selected because at the start and afterwards they are found to have or soon develop sufficient motivation to accept rehabilitation and especially prolonged group psychotherapy.

This process of self-selection, in which the patient plays the major part, continues throughout the treatment period. The center's various services are offered to the patient, beginning with case work and concluding with many months of group psychotherapy. The patient continues to make known his preferences throughout, either by being present and participating, or absent.

Once again let us stress the necessity for both the professional and nonprofessional staff member to convey to the alcoholic their interest and deep concern. The wholesome atmosphere that this engenders helps to build a secure tie between the patient and the center. Staff members must in all practical ways foster this sense of belonging in the patient so that he will continue to choose to return to whatever service he has been assigned to and will continue in his group until the appropriate time of termination.

In the out-patient treatment of the alcoholic, the willingness of the patient to participate in his rehabilitation—regardless of his reason—takes on tremendous importance. Handicapped as he is by his inability to form and maintain a therapeutic relationship (transference), particularly at first, and also by his crippling irresponsibility for himself and others, including the group therapist, the alcoholic's success in treatment depends on his day-to-day or even moment-to-moment decision to be present and sober. Zax, in describing the fate of reopened cases in an alcoholism center, indicates the questionable motives which have brought the patient back, points up the lack of a workable relationship and the absence of a bridge of understanding between the patient and the staff.

> This finding suggests that nearly half of those who reopened their cases did so with little conviction that they would be making a fresh start at conquering their drinking problem. Instead they seemed to be using the clinic almost impulsively, as one more place to go to, perhaps in the vain hope of being given a quick panacea, perhaps to obtain drugs when alcohol could not be procured, but very likely not with the serious intention of working over an extended period of time to overcome addiction... Apparently alcoholics vary in their capacity to make and sustain relationships with the clinic and in large measure this probably determines their pattern of contact... (4, p. 637).

Objective Criteria for Selection

In determining the kinds of patients who will profit from group treatment, the psychotherapist cannot separate the technical practices of selection from those of preparation. Selection is a function of the therapist's gradual preparation of the patient for group psychotherapy. Preparation and selection start when the group therapist establishes an individual treatment relation with the patient, and encourages the alcoholic to attend private sessions. The placement of the patient in his group becomes the end point in this preparatory phase. All three duties, those of preparation, selection, and introduction, come together as the therapist carefully and individually readies the patient for interaction in a group which also stands to benefit from the presence of *this* new member.

By singling out an alcoholic patient for eventual placement in an alcoholic treatment group, the therapist seems to imply to the patient that alcoholics can help other alcoholics. This may be true up to a certain point, and is one of the bases for the reparative value of A. A., but it is much less true in a setting of intensive group psychotherapy. The similar histories and experiences of the patients in alcoholic treatment groups, and their similar symptoms and behavior allow for easy early meetings. Yet, this same set of characteristics, which brings about an early cohesion, delays therapeutic change for months (see Chapter IX). It would be more accurate if instead of saying "alcoholics can help other alcoholics," we made the statement applicable to the treatment group: "alcoholics, with certain constructive traits or potentials can, in a properly constituted treatment group, help other alcoholics with similar or different constructive traits." In the light of this viewpoint, then, selection for any particular group would depend on discovering the positive factors present in the personality of the alcoholic person and the possibility for their extension. Conversely, selection should not focus upon the symptom complex and the destructive behavior which the alcoholic exhibits in common with all alcoholics.

It is erroneous to think that it is a simple matter to determine who should enter any one homogeneous group of alcoholics. The assumption usually made is that the prospective member need have only the same defect, the same behavioral problem, or the same disease process; but therapists who operate with this assumption are wrong, because they will tend to overlook those healthy elements in the patient which must be used in properly fitting the new incoming patient and the group together. *When a poorly-composed group is interrupted by a poorly-selected and unprepared patient, treatment comes to a standstill and the inadequately motivated and insufficiently related patients tend to drop out of the group.*

The rationale for using group psychotherapy with the alcoholic is not solely the attainment of sobriety, but rather to enable him to choose his own fate and no longer be driven to drink. (The physical aspects of his treatment, which we cannot discuss in this text, are implemented by medical measures and most importantly by the patient's abstinence from alcohol.) The evaluation of the patient's motivation for group psychotherapy must therefore be the first step in the selection process. Motivation, however, strongly hinges on the patient's freedom to choose—that is, the freedom to *not* drink—which in turn depends upon the alcoholic's acceptance (without reservation or rationalization) of himself as *alcoholic*. The first and very necessary step, therefore, in the center's program is to obtain the patient's recognition that he is an alcoholic. If this point can be achieved, rehabilitation and also group psychotherapy may be successful. Objective data—psychiatric diagnosis, a description of the acuteness of the alcoholism, a detailed account of the extent of the drinking or of the sobriety—although they are important in getting to know and to understand the patient, reveal little about the potential outcome of his rehabilitation and give few indications as to whether he will leave or stay in the center.

It is true for any patient, and particularly true for the alcoholic, that an initial acknowledgement of *who he is* becomes the basis for his cooperation in treatment. A patient who admits that excessive drinking "is a problem in my life," or who says that "alcohol spells trouble for me" usually stands a better chance in group psychotherapy than an alcoholic who makes no such admission. Even if the group psychotherapist considers drinking as *only* a symptom of the patient's more total organismic malfunction, it is still imperative for the patient to realize that he is truly alcoholic. The immediate and the lasting effects of drinking, whether drinking is considered to be simply an effect or the disease itself, are dangerous psychopathological and pathophysical indices of disease, and require direct and immediate intervention and correction through abstinence.

Orientation lectures offered to alcoholic patients, members of their families, and concerned close friends may produce a clue to the patient's motivation (see Chapter V). The patient's interest and concern in himself and his behavior in behalf of himself can be judged by his attendance at and attention and response to these meetings. The absence of patients from these didactic sessions indicates a paucity of motivation, so that they may therefore be considered poor risks for intensive group psychotherapy. In some cases, however, such absentees may fear disclosing to the large group their drinking problems, and if this is the problem, intensive case work supplementing the duties of the orientator may be helpful.

Later, in rehabilitation, patients may be partially screened for group psychotherapy in other practical ways. For example, the alcoholic's willingness to be evaluated by the social worker at intake, and then by the vocational counselor and the psychologist later, indicates some motivation for treatment and is a positive factor in evaluating him for group therapy. Responsible attendance at appointment hours, and participation with some spontaneity are perhaps indicative of a future potential for responsible activity in the therapy group. On the other hand, if the patient continuously breaks appointments, and is frequently late, the therapist may infer he has little real incentive to be helped, and therefore question his suitability for group therapy.

When time does not permit prolonged preparatory sessions prior to group placement, the patient's suitability and motivation for treatment can be grossly gauged to rule out poor treatment risks. Valuable information can be obtained from a knowledge of the patient's past history as well as from his current functioning in the community. Listed below are factors in the patient's work-up that will be discernible to the entire staff and which, when carefully weighed by the group therapist, will assist him in selection. These factors, therefore, attest to the nature of the patient's motivation. The better therapeutic risk, broadly, may be said to be the patient who gives indications of a general dissatisfaction with his life as a whole, as well as having made concrete efforts toward the attainment of sobriety.

Specifically, selection for group psychotherapy is indicated when patients:

1. Seek group psychotherapy in addition to AA, and acknowledge that they need a "deeper" or different experience from the one provided by AA.
2. Have had previous individual or group therapy.
3. Have accepted other forms of rehabilitation—AA, antabuse treatment, physical help, or pastoral counseling.
4. Show some degree of insight, dynamic activity, and of commitment to appointment hours.
5. Show a high level of anxiety and affect, and at the same time attempt to remain sober.
6. Accept the agency or the clinic, and realize that the staff is there to help them.
7. Accept orientation meetings.

8. Show change during orientation or individual sessions of preparation.

Selection for group psychotherapy is generally contra-indicated when the patient:

1. Expresses overt psychotic behavior.
2. Is unable to form any kind of relationship with the admission worker, with the therapist, or with any other staff member.
3. Presents severe psychopathic behavior.
4. Presents severe physical impairment.

Selection Criteria Based upon the Dynamics of Preparation

In selecting patients and introducing them into their group, the group therapist should be allowed the final decision—which he should make on the basis of his experience and judgment, and after weighing the observations and evaluations of other staff members. When decisions about selection and time of group entrance are determined by administrative needs or by a staff member other than the therapist who conducts the group, unfortunate and unnecessary repercussions will occur. The dynamics are disturbed and the therapeutic essence of the preparatory phase is obliterated. The patient's relationship to the therapist is completely incorrect, in that the therapist is not the *real leader* of the group, not being able to control who enters. Group psychotherapy is an interactional process in which the therapist must originally select the members and bring them together, and then at the end of treatment, give their autonomy back and allow them to leave.

During the preparatory phase, testing procedures other than the social-work evaluation are usually omitted. The physical examination and laboratory tests, the psychological examination, and the vocational evaluation, although of great significance, are to be administered *after* the patient has been prepared and placed in his group. To make the demand that these routine procedures be undergone before the patient has a foothold in his group usually so discourages him that he fails to return to treatment (5). Of course there can be no hard-and-fast rule about physical examination: the patient should be immediately referred to a physician or be hospitalized if he needs to be.

Staff unanimity concerning the patient's personality and a joint understanding of the patient's early group behavior can be more effectively achieved only after placement has successfully occured. After the patient's psychological and vocational tests have been given, scored, and evaluated, the therapist's course of treatment may be altered in the light of this information about the patient's personality dynamics, his strengths and weaknesses, and his growth potential.

In a series of private sessions, whose number and content are geared to the patient's individual needs, the group psychotherapist seeks to find out if the patient is suited and ready for group placement, and if he is not, to so change him and the treatment relationship that group introduction is possible. Group psychotherapists have long realized that a patient who initially is not ready for group placement may be made ready if he is given weeks (sometimes months) of preparation for entering and participating. Also they have learned that even a patient who is prepared may not enter one group successfully, but may very well enter another more suited to his needs. Even the ineligible patient who will accept private treatment hours may in the long run become eligible if there is a group properly constituted for him.

There are two related criteria which are most important for the group therapist who is evaluating and then preparing the patient to keep in mind: one is the therapist's total emotional and intellectual response to the patient; the second and more important, must be *any alterations in this response to the patient.* This point of view is consistent with that of those therapists who have an over-all esteem for the subjective and the experiential in psychotherapy (6, 7). The major selection factor is then the ability of the therapist and patient to be together and change together, no matter how subtle the evidence of change may be (8, 9). This desire to relate one to another has an evanescent quality which some studies have attempted to describe as a "mutual liking" between the therapist and the patient (10). It is our view that in working with all patients, including alcoholics, the unconscious and purely subjective reaction felt by both therapist and patient, that there is a potential for mutual growth, is most significant. In a sense, therefore, the therapist and the alcoholic patient choose to be together, not so much because "they like each other" as because they feel that they "can do something together." And it is in the early interviews of preparation that the two, therapist and patient, test their potential for mutual growth and find it present, hidden, or absent.

These initial therapeutic sessions must differ from the more traditional history-taking periods that are accepted for nonalcoholic patients. The group psychotherapist uses an interactional approach that determines the patient's strengths and weaknesses (11). The preparatory sessions become miniature forecasts of group activity by virtue of the fact that the therapist seeks the patient's response and capacity to change within the session, rather than looking for historical data. If the patient can effectively respond to the affective confrontation of the therapist, he will many times, with the support of the therapist, be able to profit by and withstand the spontaneous interplay within the treatment group. The following case history illustrates interaction during a preparatory interview.

Miss G. had attained several years of sobriety. Her entire demeanor as she came into the office and sat down was colored by an extreme lassitude. Her speech was hesitant and faltering; her words carefully chosen. She complained of feeling blocked and feelings of inertia. She began by rather mechanically reciting her drinking history, and spoke of an ever-present fear of resuming drinking. Despite her seeming indifference and lassitude, she engendered a feeling of a deeply-contained despair. The therapist ignored the specifics of her history, and immediately responded to this hidden despair. The therapist wondered why the patient wasn't connected to life, wasn't married, and wasn't having children. This expression of interest and support unleashed much affect. Miss G. began to cry over the unsatisfactory and empty nature of her relationships, and spoke of the torturous possessiveness and jealousy which overcame her in her relationships to women. She had been deprived of the basic familial relationships; her father was unknown to her and her mother was alcoholic.

Despite the patient's immobilization, deep depression, and apparent emotional deprivation, the rather striking change observed in the interaction between the therapist and patient from the beginning to the close of the session suggested the possibility for forming a good relationship and an ability to participate and change thru the interaction. The therapist's affect also changed during this private preparatory session, increasing from start to finish in interest and feeling for the patient. The therapist felt that this woman would participate with her in the mutual change required in intensive therapy.

It is to be noted that alcoholism as a disease and all that this implies is not focused upon. This is left up to the orientator who during a number of hours previous to preparation has explained and instructed the patient on the dynamics of alcoholism.

As the therapist readies the patient for group participation, he endeavors to reach through the protective layer of the patient's detachment. The almost total alienation rooted deep in the alcoholic's personality is made considerably worse by his drinking. If the patient is drinking while he is being seen by the preparing therapist, it must be pointed out to him that the drinking must stop because it is destructive, retards therapy, and interrupts the therapeutic relationships. The therapist and patient should discuss and analyze the many ways that the patient's drinking cushions his life experiences. Very gradually the patient's basic life dilemma must be identified and described to him. The following are oversimplified versions of common themes: "I did not choose to be born, so I drink." "What's in it for me? Nothing. So why stay sober?" "You don't know what it's like. You don't have to drink because you're not alcoholic." "I didn't ask to be brought into the world."

During these initial sessions, therapist and patient also begin to investigate, at first carefully, their feelings for one another and about being together. The therapist soon becomes aware of the patient's life style, the characteristic manner in which he handles anxiety, and especially the signs which might indicate discouragement and signal the patient's untimely departure from treatment. Two indices bode well for the patient's future entrance into the group: (1) the patient can be shifted from his fixed, rationalized, and evasive productions to more appropriate and affective ones, and (2) the patient is able to relinquish some of his infantile omnipotence, his fantasy of being in supreme control of everyone and everything, including his alcoholism, and even his own death.

Three definite criteria affect selection and placement, then: (1) the needs and responses of the patient; (2) the needs and the responses of the therapist, and (3) the needs and the (expected) responses of the group members. It is important to realize that the weight given each of these general criteria, as well as specific elements within them, is assigned empirically by each therapist and differs for every patient.

At the beginning, and during the individual sessions of preparation, patients exhibit characteristic behaviors and emotional responses. As these change in a positive manner or remain fixed, as the case may be, a point is reached where the therapist must decide that the patient is ready to be moved into a beginning or an on-going group, or perhaps is not to be considered for group psychotherapy at all. In Table III, at the left are listed early behaviors and moods that can be expected. Listed to the right are pregroup placement behaviors and moods that indicate sufficient change has occurred in the patient so that he may be considered for placement.

TABLE III
PATIENT BEHAVIOR AND RESPONSE DURING
PERIOD OF INDIVIDUAL PREPARATION

Initial Behavior or Mood	*Pre-group Placement Behavior or Mood*
Withdrawal of emotion, flatness, and general lack of interest	Some emotional response, less flatness, and some general interest
Depression	Less depression
Rigid behavior	Less rigid behavior
Overly defensive behavior	Less defensive behavior, with some ability for self-investigation
Inability to grasp most interpretations	Ability to grasp some interpretations
Inability to relate to the group psychotherapist	Minimal to moderate ability to relate to the psychotherapist
Frequent use of rationalizations	Less frequent use of rationalizations

During the preparatory phase, as we have said, the therapist's mood and behavior will also alter to a degree and in a generally positive direction. The inherent dynamics of this treatment situation in which the therapist and patient affectively and intellectually come together require considerable change, as time goes on, not only in the patient but in the *therapist* as well. Listed below in Table IV, on the left are the therapist's initial behaviors or moods; on the right, the expected pregroup placement behaviors and moods as they pertain to each patient, individually.

As preparation and selection continue, and particularly as the time for placement of the patient draws near, the therapist must consider

TABLE IV

Therapist Behavior and Response
During the Period of Individual Preparation

Initial Therapist Behavior or Mood	*Pre-group Placement Behavior or Mood*
The therapist is:	The therapist is:
disinterested and indifferent to the patient;	interested in and concerned with the patient;
annoyed and irritated with the patient;	less annoyed and less irritated with the patient;
slightly compassionate about the patient;	more compassionate about the patient;
detached, with little affect for the patient;	is less detached, with more affect for the patient;
unable to risk greater involvement with the patient.	is able to risk greater personal involvement with the patient.

not only the patient and his feelings for the patient but also what response the group may have to this new member. It is true that the impact of the new member cannot be definitively known until after he is introduced into the group; nevertheless it is important for the therapist to consider carefully what reaction might be expected. A therapist who believes that the patient has a "right" to belong to the group merely because he is alcoholic is apt to overlook the emergent group dynamics. On the other hand, if placement of a particular patient is made on the basis of psychodynamic principals, and if the therapist expects that certain psychotherapeutic benefits are to be derived from this shift in composition in a group whose structure and characteristics are known, then the therapist is more likely to be able to predict and observe the group's favorable or unfavorable response to the newcomer.

Table V indicates the expected group members' response to a new member depending upon the group and the incoming patient's needs. Side-by-side are listed some group factors and prominent characteristics of patients which should be taken into consideration in placement. Untimely placement of the patient—introducing him into the group at a time when the group cannot cope with a newcomer—may cause the group members to resist their treatment, to begin drinking again, to expel the new member, or perhaps even to leave therapy themselves.

TABLE V
PREDICTABLE GROUP BEHAVIOR AND RESPONSE TO THE
ADMISSION OF A NEW PATIENT

Untimely Placement
The group is:

    full, with eight to ten members; and will attempt to reject a new member.

    composed mostly of women. It will attempt to reject a new woman.

    composed mostly of men. It will attempt to reject a new man.

    in an emergency situation, and cannot attend to the needs of a new patient.

    too deeply involved in unconscious material, and cannot attend to another patient.

* * * * *

The prospective patient cannot contribute to the group because:

    he is not committed to therapy.

    he cannot face himself sufficiently.

    he desires to escape treatment through entering the group and is generally confused about group psychotherapy.

    he continues his uncontrolled drinking.

    he exhibits continuing very neurotic or even psychotic behavior including suicidal tendencies.

    he continues to need individual attention which he cannot get in the group.

Timely Placement
The group is:

    not full; it will accept a new member.

    composed about equally with men and women. It will accept a new woman.

    composed about equally with men and women. It will accept a new man.

    is not facing any emergency of its own, and can accept a new patient.

    not too deeply involved in unconscious material, and can attend to another patient.

* * * * *

The prospective patient can contribute to the group because:

    he is committed to therapy.

    he can face himself sufficiently.

    he desires to stay in treatment and does not use the group to escape from revelations and evaluations.

    he controls his drinking or is now sober.

    he does not exhibit extremely neurotic or psychotic behavior. And he is not suicidal.

    he no longer needs individual attention to the extent that he once did.

THE PATIENT'S PLACEMENT IN THE GROUP
General

The private preparatory phase of the group treatment of the alcoholic patient, conducted in individual sessions, comes to an end with the introduction of the alcoholic patient to his group. Certainly a common goal of both the professional and nonprofessional staff members is realized when the group therapist ushers in a new patient and introduces him to the seven or eight men and women who already know each other so well. If the patient has been carefully prepared over a moderate period of time, his chances of remaining in the group and of fruitfully participating are better than if he is not at all prepared, haphazardly prepared in a few sessions, or prepared by someone other than the group therapist. The bond between the patient and therapist established in the preparatory sessions continues in force in these early moments and gives the patient a real sense of security as he starts to make a few hesitant remarks about himself or someone else to the assembled group. The patient readied for the group is never a complete isolate; in a sense he has learned how to interact at the group's level, and, in contrast to the unprepared beginner, is therefore less likely to seek an immediate group identity by maintaining that he is "only an alcoholic" or that he is "alcoholic first and a human being second."

The Timing of Introduction

The patient's properly timed entrance into the group takes into account not only the patient's readiness to enter but also the group's readiness to receive him and the members' emotional availability to meet the challenge of a new troubled member (see page 225, this chapter). The optimum times for the new patient's reception is when the interaction is not so intense and so group-centered as to exclude the new member from inserting himself in the give and take, when the group needs an additional member to take the place of one who has just left, and when the new member will correct a sex imbalance in the group. Therapy groups with alcoholics should be mixed male and female and have between seven to nine members. Because of the large numbers of dropouts, a constant influx of prepared patients will be needed to keep the group up to strength and to develop a stable subgroup, a core of more or less committed patients. Some group therapists have had success in preparing two, three or four patients together for an extended time. To this small "group" then are added prepared patients individually placed at appropriate times until the group contains seven or eight members.

Homogeniety and Heterogeneity as Factors in the Timing of Group Placement

Many therapists using the group method to treat alcoholics omit a protracted period of private preparatory sessions and instead almost immediately place the alcoholic patient into a group. This approach however, ignores the heterogeneous factors actually present in the experiences and personalities of the group members. In other words, the alcoholic himself, the group therapist, and the group members for a prolonged time and perhaps even for the duration of the treatment period *only* concern themselves with the question of alcoholism, the alcoholic's behavior, and the means to maintain sobriety. Because of this single preoccupation, these groups often resemble orientation or A. A. groups. The unprepared patient who enters this kind of group finds a kind of security, not in his tie with the nonalcoholic therapist, but in his identification with the more active drinkers in the group. His sense of belonging and indeed of being entitled to membership then comes from sharing certain negative experiences and pathological personality characteristics with the others. For example, such an unprepared patient is prone to remark, especially at the start, that psychological treatment is not essential; he may reinforce this by denial of his illness and its consequences, by concrete thinking, and by relating and participating in escapades of destructive behavior. These operations tends to make him feel one with the group; but simultaneously they also tend to make him alienate himself from the group psychotherapist and from family and society in general.

Therapeutic groups composed of alcoholics, however, should in time come to resemble heterogeneous nonalcoholic patient groups (see Chapter X). This change—from the patients' considering only their alcoholism to talking about diverse experiences and dissimilar personality characteristics—is made more quickly when the group therapist has properly prepared and timed the introduction of the patient into his group. Proper preparation and selection helps the patient identify himself, his constructive adaptations and his strengths as well as the destructive theme in his life based upon drinking, the amount of alcohol he consumes and the behavior which is connected with this indulgence.

Heterogeneity is also fostered when the therapist leaves the didactic function of orientation to others in the clinic, and focuses instead on the group members' affective responses to one another and to himself. Although this therapist is just as aware of the ravages of alcohol on the patient as others who work in treatment and rehabilitation, he should not use the psychotherapeutic group to explain or teach but rather to bring about intense relationships so that these and the resulting behavior can be analyzed.

A simple rule of thumb can be used to help the therapist determine which alcoholic patient should go into which group. The well-prepared, sober patient who is able to feel and to acknowledge his relationship with his therapist and who views his life in relation to others with some emotion and sensitivity, can be placed in an on-going group whose members have become quite different in their behaviors and whose personalities have been revealed as quite unlike. The group that has become heterogeneous emphasizing its members' uniqueness and its processes will usually have a core group of patients: three to five persons, who can be identified easily. Their interaction resembles that of nonalcoholic patients, since they are capable of great intensity and trust. In addition, their attendance is consistent, their slips into acute alcoholism few, and their tendency to destructively act out markedly reduced.

A patient who has a rather tenuous grip on himself, who is sober one day and drunk the next, who will not accept the rigors of self-evaluation or the arousal of feelings for the therapist that the one-to-one preparatory sessions provoke—this patient can be placed either in a beginning group of all new members, or in a group in which the homogeneous aspects of alcoholism are still being considered by the members. This kind of alcoholic patient group lacks the core of consistent members who are present in the more diffuse, heterogeneous group; instead, it has an unstable membership characterized by high attrition, high absenteeism, and frequency of insobriety. At times acting out behavior tends to dominate these groups and the therapist may be hard pressed to control the patients. It is difficult to bring about a more stable composition because the commitment to therapy is usually lacking. The therapist must necessarily be more directive and supportive in this kind of group; in addition he will find that the role of director or teacher is mandatory at least for a while, since he must act in a way similar to the orientator, particularly if the patients have not had the benefit of systematic orientation as described in Chapter V.

Combined Group and Individual Psychothrapy

One of the advantages of group psychotherapy is that individual supplementary sessions, if required, can be used together with the group meetings, and that this combination fulfills the treatment aims. This merging of the group sessions with private sessions carefully spaced and individualized, is called *combined psychotherapy*. Combined psychotherapy, like the other services in the treatment center, may provide a rehabilitative milieu and definitive assistance by both individual and group contact with the patient.

In this chapter, we have confined ourselves to individual sessions of preparation. However, some few alcoholic patients who desperately need and will accept the closeness of private sessions combined therapy might be continued for either a short or long time after group placement. Or, individual sessions may be reintroduced for a particular patient, as needed, while still attending his group, during any time of emergency, intense acting out and so forth.

Patients are more prone to accept and to be aware of their great need for continuing individual sessions if the alcoholic group is focused upon personal conflicts rather than upon alcoholism. The intensity of the interaction and the depth of commitment to treatment permit the long standing, sober group members, especially when quite anxious to seek private hours during which new feelings and insights may emerge.

Frequently, when the patient has been sober for months, and when he begins to alter his theme of life, he appears to overextend himself or perhaps to risk too much. At times like these, when he is upset, confused and anxious, he may be tempted to resort to drink. However, should he give any indication that he is so tempted, should he ask for or manifest the need for individual hours, these should be forthcoming as soon as possible. If these private hours are instituted, their overt and covert meanings to both patient and therapist and also if possible their content should be *cautiously* relayed to the patients in the treatment group. This allows further interaction and the analysis of the very significant unfolding relationship between the needful group member and the therapist and the meaning of this event to all the others in the group.

Patient Movement from One Treatment Group to Another

In a center devoted to the treatment of alcoholics where there are many groups in progress, it may become necessary either for therapeutic or for administrative reasons to transfer a patient from one alcohol treatment group to another. If this should happen, the patient should be prepared for the transition and as far as possible told what the difficulties are and the advantages of the move. In general, the move can be made more easily from the beginning group where homogeneous (alcoholic) factors are emphasized to a similar beginning group. Because the subject matter—alcoholism—and kind of authoritarian leadership are similar in each of these groups the transition is relatively easy for the alcoholic patient who sees himself as "only alcoholic." However, a move is much more difficult if a patient must be transferred from a long-standing group which is largely heterogeneous, in its focus, to another similar group. Here, the difficulty lies in the degree of relatedness between the members who have been together for some time, their mutual trust, and their warm feelings for each other. In any situation where a move is essential for whatever reason, if possible the patient should be moved to another group with the *same* therapist. Treatment by the same therapist should be our objective throughout the duration of therapy, for in the last analysis it is the distortions in this relationship that must be lessened or finally resolved.

Placement of an Alcoholic in a Nonalcoholic Group

The alcoholic patient who has been sober for a considerable length of time and in addition who has achieved a very strong positive relationship with the therapist can very occasionally be placed in a nonalcoholic treatment group with other kinds of patients. In this instance, a successful outcome always depends upon the patient's inherent and developing character strength, plus his ability to withstand anxiety without recourse either to drinking or to a fallacious over-identification which suggests that he is *only* alcoholic. This patient can be introduced into the nonalcoholic patient group either from individual private sessions or from consistent membership in a long standing, deeply involved, heterogeneous group of alcoholics where he has been a stable member for some time.

The usual difficulty in placing an alcoholic in a nonalcoholic heterogeneous group is that very soon during the first session, it is seen that he is unable to fit in with the others. Rather than get involved with them, the alcoholic stays on the periphery of the group attempting to tell the other members why he is present. He often says things like, "I've come to this group to learn how to live. I am alcoholic." Or, "You are different from me. I am alcoholic." However, the group members, not having a drinking problem, pay scant attention to these preliminaries. A member may respond with, "I like you. We need a man in this group. Thanks for coming." Or another may say, "How do you feel about us? After all, you've been here for two sessions and you haven't said anything yet." In a deeply involved group which has been working on unconscious material for some time, a member may ask, "Did you dream about us last night? All the rest of us dream about each other from time to time. You can dream about us, you know."

The heterogeneous members who accept their diverse origins, different experiences, and unique likes and dislikes will eventually respond that he is alcoholic. They become tense and upset, even confront the patient and demand to know who he *is*. They are hardly satisfied when a fellow member, the alcoholic patient, is only able to angry, if the new patient continues to relate only his experiences and troubles with alcohol. However compassionate they are at first, the group members become listless when the alcoholic only trusts them with repetitions of his irresponsible and destructive life. At this point, if the alcoholic patient comes into the group drunk, as a way of further describing and acting out his problem and at the same time asking for help for his condition, many of the members may become angry, feel abused, and look to the therapist to control the situation. Some very irate member may even demand that the therapist evict the alcoholic, and threaten to leave himself if the therapist does not (see Chapter IX).

> A married male alcoholic patient was referred to the group psychotherapist in private practice. After a number of individual sessions of preparation the patient was placed in a long-standing group which was both nonalcoholic in membership and which had an additional therapist.
>
> At the time when the man entered the group, the members were involved with their childhoods and expressing many negative and angry feelings toward adults, their parents, and the two

therapists. At once it could be observed that the newcomer was at a loss. He apparently could not be overtly angry with his father who had been alcoholic and had sorely neglected his son, nor could he allow himself mixed angry and loving feelings for his two therapists. He attempted to convert the sessions into social meetings and continued this effort, with some success, after the sessions terminated and the patients left the office. He soon was not only inviting the group to his apartment, but also having the majority turn up.

For a while during these postgroup meetings, he remained sober while his wife offered the other group members drinks. Very soon it became noticeable that the alcoholic had singled out a younger unmarried man in the group for homosexual attention. Although this was immediately pointed out, and interpreted, the aggressive behavior persisted on the part of the alcoholic patient. He became drunk after a session, made homosexual advances to the young man, and so terrified him that he terminated all treatment and association with his group. The alcoholic continued to come to his sessions, but had begun to drink steadily. At the sessions he abused everyone, claiming that they were taking sides with the younger man. Eventually he pointed out quite blatantly, "This is the way alcoholics are. They are all homosexual underneath. What did you expect, anyway?" Soon after this explanation he left the group and would not return.

Alternate Sessions Contraindicated in Alcoholic Groups

Many group therapists who treat patients other than alcoholics, particularly those group therapists in private practice and in outpatient departments, use an *alternate* session. An alternate session is one sanctioned by the therapist but conducted by the group members themselves in the absence of the group therapist. The group members meet on a regular basis at a place and time of their own choice. The alternate session is usually held once a week and everything that happens in it is brought back to the regular session where the therapist is present. The main function of this session is to radically alter the behavior of the members by letting them conduct the meeting without the restraining or restricting influences of the therapist.

Members of the alcoholic therapy group, however, are not able to use the alternate session to their advantage. As a matter of fact, trying to use this method to complement the regular sessions is harmful, and acts to defeat the aims of treatment. The alcoholic's noncommitment to treatment precludes his having sufficient strength to cope with the session without a therapist present. The alcoholic's tendency to act out, rather than to express and talk about his feelings, makes such a meeting harmful because there is little or no control. And, finally, with the alcoholic group there is the everpresent danger that some of the patients may drink in the sessions, and this may spread. A session without the therapist may result in such damaging, destructive behavior, that the group may be adversely affected (see Chapter XI).

REFERENCES

1. Tiebout, Harry M.: The role of psychiatry in the field of alcoholism, *Quart. J. Stud. Alcohol, 12*(1):52-57, 1951.
2. Mullan, H. and Rosenbaum, M.: Group Psychotherapy: Theory and practice. New York, The Free Press (MacMillan), 1962.
3. Kjolstad, Hr.: Group psychotherapy with alcoholics. Inventory North Carolina Alcoholic Rehabilitation Program, *12*:1-33, 1963.
4. Zax, M.: The incidence and fate of the reopened case in an alcoholism outpatient treatment center. *Quart. J. Stud. Alcohol, 23*:634-639, 1962.
5. Vogel, S.: Some aspects of group psychotherapy with alcoholics, *Internat. J. Group Psychother. 7*:302-309, 1957.
6. Mullan, H., Existential factors in group psychother., *Internat. J. Group Psychother., 11*:449-455, 1961.
7. Mullan, H. and Sanguiliano, I.: The subjective phenomenon in existential psychotherapy. *J. Existent. Psychiat., 2*:17-34, 1961.
8. Graham, S. R.: The influence of therapist character structure upon rorschach changes in the course of psychotherapy. Presented at the Amer. Psychol. Assoc. meetings, September, 1960.
9. Strupp, H. H.: The psychotherapist's contribution to the treatment process, Behavioral Science. *3*:34-67, 1958.
10. Garfield, S. L., and Affleck, D. C.: Therapist's judgments concerning patients considered for psychotherapy, Presented at the American Psychological Association's Annual Meeting, September, 1960.
11. Sanguiliano, I.: Transactional history taking. Unpublished.

CHAPTER IX

QUASI-GROUP COHESION:
EARLY ANTI-THERAPEUTIC TRENDS

IRIS SANGIULIANO, Ph.D.

(In describing group psychotherapy with the alcoholic in this chapter, we present summaries of group sessions together with an analysis of their dynamics. The initial group participation of the alcoholic patient is characterized by a superficial camaraderie, singular responses, and resistances that result in a quasi-cohesive group structure which should not be confused with a more genuine group cohesion. The group psychotherapist, the nonalcoholic member of the group, is excluded from the group at the beginning, so that he must gradually introduce himself into the group which he is conducting. Only after he does this will the quasi-group cohesion develop into a more genuine cohesion based upon the uniqueness of each member.)

INTRODUCTION

The Alcoholic's Resistance to the Newness of Psychotherapy

The alcoholic's resistance to psychotherapy is great and can be equated to his resistance to change and, indeed, to anything that is new or unfamiliar; for although alcohol assuages everyday anxieties and permits the acceptance of the irrational, it also induces a state of artificial stasis. In treating the alcoholic, therefore, the therapist must learn to contend with considerably less than an ideal treatment situation. Diagnostically, alcoholics exhibit the entire range of pathological malfunctioning encompassing neurotic and psychotic disorders; but regardless of the extent of personality damage, the therapist will always encounter implusive acting out, low tolerance for frustration, and a tendency toward the immediate gratification of a momentary need, all of which are characteristic of alcoholic behavior.

The beginning of a psychotherapeutic treatment for any patient requires that he be willing to risk, have some motivation for change, and some commitment to self and therapist. The risk involved is the move into the new and unknown; the motivation must arise out of the desperate quality of his struggle for greater fulfillment; and the commitment is to remain in therapy despite the lack of immediate gratification until his manner of coping with his world is radically altered. Although the alcoholic may enter treatment in a desperate moment of need, he lacks these attributes that are necessary if he is to continue. With the patient whose presenting symptom is alcoholism (and perhaps *any* patient who suggests that any one symptom-complex is *the* problem) the very seeking of, and exclusive identification with a group characterized solely by his symptom is a denial of the new, and an avoidance of the genuine responsibility for his uniqueness as a total person. He implies in this request for therapy, "If you will help rid me of my symptom, then I can be my *old* self again."

Because of his pervasive security operations the therapist finds himself in the unfortunate position of having to build single handedly the very foundations of treatment with the alcoholic patient. He must, in addition, assist the patient in attaining sobriety, and also begin a careful undermining of the alcoholic's fantastic concept of himself and his life.

Treating the alcoholic in a group - more specifically, in a homogeneous alcoholic group - helps him accept psychotherapy more readily, despite the fact that the therapist is going along with his resistance. However, for treatment to be effective the patient must come to experience the difference between supportive groups whose main goal is the attainment of his sobriety and intensive psychotherapy. Supportive groups tend to focus on the common alcoholic symptoms exclusively without any change in emphasis; psychotherapy, while initially concerned with the alcoholic symptom, is interested in the individual differences and the uniqueness of each patient. Although attaining sobriety is a major therapeutic goal, it is not considered to be the total solution to the alcoholic's problems (see Chapter III). Sobriety is an immediate goal in therapy since without it the patient's extensive malfunctioning in relationship to self, to others, and to society can neither be experienced nor acknowledged, and without this awareness little cooperation and meaningful participation can be expected of him.

Early "Identifications" are Resistances in the Alcoholic Group

In treating the acoholic, the group psychotherapist is confronted with two facts: (a) that the alcoholic treatment group is different from all other patient groups (1), and (b) that he will usually have to modify his method of practice in order to treat these groups satisfactorily (2). The fact that all the group members have a common drinking problem provides a strong incentive for discussion and rumination. Initially with this kind of group, therefore, bonds spring up between members, on the basis of an immediate identification with a symptom. Beginning group discussions describe shared destructive experiences due to the use of alcohol: for example, more often than not, each member has suffered physical and emotional symptoms; the result of the ravages of alcoholism. Not infrequently their discussions reveal a common history of repeated attempts to get help, all of which ended in failure. Usually, too, most group members are full of "facts" and, at times, "fictions" concerning the causes and cure of alcoholism. A distinct and routine orientation period as was indicated can be of considerable help in attenuating the impact of many of these misconceptions.

In summary, then, we may say that although each patient is quite unique and individual, he also has in common, by virtue of his use of alcohol as a major defense, certain stereotyped modes of coping with his environment, including the environment of the therapy group. Almost immediately the therapist is therefore confronted with patient behavior which alienates him from them and excludes him from their shared experiences.

The Phenomenological Orientation of the Interpretation

A rigid use of formalized techniques cannot be employed with group members who are so little motivated for therapy and so prone to act out as alcoholics are. Although the group format may be based upon psychoanalytic concept and theory, great stress must be placed on the immediate group experience, and less emphasis put on casual ruminations. The relationships which evolve, the beginning questioning as to who they and the therapist are, the feelings which these experiences elicit, and the consequent emergence of a unique group culture with its own vernacular, all must be encouraged. The analytic interpretation must be more than a search for causes, it must do more than relate the patient's present to his past. The interpretive method must rather center upon each group member's manner of existence in *his* group, and in *his* life, and on *his* responsibility for what is taking place. The emphasis upon the immediate phenomenon, the "here and now" in the existence of each group participant makes for a more immediate and meaningful interpretive intervention with the alcoholic patient.

GROUP INTERACTION: THE FIRST SIX MONTHS

Indications Of "Quasi-Cohesion" in the Alcoholic Therapy Group

To describe the phenomenological group process with alcoholic members, an abbreviated actual account of a number of critical group sessions* will be reported; this is followed by a retrospective analysis of the alcoholics' initial resistance - and how that resistance was gradually resolved.

The alcoholic group assembles quickly with relative ease, and immediately forms what appears to be a cohesive unit. This fact is thought provoking, since the natural cautiousness of newly-formed groups *of other kinds of patients* is nowhere to be discerned. Questions of trust do not arise, it is assumed that all the participants are alcoholics and probably A. A. members, and this "identity" seems to offer sufficient reassurance for the suspension of caution. The psychotherapist, however, learns to question whether this is a genuine cohesion with meaningful relatedness, or whether it is another aspect of the alcoholic's penchant for symbiotic closeness. If it is the latter, the group's seeming cohesion emphasizes a pathological condition, the

---

*Much of this material is based upon a demonstration and research project (#418) in the group treatment and vocational rehabilitation of the alcoholic. Case illustrations and observations are derived from six therapy groups which ran for a two year period and were conducted by three different group psychotherapists. This study was conducted by the Office of Vocational Rehabilitation, United States Department of Health, Education and Welfare, Washington, D.C. and the National Council on Alcoholism, New York City (3, 4).

denial of the unique and constructive aspects not only of the other members but also of the individual patient himself. The therapist must therefore ask himself if this beginning group phenomena is something to be supported or even cultivated, or is it something to be vitiated or diverted? Certainly, if it is a denial of self, therapeutic group process over the long run will be defeated. If this pathological interaction is, moreover, permitted without interruption, the group member will not become sufficiently engaged with his peers and the group therapist to remain in therapy.

Because of the reality factors involved in alcohol addiction, an orientation group, organized to clarify problems specific to alcoholism, is a good precursor to beginning group therapy treatment (see Chapter V). A patient may meet with such a group prior to, or concomitant with his entrance into the psychotherapy group. It is best that the orientation discussions be separate and distinct from the actual group therapy meetings, and they may therefore be more effective if they are conducted by someone other than the group psychotherapist.

When time and expense prohibit prolonged individual preparatory sessions before a patient enters a psychotherapy group, placing him in a smaller beginning group of, for example, five carefully selected members may serve the same purpose. This smaller group of five members may subsequently serve as a core group into which new members can be gradually added. The smaller membership, after a few months, is initiated into the workings of an interactional psycho-analytic experience and not only do they offer less resistance to group therapy but they can also be counted on to help the newcomer in his beginning efforts. In these early meetings, the alcoholic's wish for and yet fear of authenticating *his* total identity, and of genuinely belonging to *his* therapy group are manifested in a number of ways. In one group that is discussed at length in this chapter, the atmosphere was set in the very first session. It is characteristic of the alcoholic's non-commitment that although five members were scheduled for this first session, only two attended. These two, nonetheless, represent in minia-ture what has been observed many times over with larger alcoholic groups. An easy exchange and seeming cohesiveness began to emerge based upon identification with a sympton. This kind of identification, however, obliterated the existence of all those present in the sense that it denied the immediate experience of being together intimately with a group of complete strangers for the first time. They all tried to mold this new and different experience into something familiar and in this way to avoid the anxiety of what was novel in this meeting (5,6). In the following pages is presented a running account of this group.

Five new members were scheduled for their first group meeting. These patients did not have the customary period of individual preparation before group placement. This smaller group membership was used a preparatory period, in addition to forming a core group membership into which other alcoholic patients could subsequently be added. The first session of this group consisted of the therapist, a vocational counselor, and, for the first forty-five minutes, only one patient, George. Later, the second member, Dora, came in. George was mostly silent during this session. The therapist spent the major portion of the time openly expressing her feelings about the absence of the other four members scheduled for the meeting. This succeeded in involving George to the extent of his having a fantasy that the others were all at some bar. He then attempted to reassure the therapist and stated if ever he weren't coming he would write. Dora arrived on the scene winded and harassed. She completely ignored the therapist and vocational counselor, sat next to George, and breezily announced, "You look familiar." She spent some time in an attempt to ferret out the reason for his familiarity, which was determined by the fact that he too was alcoholic and occasionally participated in A. A. meetings. Dora monopolized the remaining portion of the session. She was visibly anxious and tried to focus this new group completely on *the problem of alcoholism.* She became defensive, felt attacked, and was mystified by any attempt to relate to her as more than an alcoholic. Dora felt secure only in relating to George, the familiar one. The contradiction in her attitude was pointed out by the therapist. She had come to group supposedly seeking something different from A. A., and yet here she was, attempting to make group therapy into an A. A. meeting. George made some general comment; Dora again felt attacked, but directed her anger only toward George, ignoring the therapist and vocational counselor. She finally conceded that she would accept George's comments only if he were "identifying" with her and was not "accusing" her. In her words, "Maybe that's it; you're not attacking me at all, you're identifying with me." When the matter of the absent members was brought up, Dora turned to the therapist for the first time, and commented, "This isn't anything personal, *this is the way alcoholics are.*"

The same kind of apparent cohesiveness between patients was evidenced even more pointedly in the second session in which the full membership of five was present. The atmosphere was one of forced comaraderie; comments were all generalizations, and an intellectualized seeking out of causes for their alcoholism. However, of major significance is the fact that even in this initial period a genuine self-searching was also expressed, which involved them in a more subtle quest for the meaning of their own roots, as well as of the therapist's identity and purpose. These seeds of self-awareness are what must be cultivated in any group psychotherapy, and work with alcoholics is no exception. During this second session, a beginning glimmer of the therapeutic potential of the group could be seen and a beginning identification emerged which had subsequently to be broadened so that it became based on more than the alcoholic symptom. Questions about family ties and early identifications were aired which expressed their fundamental nonacceptance of themselves as separate individuals with unique origins and life experiences.

Salvadore insisted on being called Sy, since this sounded less Italian. Pat preferred to be referred to as Cecily since this was more British and less Irish. Rosalie rechristened herself Leslie: it was more "sophisticated." Prejudices were gingerly broached: one member quipped, "What's wrong with being Irish?" This kind of interaction also provoked questioning about the therapist's identity. "Who is she? Why is she with us?" "Is she married? Does she have children?" "Is she living a fulfilled life or is she another do-gooder, another martyr?" "Does she really give a damn?"

This more meaningful excursion into their feelings about their origins, was shortlived. For the most part the second session was concerned with explanations of their compulsive behavior rather than a more personal interaction. Any therapist, for example, who has made known his interest in fantasy material may be inundated with dreams but they will be told in such a way as to prevent response. The general atmosphere will still be that of a parlor game. Dreams are apt to be universalized because the alcoholic patient needs to deny his dreams have any personal significance and therefore abstracts and generalizes them. He cannot permit the dream to remain as a unique presentation of himself which would identify him apart from his alcoholism. For instance if the group members question each other about whether they have ever had drinking dreams a number of drinking dreams will be offered in rapid succession. Implicit still in these early sessions, is the all-pervading theme, *All alcoholics are alike.* Vogel reports similar experiences as he describes the "broad generalities" and "cliches" of the alcoholic patient (7).

In the third session, further manifestations of quasi-contact and interaction in the abstract became evident in the group's overconcern about the member who had attended a single session, who had remained silent throughout, and who had then dropped out. One member, Jim, suggested phoning and arranging a house call so that the absent person could be brought back into the group. The fact that Jim made this suggestion was significant since he had had no association with A. A. and their methods; his concern perhaps indicates a projection of interest and compassion away from the alcoholic's self onto the abstracted object, "the alcoholic."

Early Indices of Concern for Self and Others

By the sixth session, a subtle and yet radical change in the group atmosphere had occurred, for in this meeting the first need to be identified and accepted as more than alcoholic was expressed. Genuine interaction based upon feelings of self-worth and uniqueness had begun to emerge, so that the group began seriously to question their feelings for one another.

> One member, Rose, who had come relatively recently into the group, was very late for this session. Rose is a dramatic-looking woman, who speaks with a definitely British accent and always wears large picture hats. For the most part in the therapy session she sat silent, listening attentively but with a rather superior air. The group had done nothing to include her and Rose had done nothing to participate. The covert hostility of the group toward her came out in the fantasied fear expressed by one member about the possibility of introducing new members because they "may be people we wouldn't like." Lena was the first to attack Rose in

her absence. She explained that she hated "superior" people; as she continued to speak it became apparent that Lena believed Rose was not an alcoholic. When Rose finally arrived, Lena began questioning her immediately about whether or not she actually was alcoholic. On ascertaining that she was, Lena's demeanor changed, and her hostility abated. She then turned to the therapist and began to question her about scientific theories of alcoholism. When the therapist responded to Lena by stating, "You are so full of feeling tonight," Lena burst into heartrending sobs, and related that earlier in the day her supervisor had reprimanded her, and in the midst of her tirade against Lena, she had said that Lena would have been fired years ago except that someone felt compassion for her because she was a "boozer." Lena experienced herself as a total failure, and felt that her existence and genuine worth were completely denied. She was being paid each week not because of what she could do but out of pity because she was an alcoholic. Lena had dramatically reenacted within the the group session in her behavior toward Rose what she had experienced at work. Once Lena had established Rose as an alcoholic her attitude also changed toward her and she dared not dislike her. Alice, very much disturbed when this was pointed out, turned to Lena and said, "Now I feel as though you like me and we have become friends not because I'm me, but because I'm also an alcoholic." When the therapist suggested the possibility of a genuine "love" for self and other, Dora commented, "I don't know what love is. I guess it's because I never had children and I feel it's something only between mother and child."

The need for self-affirmation and recognition on grounds other than the commonality of symptom becomes expressed fully only after several months of treatment. One woman group member had experienced a severe emotional upheaval. Much to the group's consternation and concern she had become involved with a man in the group in acting out a deep fantasy relationship, and for many sessions the relationship between these two was the focus of the group's interaction. Finally, the woman expressed considerable guilt at taking "so much of the group's time," especially since she did not consider herself primarily alcoholic. The response to her remark, made by another woman in the group, epitomized the degree to which these "alcoholics" had changed. "I've learned," she said, "that there are far more serious problems in life than alcoholism. You most certainly do belong in the group."

As the character of the group interaction changes in this direction, new members are no longer so easily assimilated. As the group becomes more genuinely engaged the issue of trust arises. For example, a fear of revealing oneself may be expressed if many group members are also members of A. A.; the fear being that gossip may occur concerning intimate details revealed in the group which might be damaging. Or, concern may be voiced regarding the irresponsibility of another member who may in his alcoholic stupor reveal incidents which take place in the group meetings. The nature of the resistances thus change as the group engagement changes. However, despite the resistances involved with these new concerns, the resistances are now more realistically based than were the earlier fears. The deeply-engaged group, therefore, accepts any new alcoholic member with great reluctance, and a new patient who is to be introduced into an established, ongoing and cohesive alcoholic group thus requires a longer period of preparation before entering the group and an extended period of continuous support in the meetings from the group psychotherapist.

THE DYNAMICS OF QUASI-GROUP COHESION

Introduction: The Exclusion of the Therapist

During the beginning months of treatment, the forces toward quasi-group cohesion are strongly in evidence, and produce common resistance to therapeutic change. Although these forces are expected even in heterogeneous nonalcoholic groups of patients, they are more marked and have greater intensity in a homogeneously alcoholic group. In heterogeneous groups this quasi, superficial cohesion may be desirable, because it can be useful to bring the group together with some sense of belonging at the inception of therapy; with the alcoholic group, however, it appears to be a definite obstacle and one that may prevent genuine interaction, spontaneity, and personal contact if it is permitted to continue.

It is not unusual that when the group is formed the patients immediately come together around the subject which most preoccupies them, alcoholism. This stimulus toward union is, however, believed to be mostly defensive. It may be based upon a mutual uniqueness, but because this uniqueness is pathological, the common focus of interest merely emphasizes the group member's disease and his maladjustment to society.

In any "alcoholic" group coming events cast their shadow. In a very few sessions the group atmosphere will be rigidly determined by a series of forces which affect adversely the therapist's attempts to relate therapeutically to the group members. An analysis of the first six months of treatment will reveal the following five factors all of which knit the group together in a quasi-cohesion while at the same time act to exclude the nonalcoholic member, the group psychotherapist:

(a) The availability and the use of alcohol; (b) the alcoholic's essential noncommitment to reality; (c) the misinterpretation of the therapeutic group and its ultimate purpose; (d) the use of a pseudo-identification as a defense against contact, and (e) the alcoholic's universalization and abstraction of the unique in order to obliterate the personal and the new.

The group psychotherapist at first naturally must go along with these forces. He may even to some extent be able to use them for therapeutic ends, but in the long run a cohesion must develop that is based upon the patients' and the therapist's mutual and more authentic attempts to deal with the struggles inherent in living. The therapist's interruption of this state of quasi-cohesion will frustrate the alcoholic's limited identification, but at the same time will offer him support of another kind. That is, the therapist must endeavor to interrupt the pseudo-identification but in so doing offer himself, his concern, interest and person. In this way it is made possible for the alcoholic to broaden his base of identification since he is being treated as more than just an alcoholic.

The Availablity and the Use of Alcohol

In private practice, out-patient clinic, and agency treatment, the alcoholic patient, no less than everybody else in our society is exposed to the temptation implicit in the easy availbility of alcohol.*

---

*This same problem of accessibility of alcohol is present in General, State and Federal hospitals which grant passes and furloughs to their alcoholic patients.

Alcoholic patients of psychotherapeutic groups will, therefore, sometimes succumb and drink, and then either stay away from therapy or come and disrupt the group. The alcoholic binge has a different affect on and meaning for each patient, the general effect of this behavior is to interrupt the group process. The attention of the group members and therapist becomes riveted not only upon the inebriated one but also upon those destructive aspects of themselves which are related to alcohol.

These alcoholic slips are not completely negative for the therapy but it is true that to have a member in the group who is inebriated benefits himself or the others very little. The intoxicated member will have little if any recall for the events of the session so that the possibility for engagement is nonexistent, while the others, once more, have to be concerned with some aspect of their compulsive pattern (i.e. feelings of guilt, reparation and so on).

For this reason, establishing and maintaining nondistorted relatedness patterns among group members if they continue to drink becomes untenable. The roles of the sober versus the inebriated members become fixed once again. There is an immediate reaching out toward the disruptive inebriate by the others who want to help him, cure him, and take care of him, which may seem to be a move toward cohesion, but because their interest is an abstract "helping," quite apart from the person, it is actually a denial of the group members' inner conflicts and intrapsychic problems. This unfortunate reversion to the kind of quasi-cohesion present in the early sessions was apparent in the group when Sy, for example, showed up one night in an intoxicated condition. Some members attempted to help him because they would do "the same for anybody," while others were immobilized by their feelings of hostility and fear. Little could be done for him at the time beyond custodial care, and in the meantime the therapeutic process all but came to a halt. In addition, and this is of crucial importance, the nonalcoholic therapist was all but excluded from the group interaction.

The Alcoholic Patient's Essential Noncommitment to Reality

Initially and for an indefinite time thereafter, the psychotherapist who treats a group of alcoholic patients confronts men and women who identify themselves *primarily* in terms of a drinking problem. Unlike nonalcoholic patients, who see themselves as being both the same and different from their fellow group members, alcoholics view themselves as being very much the same. This "self-labeling" binds these patients together and sets them apart, in their own minds, from an nonalcoholic society. What is most important about their self-labeling, though, is that it divests them of the need to assume responsibility, and allows them to ignore the demands inherent in an awareness of time, place and person. Absences, lateness, and abrupt leavetaking are characteristic of their way of life and these continue to appear in the treatment situation; indeed, they become even more common as anxiety mounts. In the very first group session described previously, for instance, three of the five members scheduled to attend failed to appear. This kind of behavior is taken for granted at the beginning. As Dora put it, "This is the way alcoholics are." Rather than be responsible for their behavior, and accept the fact that how they behave is *personally* motivated, they cling to the illusion that what they do is solely a function of their alcoholism. A pervasive and persistent acting out which is characteristic of the alcoholic is the result.

Paradoxically, although the group members label themselves alcoholics to begin with, very few genuinely experience themselves as such. The group member who genuinely expriences his alcoholism stops drinking. Other evidences of his awareness may, for example, be a decision to join Alcoholics Anonymous, to accept Antabue medication, or to acknowledge the fact that he cannot drink again. The group member who at the inception of therapy states that he has a drinking problem is very often using his symptom to focus upon a general conflict and to avoid his more specific intrapsychic struggles. His alcoholism is a calling card which enables the group member to enter the group readily in an easy and superficial manner and at the same time it does not affect his isolation from others and his alienation from himself.

Misinterpretation of the Therapeutic Group and Its Ultimate Purpose

Society's way of approaching the alcoholic has been to try to educate him. The Socratic belief that knowledge is virtue still holds sway. The alcoholic treated much like a child in need of correction is encouraged to understand his addiction and its destructive implications. This didactic approach to control alcoholism is easily understandable. The fact that drunkenness is a socially destructive force has been acknowledged and discussed ever since the writings of Plato and Aristotle. An exclusively educational approach, however, without psychotherapeutic repair, has limited value. It may be effective in restraining excessive drinking for a time but how efficacious it is in helping to restore a disrupted life, treat deep-seated personality problems, or maintain sobriety is open to question.

Considering the prevalent educational attitude toward drinking, it is not surprising that the alcoholic patient, sometimes even a patient who has been prepared for group therapy expects the function of his therapy group to be exclusively didactic. This expectation is manifested in the many theoretical questions about alcoholism that are posed in the initial phase of therapy. Not infrequently, members request an agenda for the evening's discussion, and only later on acknowledge the anxiety which is engendered in them by an unstructured situation with limitless possibilities. Thus, during the beginning phase of therapy, the alcoholic patients demand that the nonalcoholic therapist teach them *about* alcoholism, its cause and cure. This demand serves a dual purpose, however, since it also is intended to keep the therapist and patients at a distance, so that their relationship is impersonal, and uninvolved. Interestingly enough, theoretical questions diminish as therapy proceeds, except that they do reappear at times of particular stress.

Most alcoholic patients have an authoritative knowledge of alcoholism. They can recite statistics, they are aware of alcohol's immediate and long term effects, and they can describe the certain outcome of continued inebriation. They use their knowledge, however, not to supplement the treatment efforts of the therapist but instead to deny them. The alcoholic group member claims he wants to learn new facts about alcoholism, but the therapist soon realizes that the group patient considers alcohol to be *his* province, about which he possesses exclusive knowledge and whose rituals only he understands. This general desire to learn about themselves as alcoholics is therefore another force toward quasi group cohesion. This common interest seems to act to bring the group together as novices eager to learn, but actually this is hardly the case at all. The underlying dynamic which is operating in most instances is rather the firm belief held by most alcoholic patients, that *alcohol's magic power over their lives is greater than the therapist's potential to help them.*

Pseudo-identification as a Defense Against Contact

The alcoholic's beginning identification in the group is only with the pathological condition of alcoholism. By identifying only his and the other members' alcoholism, each patient denies the individual and constructive aspects in the others in the group, as well as the constructive strivings in himself. This identification precludes a genuine engagement between member and member, and between member and therapist. In addition, as has been pointed out, it adversely effects the therapeutic process by excluding or even at times eliminating the nonalcoholic therapist.

In the very first session of the group, this pseudo-contact was epitomized by Dora's initial comment to George: "You look familiar," and continuous inquiry, "Are all alcoholics this way?" In the sessions which followed, genuine contact was avoided through their universalization of their dreams, and their questioning each other about drinking dreams. The nondiscriminative response which is an all-pervasive aspect of alcoholism, could be seen also in the group's efforts to retrieve a member who left, despite the fact that he had attended only one session and was virtually a nonparticipant! Montaigne in his essay on drunkenness interestingly points out the indifference of the palate necessary to make a "good toper" (8).

The more differentiated and meaningful feelings in peer relationships are apparently incomprehensible to the alcoholic. Any adult relationship in which there is an experience of difference or separateness is often felt by the alcoholic as threatening or even hostile. Dora's statement that love is something that exists for her *only* between mother and child depicts the alcoholic's essentially symbiotic manner of relating to the other. Love, or more specifically their very survival, is seen only in terms of connection with the nurturing mother. This limited capacity for involvement does have serious consequences for the formation of a genuine therapeutic relationship. In any effective therapeutic treatment, the individual's horizons must grow beyond the limited scope encompassed by the mother's breast. However, in the treatment of the alcoholic the therapist is again at cross purposes. He must learn to use at first what in the end may prove to be the very cause of a therapeutic impasse. The alcoholic's capacity to form this dependent relationship despite its limitation is still an opening for the beginning of therapy. Unfortunately, there are some alcoholics who resist even the maternal tie and so deny the beginning possibility for any contact. They are usually the ones who are vehemently reacting against their passive dependency needs (see Chapter XIII).

The greatest hazard in the formation of these symbiotic patterns of relating is that they can result in the exclusion of the therapist. This is most often observed in the beginning group patient who will indiscriminately relate only to the other group members simply because they are alcoholic and therefore not separate or different from him. It is incumbent upon the psychotherapist then gradually to intervene in these relationships. This, however, must be done with care and sensitivity. The psychotherapist must at first use the alcoholic's need and desire for the symbiotic union, in the activation and directing of these dependency needs toward *the therapist* and the psychotherapy group as a whole. It is only in this way that the therapist can be included so that hopefully the relationship can change and grow. The therapist may begin his task by interrupting the alcoholic group member's tendency to assume an objective, over-intellectualized, analytic view *about* himself and others. To do this, the therapist begins to feelingly respond to each member in the group as separate and unique individuals. Because the alcoholic patient continues for an indefinite time to need an all-accepting and all-giving relationship, he will naturally consider that the therapist is there solely to gratify his demands. If the therapist expresses his own requirements too early in the formation of the treatment group, any such statement is likely to be experienced as a rejection by the patients. For these reasons, the issues of the scheduling of appointments, the demands relating to the keeping of appointments, the payment of fees, and so forth will become critical aspects of the therapeutic relationship. If the therapist requests committed attendance or objects to lateness to precipitously, an alcoholic patient may respond by a premature termination of treatment. Indeed, any expression of need for satisfaction or fulfillment by the therapist during the early part of group treatment is immediately threatening to the alcoholic patient.

In passing, we might add that this kind of dependent union continues to operate in the remitted alcoholic. In order to maintain his sobriety he seems to enter upon the other aspect of the symbiosis; that is, he becomes the nursing "mother." The later steps of Alcoholics Anonymous, the neccessity for life-long membership in A.A., and also the large number of alcoholics who marry other alcoholics lends support to this view. Generally then, the alcoholic grouping initially can tolerate only pseudo-identification, or more specifically a symbiotic relationship to a "mother" figure. Differentiated and genuinely peer relationships between the patient and the other group members is minimal. Thus, self-definition is avoided.

The Alcoholic's Universalization and Abstraction of the Unique in Order to Obliterate the Personal and the New

The alcoholic patient in the therapy group has great difficulty in facing *his* responsibility for the immediate and passing moment. He refuses to see the part he plays in the day-to-day or the week-to-week therapeutic process. In denying the immediate experience, he repeatedly universalizes and abstracts anything which would identify him as a unique person. His preference for group meetings with fixed agendas of fixed membership of only alcoholics, and a fixed recounting of symptoms, is an attempt at control of anxiety by obliterating what is new or unknown. This denial of self, and personal meaning, moreover, is supported by the alcoholic group membership. Most often the therapist's responses and interpretations are met with a nondiscriminative retort such as "all alcoholics are like that."

The group's need, cited above, to determine whether or not any new member is alcoholic, illustrates the anxiety inherent in unfamiliarity. The fear which was expressed by one member of his possibly disliking new members was another example. Risk becomes minimal when the group constellation is alcoholic. One member openly voiced this feeling when she stated, "If we know someone is alcoholic, we know something about him, his weaknesses and vulnerability." Turning to the therapist, she added, "We don't know yours." Or again, Lena's attempt to theorize about alcoholism expressed her efforts to escape her own desperation, and her sense of abject failure and inadequacy aroused by her exchange with her supervisor.

The alcoholic group members' attempt to abstract their dreams, is one more illustration of how they minimize their responsibility for themselves. With the denial of their dreams, there is an implicit denial of uniqueness. The existence of each of the participants is ignored. The therapist as a total, feeling person rather than just an objective observer is denied in Dora's comments about the absent members, "It's nothing personal, that's how alcoholics are." Dora denied George, another group member, also, when she responded only to his alcoholism. It may well be that what the alcoholic is telling us is that it is easier to be alcoholic than personally disturbed. As one member stated, "I'd rather be crazy, drunk than crazy, sober," and then added, "I've forgotten how I think when I'm sober."

THE ALCOHOLIC MEMBER IN AN NONALCOHOLIC GROUP

The response of a nonalcoholic patient group to the alcoholic group member generally serves to support the alcoholic at first. As a whole, the nonalcoholic group members treat the problem drinker with far more compassion and less contempt than do members in a homogeneous group. However, the heterogeneous patient group is apt to be far less tolerant of the alcoholic's continuous nondiscriminative responsiveness. Attempts are often made in the heterogeneous patient group to dislodge the alcoholic from his specialness as a minority. The therapist in such a group is also confronted with his special treatment of the alcoholic patient; and any fears that the nonalcoholic group members may have of being exploited by the alcoholism are actively and openly expressed.

> Amy and Ben both were actively drinking. After having been in an alcoholic treatment group, they were placed in a heterogeneous patient group. Both were active in A.A. and had been on Antabuse therapy. Their new group at first welcomed them warmly, and supported their efforts. However, after several weeks of rather characteristic behavior, the heterogeneous group began to object. Ben was frequently absent, came drunk, and insisted on speaking in generalities and cliches. Amy also absented herself frequently, and

preferred abstractions about herself, to any genuine interaction with the others. She openly admitted that she was afraid of the possible involvements in a group of this kind. Both Ben and Amy voiced a preference for the previous homogeneous group. Ruth, a nonalcoholic, finally turned to Amy and expressed her sense of impotent frustration by saying, "You want to be an alcoholic because you want to be exclusive. You don't want to be faced with the truth that you are more than a drunk." Ruth then turned to the therapist, whom she experienced as both impotent and exploited by the alcoholism, and added angrily, "Why are these two non-sequitors in our group? If all they are are alcoholics and not human beings like the rest of us, then they shouldn't be with us, let them stay only with A.A." Another group member, Joshua, then related a dream in which "A young boy is badly in need of help. He can't communicate. We try to help but suddenly we are called away. Someone has been heavily drinking and we all have to leave the young boy to help the drunken one."

It is apparent from this dream that Joshua experienced Amy's and Ben's alcoholism both as an exploitation and distraction from the more urgent human struggle, the inability to communicate. The group described, despaired over the impossibility of truly belonging and identifying when some group members are specifically and exclusively symptom-oriented. The underlying contempt of the alcoholic which is implicit in the development of a homogeneous group, was expressed in Ben's preference for the alcoholic group. "I like the alcoholic group better. It made me feel stronger. I guess I felt above the others."

There is little question that a homogeneously alcoholic treatment group is construed by the alcoholic patient as less threatening than a heterogeneous group. For this reason, it may well be considered the preferred means of introducing the patient to psychotherapy. The immediate common identification with a symptom permits alcoholic patients to have a motive for beginning treatment. Although such a limited identification can later become a major obstacle to treatment, it often does permit the patient to remain in a therapeutic environment long enough so that the possibility for deeper and more committed participation increases.

REFERENCES

1. Feibel, C.: The archaic personality structure of alcoholic: and its implications for group psychotherapy. *Int. J. Group Psychoth., 10*:39-45, 1960.

2. Mullan, H., and Rosenbaum, M.: *Group Psychotherapy: Theory and Practice.* New York, Free Press of Glencoe, 1962.
3. Mullan, H., and Sangiuliano, I.: *Group psychotherapy and the alcoholic.* 1. Early therapeutic moves. Presented at the Third World Congress of Psychiatry, Montreal, Canada, June 3-10, 1961.
4. Mullan, H., and Sangiuliano, I.: Group psychotherapy and the alcoholic. 2. The phenomenology of early group interaction. Reprint from Nat'l Council on Alcoholism, New York City.
5. Jaspers, K.: *Way to Wisdom.* New Haven, Yale University Press, 1951.
6. Maslow, A.: *Article in Existential Inquiries, 1:* 1959.
7. Vogel, S.: Some aspects of group psychotherapy with alcoholics. *Int. J. Group Psychoth., 7*:302-309, 1957.
8. Montaigne, M.: *The Essays.* Book the Second: Of drunkenness.

CHAPTER X

AUTHENTIC COHESION:
THE INTERVENTION
BY THE NONALCOHOLIC MEMBER,
THE GROUP PSYCHOTHERAPIST

IRIS SANGIULIANO, Ph.D.

(A paradoxical situation exists during the early months of group psychotherapy with the alcoholic, which is the result of the tendency that group members have to exclude the therapist because he is nonalcoholic while at the same time the therapist continues to conduct the group. As long as this exclusion occurs the group is not truly cohesive. The therapist who at the beginning is considered an intruder by the alcoholic group members must use a treatment approach which insures their more complete participation and at the same time their greater acceptance of him.)

INTRODUCTION

Early in the group treatment of alcoholics, each patient in the group regards the therapist as antithetical to himself and to the other patients. The nonalcoholic therapist is almost brushed aside; the group members ignore him, speak only to each other and then only about their common experiences with alcohol. This situation in which the leader is excluded from his group reflects the belief held by most alcoholics that "only an alcoholic can help another alcoholic." Initially then, the therapist's method must be directed toward including enough of his thoughts and feelings that are relevant to the group interaction, for his presence to begin to be felt and acknowledged by the group.

Peggy had attended group a few sessions when she announced that she was getting a two week vacation and she was not coming to group even though she intended to remain in the city. The therapist responded, "I make certain to be here each week and I'm anxious about getting here on time, why do you want a vacation from us? I intend to be here for the next two weeks."

However, coincident with the therapist's endeavor to achieve a genuine acceptance by the alcoholic members, he must also be actively concerned with the patients' uncontrolled drinking. This is of primary importance. Unless the alcoholic patients are able to attain some degree of sobriety, even though they attend group sessions the psychotherapy offered is unavailable to them. The psychotherapist must therefore use all available methods to interrupt the compulsive drinking of each patient. The sphere of activity of the group therapist conducting alcoholic groups is necessarily extensive. He must be informed about and able to utilize, when necessary, all community facilities—medical, psychiatric, and social—that can assist the alcoholic to attain sobriety (1, 2). The therapist may suggest that the patient consult a physician for aversion drugs, such as Antabuse, or for physical rehabilitation; he may hospitalize for emergency physical support and drying-out; he may direct the patient to Alcoholics Anonymous. In the group, he interprets directly, counsels, makes definite suggestions, and indicates his concern in many ways. Unlike group psychotherapy with other patients, group treatment with alcoholics should help them to cope with the every day reality problems which were avoided in their alcoholic state and which loom large in their new found sobriety. This must be done in addition to the more usual analytic method of interpretation which is aimed at discovering and altering the fantasy involved in their distorted perception of reality. Although direct counseling, when used, limits the depth of the therapist's analytical function, it must be assumed in the early relationship because a patient who is actively drinking is often incapable of sound judgment. The therapist thus may temporarily have to assume the role of counselor and assist the patient with any number of pressing reality problems—such as the disruption of vocational, social, and familial ties—for any kind of future rehabilitative effort to be effective. The alcoholic is at odds with his society. He cannot, as long as he drinks, participate satisfactorily in its culture. The group psychotherapist therefore must mediate between the antisocial or asocial patient and his society.

General Methods of Therapist Participation:
The Availability of the Group Therapist

At the beginning, the alcoholic group member all but ignores the therapist. Later, when patients do reluctantly attempt to include him, it is as a peer—which is also quite unreal. Questions posed by the alcoholic, often embarrassingly frank, are aimed at discovering why the therapist is present and how he can help. Is he a do-gooder or is he another martyr? Often these queries refer to the therapist's personal life, family and background: for instance, "Are you, or is any member of your family, alcoholic?" These questions with a seeming interest in the therapist both include and exclude him since they imply that the therapist can only help if he has been personally disrupted by alcoholism. However personal they may be, these questions—when responded to by the therapist with an awareness of their real meaning— offer a beginning therapeutic engagement between the nonalcoholic therapist and the alcoholic patient. Rather than taking these questions at face value, that is, dealing with their manifest content, the therapist should attempt to discern their genuine intent (latent content) so that he can respond to them relevantly.

> For example, to the question, "Are you or members of your family alcoholic?", the psychotherapist rather than simply give the factual reply of "no," answered, "If I haven't known conflict, suffering and anxiety personally I couldn't have become a psychotherapist. If I had gotten all I needed in my life, I wouldn't be here with you tonight."

Insofar as the alcoholic is not committed to the therapeutic relationship, the group therapist must be fully committed to it. The alcoholic's isolation, his repressed feelings, his lack of spontaneity, and his unwillingness to risk contact must be counterbalanced by the therapist's availability and his willingness to be affectively responsive, spontaneous, and concerned. It is crucial with this kind of patient for the therapist to communicate his deep interest through full participation in the group; and he may even find it necessary to be available after clinic hours on occasion. The early aim of the therapist is to form a responsive and stable core group of four or five members that fills the necessary function of offsetting each individual member's inclination to be absent, late, or even to leave therapy abruptly. From this group, a larger number can be added to make a total group membership of from seven to nine. The alcoholic patient must eventually come to experience the treatment group as different from any other group he has known. The group meetings cannot continue to be just a place to go because there is no other place; and the patient's presence in the group must be promoted into a mutually-stimulating experience for both patient and therapist. The responsibility for achieving this stable group does not rest solely with the patients; the therapist must be able to provide the setting for this new experience.

In a sense, in the therapeutic group the patient finds an integral part of himself, a part that can best be described as that one which is striving for health. It is this part which first allows him to contact the others, and it is that part that allows him to commit himself to newness and change. As the gestalt of the group changes, so does the individual patient. Originally the therapist must assume total responsibility for the establishment of this therapeutic milieu. This also changes as time goes on, and the group as a whole, begins to form sufficent group ego to complement and support the therapist's effort. The curative activity becomes a shared experience between the therapist and the constructive forces of the interacting therapeutic group.

Since in the early group meetings the therapist must orient the group toward eventually including him, a positive relationship must be encouraged between the members and the therapist. This is an attempt on the therapist's part to begin to replace the symbiotic bond betweent parent and patient with a more realistic tie between the patient and himself, which is possible only as the alcoholic attains sobriety. A therapeutic gestalt eventually forms between patients and therapist and at this point the therapist is able to permit himself a fuller range of response which include his feelings and fantasies. This does not suggest that the therapist take on the image of an all-accepting and all-embracing parent. In view of the definite limits which the alcoholic requires this would be quite unreal and indeed uncalled for.

It is also unreal and therapeutically unsound for the psychotherapist to attempt to show equal and similar feelings to or respond in the same manner to each patient. "The crucial agency in psychotherapy is not so much the method but rather the relationship between the patient and his doctor . . . it is individualization and improvisation which must be taught and must be learned" (3, p. 520).

The group psychotherapist is called upon to respond to, rather than interpret and analyze, the alcoholics' behavior, including his drinking and his frequent absences from the group. Unlike the usual representative of society, the therapist responds neither as a martyr nor as a do-gooder. The therapist is neither prohibitive nor permissive, but attempts, within the framework of the therapy group, to achieve something quite different: a mutual interchange which will be in contrast with the alcoholic's previous life experiences.

In another context, the authors' described two characteristics which are the foundation of every therapeutic relationship. These have been designated as "affective honesty and constancy"; traits especially necessary in working with the alcoholic patient. At first, these qualities more clearly typify the psychotherapist but eventually they must also come to characterize the patient. "Affective honesty involves the therapist's willingness to experience the moment with the patient and simultaneously to communicate this experience to him. Through this open and total communication, the therapist permits the other in the transaction to *know who and how he is*" (4 p. 24). Constancy "implies a willingness on the part of the therapist to remain with the patient indefinitely as both face life's paradoxes together. But constancy does not mean that the patient is given free rein to act out destructively" (4 p 28).

Specific Methods of Therapist Participation: The Achievement of Therapeutic Engagement

In order for "individualization and improvisation" to emerge in each patient's relationships with both his therapist and his group, the therapist must interrupt the quasi-cohesiveness of the beginning alcoholic group and thus reduce each patient's resistance to change. This means that the uniqueness and spontaneity of each member can flourish in the group, only if the therapist is emotionally available and genuinely participating. To bring about fruitful engagement the therapist may respond in any of the following five ways: (5, 6).

(1) The Therapist Responds Authentically to the Alcoholic

Alcoholism, viewed dynamically, may be considered as similar to suicidal preoccupation in a depressed patient, that is, it is a symptom that requires direct and immediate intervention if psychotherapy is to be effective. That is why orientation into the nature of alcoholism and possible remedial measures are given to the patient early in his rehabilitation program (see Chapter 5). In some treatment groups, the group as a whole quickly develops a commitment to change which encourages and even demands sobriety from its members and thus supports the therapist's intervention.

The therapist's response to the alcoholic, like his response to any other symptomatic behavior, must necessarily be individual and unique. If, for example, two members come into the group drunk, the therapist may respond to one with anger and frustration and to the other, with deep compassion. Or he may suggest one member use Antabuse or join Alcoholics Anonymous, and question another member's use of either of these measures when they are being used to deny his conflicts and subvert his rehabilitation.

Especially with the alcoholic, the therapist must keep the limits of his function clearly in mind if he is to avoid either too much or too little action. Alcoholism facilitates acting out, and if the therapist is not alert to this, he may be moved to respond in ways which are deleterious to treatment. Although the therapist is required to participate more actively with alcoholics than with other patients, he still should not assume the role of the all-giving, omniscient, and omnipotent figure that the patient may at times demand. Phone calls at all hours of the day and night, for example, may be appropriate between the alcoholic and family members or AA sponsors; but they should be discouraged by the group psychotherapist once the patient is participating in his group. This attitude is difficult to maintain at first, because the patient experiences it as a rejection. However, the patient must be encouraged and, in a sense, educated to bring all of his struggle and conflict to the group, so that, in the interactional milieu of the treatment process, the patient can be assured of a much more general acceptance and relevant response from both the therapist and group members. The therapist must distinguish for himself and for his patient, between acting out and a genuine change; in order to do this, the therapist must become increasingly sensitive to the group experience of the moment.

Frank had been in the group several months during which time he stopped drinking completely. His group attendance was always regular and punctual. About 2:30 one morning, the therapist received a phone message from her service that Frank was on her office wire, he had been drinking and was confused and disturbed.

The therapist returned his call and it became obvious that although the resumption of his drinking was a "slip," it was also an indication that Frank was reaching another phase in his therapy. The patient was experiencing an early struggle in which he both wanted and rejected a complete possession of his mother. The therapist supported Frank in his struggle and reassured him that she was with him, and so were his group and A.A. at this time. The patient was encouraged to bring his feelings to the group and also allow them to help him.

The therapist's over all attitude of not permitting himself to be exploited is communicated to the group members and becomes especially significant for the remitted alcoholic. The remitted alcoholic, with his desire to atone for his past "sins," is readily exploited by any active drinker's attempts to involve him in machinations; and the result is much extra group interaction which serves to divert group analysis. The therapist must intervene by refusing to allow this misuse of one member by another.

In the illustration cited above, the psychotherapist showed discrimination in responding to that particular phone call. Had the circumstances been different, the therapist's response also would have been different. For example, with another group member who periodically got drunk and phoned without any consideration for the hour of the night, or the length of the conversation, the therapist's response was quite different. The therapist's reactions to this behavior were discussed in the group, and the patient was directly confronted with her hostility and exploitation of the psychotherapist. The therapist showed her unwillingness to be subjected to this kind of behavior by refusing to accept further phone calls. Moreover, the other group members began to distinguish between a genuine call for help and exploitation. This proved exceedingly fruitful for the others in examining their own profound feelings of guilt which frequently were quite unrelated to the external reality. The patient, in addition came to experience her deep and pervasive rage which the drinking permitted her to express.

(2) The Therapist Perceives the Actual Alcoholic Symptom Phenomenologically

The patient's behavior while drinking frequently communicates his needs and also indicates the use he is making of alcohol. The therapist must view the alcoholic symptom as the individual's mode of being and of coping with his world. Thus, George drinks in order to express his anger; Ethel drinks for the "lousy feeling afterwards"; and Lena, "to talk"—Lena is usually very withdrawn, but makes continual phone calls to everyone when she is drunk. George recalls that as a child his father sent him out into the woods to find a stick with which to be beaten, as punishment for some minor infraction. Ethel used to drink for the bad feeling after a binge; now, after two years of staying sober, she eats chocolate until she vomits. Each of these experiences individualizes and personalizes these alcoholic group members. Furthermore, the patients' focus on alcoholism as the root of all their problems is rudely shaken by those group members who have attained sobriety. Ethel's experience, for example, illustrates a generalized malfunctioning which persists long after she has attained sobriety. Like many other remitted alcoholics, she has found a substitute: chocolate, in this case. Others find that the oblivion they once obtained with alcohol can be achieved through overintellectualization, rationalization and a continuing search for the right formula; and, although the least of the evils, this approach does not provide workable solutions to realistic problems, either.

(3) The Therapist Responds to the "New" and the "Now" in the Group Interaction

The ever-present tendency of alcoholics to deny and generalize their conflicts can only be overcome by focusing upon the experience of being together, at the moment. As therapist and group members respond to each other with feeling, each member experiences his unique and individual sense of self. During one session, Bill and Jim engaged in a heated and abstruse philosophical discussion. The therapist intervened merely by turning to Bill and asking, "What do you really feel about Jim?" Abandoning the character of their discussion, Bill spontaneously replied, "He gives me a pain in the ass," a remark that immediately brought the two men to another level of interaction on which questions about their adequacy as males, their attraction for one another, and their fear of homosexuality were made possible.

(4) The Therapist Responds Totally and Organically

The therapist is required to be present in the group meetings as a totally functioning human being. In view of the alcoholic's marked tendency to abstract and generalize experiences, the presence of the therapist as a thinking, feeling, and responsive person is critical. By experiencing his own manner of existence in the alcoholic group, the therapist is able to call on the patients for a genuine expression of feelings; and the differentiated responses elicited by the resulting I-Thou contacts between therapist and patient and between patient and patient further the uniqueness of each person. If, for example, several members come late for a group session, the inclination of the group is to ignore this behavior and assume that the absentees are all at some bar getting "stoned." In contrast to this generalized and impersonal response, the psychotherapist will react differently to the absence of each. He may speak about his anxiety in regard to one absent group member, adding that he will phone if the patient doesn't come at all; and then express only regret at the absence of another group member, because he really doesn't seem to care *enough* whether that patient is present or not. This kind of responsiveness on the therapist's part enables the group and therapist to explore together their feelings about missing members. Further, the therapist's anxiety concerning one person and his indifference to another, identifies the two group members as separate and unique persons and also opens the way for change in the therapeutic relationship. The therapist and group members must begin to explore the therapist's anxiety about the one patient, and his indifference to the other.

Similarly, the therapist's freedom in sharing fantasies and dreams relevant to the group interaction helps to free the group from their own superrational bonds (see Chapter 12). For example, the therapist may fantasize that George and Rose are somewhere together and involve the group in continuing that fantasy. He may also bring in a dream which may or may not directly relate to some of the group members and ask for the group's reaction to the dream. Again, the use of any such material is an effort toward a clearer delineation of each patient.

(5) The Therapist Responds with His Despair

A therapeutic dimension of consequence arises when the nonalcoholic therapist begins to question his own identity and his feelings of belonging in an alcoholic group. The therapist's feeling of exclusion (and, at times, isolation) can, if voiced, plunge the entire group into a questioning of, and concern with, new meanings. Interests other than those which are involved with their own symptoms can thus be activated; and the therapist's existence comes to the fore for the first time through his expression of frustration and human needs.

> One therapist, after some time in an alcoholic group expressed the feeling that she did not belong in this alcoholic world. Judy, visibly upset, responded by turning to another group member to whom she had become closely related, and asked to be recognized for herself, not as just another alcoholic. As a result of this interchange the therapist suddenly experienced Judy as a woman with many conflicts both as a wife and mother. She thereupon turned to Judy and sincerely commented, "I guess I know what you are feeling right now, Judy, because I know how a women feels." Jay also appeared freed by this interaction. He suddenly became much more spontaneous in his interaction with the others and for the first time relinquished his usual ponderous and overintellectualized demeanor. The therapist was also able to experience Jay differently and stated, "Suddenly I've become aware of what a very attractive man you are." The deeper group indentifications which thus emerged were in terms of the humanness of each participant—that is, each person was seen as a totality in his struggle as a man or woman, husband or wife.

Group Process with Alcoholics

In a group in which all members have the same symptom, group composition becomes a critical variable, particularly because initially-homogeneous groupings are more likely to have and therefore support similar kinds of resistances. We have observed, however, that these resistances can be more quickly overcome in some alcoholic groups than in others. Some groups can within a three-month period become deeply committed to a genuinely therapeutic process while others, even after a year's time, are still superficially engaged.

We have had the opportunity to observe* marked contrasts in over all functioning between a poorly- and an effectively-constituted group

---

*Project 418—New York Alcoholism Vocational Rehabilitation Project: The Inclusion of Vocational Counseling in an Alcoholism Rehabilitation Program, January 1963.

(see Chapter 9). These two kinds of groups can be indentified by certain characteristics that serve either to support or undermine the beginning resistances. The following table describes some of the characteristics that point to faulty or effective group interaction:

With a homogeneous alcoholic group, proper group composition becomes mandatory because such a group so readily supports its common resistances. However, it is difficult to describe the kinds of personalities which will interact to produce a genuinely growth-facilitating and cohesive milieu. Perhaps the major requirement for an effective

GROUP INTERACTION IN THE ALCOHOLIC GROUP

Effective	*Faulty*
Dilution of quasi-cohesiveness. Therapeutic experience becomes a shared experience between group and therapist.	Persistence of a quasi-cohesiveness which excludes therapist. If therapist is included, group focuses exclusively on him, using him only as a problem-solver.
Emergence of a committed group ego. Help is forthcoming from the group.	Therapist assumes too many functions for too many members.
Group members' beginning efforts toward sobriety.	Persistent alcoholic binges and group members' refusal to accept any remedial measures.
Minimal extra-group socializing except for emergency support.	Prevalence of extra-group socializing: phone-calls, dates, borrowing money, use of group members for their business affiliations, and so on.
Therapeutic confrontation and intervention by the individual group members and the therapist.	Group support of mutual resistances. Confrontation and intervention by the therapist only.
Interaction with therapist is kept within the confines of the group.	Prevalence of extra-group contacts with therapist: frequent phone-calls, communications, etc.
Content is either group-oriented or described as difficult to reveal in the group.	Attempts are made to involve therapist in special "confidences" and so isolate him from the group.
Content of the sessions is characterized by personal material: revelation of dream and fantasy material, and interaction which can potentially lead to deeper engagement.	Content of the sessions is characterized by abstract discussions, futile hyperactivity and interactions.

group is that it be composed of persons who bring enough heterogeneity in experience and behavior into the group to insure growth rather than the perpetuation of similar resistances. For example, when there is a choice, the therapist ought to make sure that a given group include both remitted and active alcoholics, rather than active alcoholics alone. Some individuals who are poorly integrated psychologically and not participating in their community can be tolerated by the group if others in it are pretty well integrated and functioning within society. Overintellectualized group members have much to gain from contact with more subjectively-responsive members.

A most significant element for effective group functioning is the presence of individuals who have a fundamental center of personal integrity. Psychopaths lacking in this integrity cannot be included; not only are they incapable of benefiting themselves in an alcoholic patient group but they are disruptive and destructive to the therapeutic process.

Genuine Therapeusis Evolves from the Humanness of the Participants; not from the Elaboration of Symptoms

One of the primary therapeutic endeavor in an alcoholic group is to broaden the patient's basis of identification. The alcoholic patient must become more than a mere aggregate of symptoms. This goal can be most effectively accomplished through the therapist's awareness and willingness to experience quite personally the ongoing group interaction. As the therapist begins to respond meaningfully to each group member, the alcoholic patient begins to realize that belonging and uniqueness are not functions of the fact that he has a disease, *alcoholism,* any more than they would be if he suffered from ulcers, headaches, or homosexuality. The struggle with disease is merely another reminder of our essential state of being human. Individuality only becomes evident in acknowledgement of the disease and the use made of this knowledge.

The genuine contact which facilitates the therapeutic transaction is born out of the struggle inherent in the fact that we are all mortal. The therapist who is aware that he too exists in a continuous paradoxical state between living and dying adheres to fewer fixed techniques, and becomes more spontaneous and responsive (7). When this awareness is expressed by the therapist with vigor, the alcoholic group member feels able to begin risking the unknown. In this connection our point of view coincides with that of Maslow, who suggests "that much of what we now call psychology is the study of tricks we use to avoid the anxiety of absolute novelty by making believe that the future will be like the past" (8).

The dynamics of alcoholism as revealed in the interacting group are more than a struggle against an addiction to drink. Alcoholism is, rather, a struggle against life and its vicissitudes, a struggle which is momentarily resolved by a recourse to oblivion. Taking part in the therapeutic group requires a willingness to risk new experiences in which choices must inevitably be made and responsibility for oneself assumed.

It is critical, therefore, that the alcoholic identify his struggle with alcohol early in group therapy. Like the psychotic or suicidal patient who must experience himself as psychotic or suicidal, the alcoholic patient must experience himself as having a problem with alcohol. This is a necessary beginning, even though this recognition of himself as alcoholic involves in some sense a self-deception since it ignores everything else that he is. Initially, this recognition need be only to the extent that it encourages the patient to take positive steps to stop drinking. Later, as a more certain identity emerges, the alcoholic group member—in concert with the others—must experience and accept life as it *is,* rather than as he believes it *should be.*

REFERENCES

1. Tarleton, C. H., and Tarnower, S. M.: The use of letters as part of the psychotherapeutic relationship. *Quart. J. Stud. on Alcohol, 21*:82-89, 1960.
2. O'Brien, C. C.: A multidisciplinary approach to the diagnosis and therapy of the nonrehabilitated alcoholic personality. *J. Psychol., 50*:377-381, 1960.
3. Frankl, V.: Paradoxical intention. *Amer. J. Psychother. 14*:520-535, 1960.
4. Mullan, H., and Sangiuliano, I.: *The Therapist's Contribution to the Treatment Process: His Person, Transactions and Treatment Methods.* Springfield, Thomas, 1964.
5. Smuts, J. C.: *Holism and Evolution.* New York, Macmillan, 1926.
6. Mullan, H.: Trends in group psychotherapy in the United States. *Int. J. Soc. Psychia., 3*:224-230, 1957.
7. Mullan, H., and Sangiuliano, I.: The subjective phenomenon in existential psychotherapy. *J. Exist. Psychia., 2*:17-34, 1961.
8. Maslow, A.: Article appearing in *Existential Inquiries, 1*: 1959.

CHAPTER XI

ACTING OUT
IN AN ALCOHOLIC TREATMENT GROUP
IRIS SANGIULIANO, Ph.D.

*(Acting out, in the form of repeated alcoholic binges, sexual in-
discriminations, or antisocial acts characteristic of this patient, although destructive per se, can be utilized to advantage in the
psychotherapeutic treatment process. Acting out may be viewed as
a preverbal form of communication. The establishment of the
archaic symbiotic bonds between the patient and his therapist, and
between the patient and his therapy group, may serve to assist in
the abatement of the acting out.
...The group therapist working with alcoholics, unlike therapists
with other patients, must be aware that acting out and its management are always the critical factors throughout the group therapeutic process. He must, therefore, have a clear sense of himself,
and a genuine tolerance of, and willingness to be with, this kind of
patient.)*

INTRODUCTION

Acting Out: General Statement

References to the problem of acting out and efficacious ways to
treat it are plentiful in professional literature (1, 2, 3, 4). This concern is understandable since acting out profoundly affects not only
the treatment process but the psychotherapist as well, and if acting
out persists, it is unlikely that the patient will benefit or even continue
in treatment. Traditionally, acting out is defined as largely-uncon-
scious, repetitive behavior, which is motivated by past conflictual
experiences. Basically, acting out expresses an intrapsychic struggle
interpersonally, and may therefore be regarded as an attempt to discharge tension and avoid anxiety. The immediate gratification which
it affords is sufficient reason for acting out to become self-perpetuating.

The nature of the psychotherapist's involvement with the patient
when he acts out has serious consequences for the therapeutic out-

come. It is almost axiomatic that acting out is behavior that *involves others;* and the therapist, regardless of his particular theoretical orientation, is no exception. Psychotherapists, notwithstanding their personal preferences for or against a nonjudgmental facade of anonymity, are forced to become engaged with the patient. Moreover, this is not only true for the psychotherapist: When treatment is taking place in other than a private-practice setting—for example, in an alcoholic treatment center—the entire staff of the institution may also become involved.

Although there has been much discussion on the subject of acting out, there is considerable difference of opinion concerning both the general concept and its most effective methods of treatment. Acting out is usually discussed in dichotomous terms: that is, either as a clearly-negative or clearly-positive phenomenon. Treatment methods also seem to fall into opposing camps, with permissiveness and a *laissez-faire* attitude on the one hand; and prohibitive and specific restrictions on the other. Acting out which is so characteristic of the alcoholic, will be considered here from a somewhat more exploratory viewpoint. A phenomenological evaluation of the alcoholic's acting out is offered as a step toward evolving a workable treatment program deemed so essential in the treatment of this patient.

Characteristics of Alcoholic Acting Out

Therapists neither originate nor stop acting out, although they may offer a patient the prerequisite conditions in the therapeutic situation for facilitating or inhibiting this behavior. Therapists who deal with the delinquent (5, 6) and addictive (7, 8, 9) personality disorders, of which alcoholism is one, experience acting out in an especially intense form.

For the alcoholic patient, acting out has become a way of life, and this behavior very directly influences every aspect of his existence—vocational, social, familial, and intrapsychic. In contrast to the non-alcoholic, the specific nature of the alcoholic's acting out—which may be expressed in sexual, drinking, antisocial, or asocial terms—seems to have little diagnostic significance. It appears to be characteristically the expression of an essentially oral demand; as such, it reflects the intrapsychic conflict of this patient with his passive-aggressive orientation. The psychotherapist thus confronted with acting out as a major character defense, complicated by drinking, must—unfortunately—almost immediately face the task of engaging the patient at this, his most vulnerable point.

Acting out in an alcoholic group presents the therapist with certain unique problems. For example, when acting out is manifested in drinking, both therapist and group are confronted with either of two different situations, each equally untenable. The group member who is acting out either absents himself from the sessions and is beyond reach; or he attends, but in so inebriated a condition that he is, in another sense, also beyond reach. How the therapist responds to either situation will vary a great deal, depending upon whether this behavior occurs at the beginning of therapy, or later. In addition, the ego strength of the acting-out patient, the strength and vulnerability of the group as a whole, and the therapist's level of tolerance for frustration and anxiety, all significantly determine the response to the inebriated member.

TOWARD AN IDENTIFICATION OF ACTING OUT IN THE ALCOHOLIC

The Phenomenon

Phenomenologically, acting out can be characterized in a variety of ways, implying also that to alter this behavior there are a *number* of treatment possibilities. Like so many other therapeutic phenomena, acting out is a communication. It is, however, a communication which seems to reflect a preverbal form of thinking and behavior, and is primarily about a past, early, fantastic, and distorted life theme (10). It differs from other fantasy material, however, in that—as a presentation of the alcoholic's "internal reality"—it is acted upon: lived out quite literally with real situations and real people (11). This activity allows the conflictual fantasy to be externalized, so that the anxiety which it might engender otherwise, is avoided. The alcoholic patient who has found he can more readily sustain conflicting fantasies when drunk is caught in a vicious circle. The alcohol enables him to act out, as for example, the release of hostility which occurs when he is drunk; while simultaneously, it engenders further acting out. The alcoholic learns to use his drinking as a *carte blanche* to excuse all his irrationalities. This knowledge is expressed in statements both explicit and implicit: for example, "I am not responsible, I can't help it, I'm alcoholic." Or, "I'm not really crazy; it's the alcohol that makes me act crazy." Characteristically, his intrapsychic struggle becomes an interpersonal one; his subjective experience is effectively objectified and alienated, lessening his feeling of responsibility and guilt.

One of the most critical aspects of acting out is that it is always translated interpersonally and always involves others. In most instances of alcoholic acting out, moreover, the nature of the involvement is such that is precipitates acting out in response. The reciprocity of the phenomenon dramatically identifies it. Some therapists go so far as to contend that acting out is "any act which threatens the therapist." It is certainly true that the patient's attemped avoidance of anxiety by acting out is reflected in a concomitant rise in anxiety in the group and in the therapist. In addition, the acting-out alcoholic's lack of risk in the face of the unknown, his limited responsibility, and limited freedom of choice in his compulsive behavior, put an added burden on the group members and psychotherapist, all of whom must assume excessive risk-taking, responsibility, and decision-making. ·

> Two group members became sexually involved in a mutually destructive relationship. The group felt trapped in the conspiracy between the two and feelings ran high. Since the two group members themselves were compulsively bound together, the group assumed the greater responsibility for interrupting this liaison. Although this couple's behavior had many different meanings for each member and in a sense it became grist for the "therapeutic mill," this compulsive acting out was not interrupted without considerable anxiety, disruption and responsibility on the part of the other group members.

Indirectly, the current research on communication theory has considerably clarified the concept of how acting out develops. Such concepts as the "double bind" and "family homeostasis," referred to by Bateson, Jackson, Weakland and Haley (12, 13) have added immeasurably to our understanding of pathological familial interactions, including one aspect of the facilitation and development of acting out in the alcoholic. Jackson and Weakland described the double-bind concept as "grounded in our most basic conception about communication as the chief means of human interaction and influence: that in actual human communication a single and simple message never occurs, but that communication always and necessarily involves a multiplicity of messages, on different levels, at once . . . The double-bind concept refers to a pattern of pairs or sets of messages, on different levels, which are closely related but sharply incongruent, occurring together with other messages which by concealment, denial, or other means seriously hinder the recipient from clearly noticing the incongruence and handling it effectively . . ." (13, p. 32). It has been clinically observed that the double-bind relationship is basic to the formation of many pathological conditions. In its more complicated aspects an "interlocking gestalt" is formed in the family unit, and the double bind becomes the critical avenue of communication between parent—most often the mother—and child (12).

The intertwining of intrapsychic and interpersonal factors are thus very clearly delineated in the double-bind communication; and with this in mind, it may be said that although acting out is personally determined and initiated, it is a response to an outer conflictual stimulus: one quite often observable in the alcoholic's familial relationships. For instance, verbal prohibition concerning drinking on the part of the family is not infrequently accompanied by subtle, nonverbal acquiescence. To cite some examples: Agnes relates her mother's marked disapproval of her drinking; she then says that her mother had recently returned from Paris, bringing her a case of liquor as a gift. In another case, although Margaret's husband and children are distressed by her binges, on her birthday and for Christmas they give her a bottle as a gift. They explain, "It's all that she really likes, and besides she's nicer when she drinks a little." The alcoholic who is burdened with guilt about exploiting society is often, paradoxically enough, very directly and intimately the victim of exploitation.

One author suggests that a factor of subtle unconscious symbiotic influence of one person upon another, is a dynamic factor in the development of the acting-out personality (4, p. 631). A symbiotic bind is the result of very early defective development in the differentiation that normally occurs between the infant's and the mother's ego, so that a sensitivity exists in the child to the unspoken fears and wishes of the mother, and this is later transferred to any significant figure. This particular way of relating in which multi-leveled communication is acted upon, is frequently observed in the alcoholic. This patient is very quick to discern and act upon any inconsistency within the therapist, or between the therapist and another staff member. It is not what is said that moves the alcoholic patient, but rather the consistency between the word and what is genuinely experienced by the therapist. This is one reason why the person of the therapist cannot be ignored in maintaining an acting out impasse.

THERAPEUTIC IMPLICATIONS OF ACTING OUT

The Treatment Paradox

In treating the alcoholic, the therapist faces a dilemma from the very beginning. If he attempts to keep the level of anxiety low and offer the kind of supportive presence that prevents real psychological change, he also is faced with the possibility that the patient's despair that "nothing is happening" will cause him to terminate prematurely. If the psychotherapist decides to risk provoking some anxiety, he may also provoke either drinking bouts or an acting out of the transference distortions without drinking. Faced with the possibility of a premature termination because either "nothing" or "too much" is happening, the therapist has little choice but to risk therapeutic engagement, while at the same time attempting to control the compulsive, repetitive behavior.

With the acting-out alcoholic, the psychotherapist's, as well as the entire staff's, role is enlarged. The professional worker in the treatment center will be involved in many facts of the patient's life—with his fantasies as well as his so-called reality problems of everyday living. This is why there must be a consensus about values, goals, and action among the other staff members and the group psychotherapist; and why interactional, interdisciplinary staff conferences are an integral part of the alcoholic treatment program (see Chapter II).

Given the therapist who is committed to forming an intense relationship within his group, aware of the possible facilitation of acting out, the question arises: How is this therapist to begin? First, he must take into account the level of tolerance for stress possessed by each patient, group, and himself. And second, the ego strength and degree of self-congruence in both patients and therapist must be the determining factor in the kind and the intensity of the interaction which is encouraged. The therapist cannot use rigid or preconceived rules as to what constitutes "good" or "bad" therapeutic practice. For example, although some regression is permitted and even engendered with the usual patient, the alcoholic patient comes to therapy already in a regressed state; rather than encourage further regression and court still more acting out, the therapist must aim toward something quite different. The psychotherapist's effectiveness with the alcoholic can be judged by his capacity to offer this patient adequate support, yet at the same time, sufficient frustration to promote genuine growth and maturity. From the very first contact, the therapist must communicate his acceptance of alcoholism as a symptom; at the same time, he must also communicate to the patient: "I want you to be sober." If a new patient acts out by drinking, the statement can be made: "I wish you could be as feeling and spontaneous, and be here with us, without alcohol."

There is certainly no one way to behave with the alcoholic patient, nor is there one way to respond to his destructive behavior. Rather, the therapeutic relationship must begin by taking into account the total patient, his willingness and ability to cooperate and his state of sobriety. With some patients this may mean direct intervention by the therapist until the patient can begin to exercise his own control. However, whatever the communication between patient and therapist, it must be different from the original communications between the parent and the patient. The therapist's direct intervention and his natural anxiety about the alcoholic who is endangering his own life, must not be like those earlier inconsistent parental prohibitions and admonitions, which carried with them the expectation that *the patient would fail*. The question must also be asked: How well can the therapist tolerate the profound egocentricity and pervasive distortion of the alcoholic patient? If the therapist tends to be masochistically inclined, his tolerance may be too great. On the other hand, if he has not yet fully come to terms with his own egocentricity, his tolerance will be too low.

Acting Out as a Preverbal Communication: Treatment Implications

Acting out, as stated above, is a communication of an early pre-verbal form of behavior. Considered in this light, it very definitely reveals something *about* the person being treated. Moreover, the fact that the patient who acts out also tries to involve others including his therapist in his behavior, gives the therapist a treatment entrée. When this occurs, it is up to the therapist to change the relationship between him and his patient from mere acting out and release of tension, to a more genuine interaction. The therapist does not shun the involvement, but, rather, enters into it on *his* terms.

The psychotherapist must be very aware of his feelings and responses to the patient in this engagement. Authentic transactions are only possible when the therapist deeply experiences the meaning of the group interaction between the group members and himself. The therapist must therefore come to question his anxiety, and his need to set up new limits. He must wonder about any overreaction or—conversely—any attempt to maintain a "neutral" position. His own role and latent fantasies must be scrutinized. Does he see himself as a saviour, a social crusader, or "the good mother?" (14)

Once a more genuine group cohesion is achieved, the patient no longer tells *about* himself. Instead, through the interaction, he actively identifies himself and the others. Who the patient is, and how he affects and is affected by the world around him, are now phenom-enologically present. Since acting out is outwardly directed, in order for any change to occur in the alcoholic, a greater internalization of his personal struggle must take place. This is no easy undertaking since the alcoholic clings very tenaciously to externalization, maintaining it through the kind of involvements he enters into with others. The psychotherapist must be very clear in his own mind about when he is genuinely responding to his alcoholic patient and when he has been duped or perhaps forced into acting out, either with or against him.

The alcoholic's refusal to accept a new way of relating to the world with responsibility forces the therapist to take a stand. The patient directly and quickly confronts the therapist and group with his drinking, sexual indiscrimination, and antisocial behavior; and asks the therapist to control him by assuming the complete responsibility for a new course of action. To the degree that he succeeds by these means in seductively enmeshing the therapist, therapy fails. The therapist who is forced into setting new limits or rigid rules in response to the manipulative patient, succeeds in alienating him and clearly establishes the battleline between two distinct camps, doctor and patient, thus threatening the alcoholic's basic narcissism. This narcissism considerably limits the extent of possible psychotherapeutic engagement since initially the alcoholic patient seems aware only of himself or duplicates of himself.

What can be offered the patient instead of an unreal, strict prohibition; or an equally unreal, all-accepting permissiveness? In reality, abstract interpretations, prohibitions, or a *laissez-faire* attitude can be sufficiently threatening to this patient so that he will terminate therapy. Rather than attack this patient's narcissism, the therapist should endeavor to use the early symbiotic bond and join forces with him. He does this by focusing upon these early feelings and directing them toward the therapeutic relationship. In a sense, the therapist is assuming the position of the original parental figure; however, instead of facilitating further acting out, he accepts his patient's attempts at seduction without acting upon them. In focusing upon the earlier parent-child relationship as currently manifested, the therapist attempts to clarify the patient's distorted relationship to him, to the group, and to the world. This is of primary importance in the treatment of acting out, when the therapist must also be aware of his own involvement with the patient and other group members. The therapist can accomplish this when he is genuinely and totally present, expressing his concerns and feelings relevant to the group quite openly (10). Instead of courting a head-on collision, he must endeavor to join the patient in his struggle for reality. The psychotherapist is placed in a position where he must accept the patient's personal inner struggle which the patient cannot accept and which he avoids through acting out; indeed, the patient's acceptance of his conflicted feelings without acting upon them is a definite indication of growth. The therapist must respond to the patient's aberrant behavior with all of himself, both with conscious and unconscious material. For example, one therapist's honest admission to an alcoholic group that she viewed alcoholic binges as destructive was followed by further identifying comments. She stated that she was not a "do-gooder," that she was a human being, and that she expected to get something for herself out of the group meetings. This total response to the alcoholic acting out altered the group atmosphere. The therapist had made it plain she was not an object, nor did she intend to treat the patients as objects—as they are prone to treat each other. In other instances, by relating pertinent dreams, the therapist not only clarified her role in the acting out, but also facilitated greater participation and identification, and communicated her genuine concern (see Chapter XII).

CLINICAL ILLUSTRATIONS

Introduction

Acting out, as stated earlier, is both an intrapsychic and interpersonal phenomenon. Characteristic of the alcoholic patient, he enters therapy with a long and involved history of acting out. Despite this, it is of interest to note that as psychotherapy proceeds, the acting-out behavior becomes more and more related to the treatment situation. Although acting out may at first reflect only the patient's intrapsychic struggle as therapy progresses it also indicates the transference impasse between therapist and patient. Thus, any significant inconsistency within the therapist is enough to facilitate further acting out in the patient. This is sometimes carried even further when the patient senses conflict in the goals and values between the psychotherapist and the Treatment Center or other members of the staff.

Three specific kinds of acting out characteristic of the alcoholic therapy group will be given.

Acting Out as Reflected in the Relationship Between the Patient and His World

When the patient enters therapy with a history of acting out, the developing transference relationship cannot be conceived of as intiating the acting out, but it can be instrumental in the abatement of acting-out behavior, if the psychotherapeutic relationship can succeed in being different from the original parental relationship. In most instances, moreover, the alcoholic patient will use his alcoholism as a rationalization for acting out.

Agnes entered group therapy with many qualms. She doubted

that she was really alcoholic. "I have never hit bottom and I don't look like a drunk." She was there, however, at her husband's insistence.

Agnes was married at the age of nineteen and had two children. Her initial group participation was tentative: She spoke of the defensive armor of the group. Gradually, however, she gained more assurance and began to risk greater interaction by becoming more personal. She related to two of the group members as parental figures, and considered one woman the "perfect mother." She also spoke of the possibility of having an affair with a young physician, which would not have been her first extra-marital experience. She related her intentions toward this man in a casual, almost business-like way. The group responded with misgivings, and expressed the fear that she would become more deeply involved than she was aware of. Agnes' sporadic drinking continued, and it became apparent that her alcoholism was used to test out her sexuality.

About six months after she had joined the group, a new member, Jonathan, came into the group. Jonathan was a latent psychotic whose behavior had psychopathic overtones. He spoke freely of his homosexual love-affairs and was very manipulative in the group. Agnes immediately became involved with his exploitations. Their relationship reached its most critical point when the therapist was on vacation and the group was continuing to meet without her. During this time, Agnes became obsessed with Jonathan's helplessness, procured an apartment for him, fed him, and assisted him to obtain some part-time work. When the regular group sessions were resumed, Agnes began to absent herself, so she could be with Jonathan, who was drinking heavily. During one of the group meetings, they both absented themselves and went on a drinking spree and Agnes attempted to seduce him.

The narcissistic nature of the relationship between Agnes and Jonathan became more and more apparent: There was a striking physical resemblance between the two, and they were frequently mistaken for siblings. They had found a destructive symbiotic-like union, and although Agnes was able to interpret her feelings for Jonathan, her behavior remained unaltered. Agnes related having similar feelings toward her father, a robust man who died of a neurological disease. She also spoke of a strong resentment toward her mother, who she viewed as frigid and unfeeling. Agnes was visibly shaken and began to question who she really was, and where she belonged. Since she did not conceive of herself as having an alcoholic problem primarily, she began to feel guilty about taking up so much of the group's time. Instead of admonishing, or attempting to prohibit or permit the destructive relationship with Jonathan, the therapist intervened by stressing *her* relationship to Agnes. This was done in many ways, one of which included relating a dream. In this dream, the therapist was an observer. She was standing by and saw a jet-propelled plane crash in midair. She ran to the scene of the crash and cried: "I too could be in that plane!" Through this dream, the therapist indicated her relationship with Agnes. At this time, Agnes began to express direct interest in the therapist and in her life. The group also reaffirmed her, perhaps in the most profound way an alcoholic group can. They pointed out to Agnes that it was her struggle in life, rather than her alcoholism, that identified her and made her "belong" to the group. Her compulsive acting out illustrated a wish to master her situation with a simultaneous fear of doing so. The lack of external opposition or attempts to castigate her made Agnes begin to experience the destructive and compulsive bind she was in, with Jonathan, until finally she was able to discontinue seeing him.

In retrospect, although Agnes' behavior was undoubtedly destructive, its development permitted the patient, the group, and the therapist to experience Jonathan's and her struggle *in vivo*. And, although as part of her acting out, Agnes momentarily withdrew from the treatment group, in the end she was brought more deeply into therapy and into experiencing her conflicts, so that she even sought additional individual therapy. Moreover, the circumstances gave the therapist the opportunity to participate intensively with Agnes in her life struggle and to establish a beginning bond between them, without having to act out in response. The therapist, however, had to have the ability and willingness to withstand the confusion and mounting anxiety of the moment.

The fact that acting out may cause a group member to withdraw from therapy cannot be ignored. Sexual acting out for Agnes was as addictive as her alcoholism; and similar situations were relived by her many times in the course of her treatment, before a definite decrease in both her drinking and indiscriminate infantile sexuality occurred.

Acting Out as a Reflection of the Relationship Between Therapist and Patient

Acting out that begins in the later phases of therapy may well be facilitated by the therapeutic process and the nature of the transferential relationship between patient and therapist. In such instances it behooves the psychotherapist to be especially alert and aware of his feelings toward the patient.

Samuel was a latent psychotic. From the beginning of his therapy, he made a strong effort to remain sober. He became an active A.A. member and had attained ten months of sobriety at the time of the incident to be described below. Despite his new-found sobriety, Samuel's mental status did not improve; on the contrary, many of his deep-seated characterological problems came more clearly into evidence. His mutually-destructive relationship with his wife seemed to be based upon pity, guilt, and atonement. In the group, he lived out an actual incestuous relationship with his sister, and incestuous fantasies about his mother. Samuel's sense of limits, of belonging, and of identification were sadly confused. With sobriety, he became overtly hostile, rebellious, and questioning. His bitterness and disillusionment were manifested in suicidal threats and, finally, one abortive attempt. He resented the therapist for being female, for smoking, and most of all for being a sexual woman. During this period of heightened turmoil for Samuel, the therapist had a dream which she reported to the group: "Samuel and I were in bed together. He was gently caressing me and started kissing me. I then said, 'No, we can't have intercourse. We will have to stop because we are related.'"

Following this session, the group met for one session without the therapist who was attending professional meetings. In the first group meeting after she returned, the group appeared strained. One member, Rebecca, an older woman who had recently been "abandoned" by her husband for another woman, seemed unusually withdrawn. The therapist showed concern for Rebecca. Samuel responded, "What Rebecca can't talk about is that we've had intercourse." The therapist merely said, "But I told you I wouldn't screw with you; pity or not, you can't sleep with your mother." Another member, Albert, retorted, "Never mind the dream; Samuel is letting you know that you're possible." Albert, visibly angered, added that the sanctity of the group had been violated. Samuel turned to the therapist and stated, "I could have had intercourse with my mother if I had tried," then adding, "Do you want me to leave?"

It became obvious that the acting out was a dual communication in the transference relationship between therapist and patient. It was both a defiance and anger against the therapist's prohibition, and also a seeking of her deepest acceptance of his incestuous past. The therapist accepted Samuel's struggle and the fact that despite this, he remained sober. His need to reach and be accepted by the therapist was actively present. Samuel was searching for limits without being rejected; and the therapist was able to support this search for boundaries while at the same time she frustrated the actual acting out. Samuel admitted he had been angry at the alternate session because the therapist was absent. He had had the fantasy that she was on her honeymoon. The acting out thus was a communication, a symbolic act that, when utilized positively and not countered with restrictions, served to deeply involve the individual members, the therapist, and the group as a whole, in the therapeutic process. A redefinition of the man-woman relationship took place for Samuel, whereby he was shown that he could have a caring relationship with a woman without offering her sexual intercourse.

Acting Out Reflected in the Relationship Between Staff and Institution

The alcoholic's penchant for the "divide-and-conquer" technique is reflected in the confusion which he is apt to engender among professional staff members and, indeed, *all* of the clinic's working personnel. Phone calls made while drinking—to the Center's secretary, social worker, or vocational counselor—complaining about the therapist and his "unavailability" are not uncommon. Demands for advice, or asking that excuses for absences be relayed, must be handled with consistent unanimity.

For example, one patient became overly friendly with the receptionist at a clinic. The patient quickly sensed that she and the receptionist had a mutual problem; and proceeded to dilute much of her own anxiety in prolonged phone conversations with the receptionist who—because of *her* involvement—was unable to terminate the relationship.

Personnel morale and efficiency can be quickly lowered, and friction among staff members easily engendered, if such dynamics are not aired and understood. To prevent the alcoholic from playing one staff member off against another, all phone-calls pertaining to the group should be referred to the group psychotherapist. For instance, if a group member calls to cancel an appointment or to complain about the group, he should be encouraged by any of the personnel to come to his regular session and talk about his feelings in the group. The unanimity of the staff is reflected in their concerted endeavor to turn as much of the interaction into *group* interaction as is possible.

The Alternate Session

The use of the alternate group meeting, in which the members meet alone without the therapist (see Chapter VIII), an acceptable practice with many groups, has particular hazards when used with an alcoholic group. Utilization of an alternate meeting requires of *any* group a degree of group-ego and genuine cohesiveness which the alcoholic group develops only in the late stages of psychotherapy, if at all. If an alternate session is introduced at the beginning of the therapeutic experience, it plays into the already-resistive group's quasi-cohesion, and encourages superficial interaction. Furthermore, it tends to exclude the therapist, who is already considered a foreigner in the homogeneous alcoholic group (see Chapter IX).

Should the alternate meeting be introduced during the mid-phase of therapy, a disruptive acting out may occur, threatening all the members and recreating a detrimental experience of limitless boundaries. When this happens, both a group contagion and splintering can be observed to take place in the group. Acting out never occurs in isolation; and the alcoholic patient will attempt to involve his fellow group members, and the therapist as well. The other members may begin to act out together, either with or against the particular member. Invariably, this kind of involvement becomes an exploitative gambit on the part of the patient who starts the acting out. The group may respond by accepting the exploitation because they misinterpret therapeutic "permissiveness" and also because of their own individual needs to atone for past transgressions. For example, it is not unusual for the alcoholic who has a similar history of unpaid debts when he was drinking, to feel that he can make amends by giving a fellow group member money, regardless of the other's intent. This sort of acceptance is likely to be shortlived, however; what is apt to follow is that the group splinters and the acting out members are quite directly ostracized and censured. This splintering adds to the already considerable guilt and increases the possibility in each member of his premature termination. What is more, the use of alternate sessions brings up issues of secrecy and reporting back to the therapist; these too, tend to add to already-substantial group resistances and anxieties. The group may then appeal to the therapist to define boundaries and set limits. Ordinarily, with other kinds of patients, circumstances like these may be once again considered grist for the treatment mill; for alcoholics, already so intolerant of stress, they can prove too burdensome. Another danger in using alternate meetings with alcoholics is that an occasional member may attend only the alternate meetings and skip his regular sessions. This is not as strange as it may seem: Alcoholics are firm believers in self-help, and in the superiority of help from similarly-afflicted peers; and alcoholic patients are so adept at rationalization that this kind of behavior is very difficult to control.

One of the many advantages of the alternate meetings is that they give continuity to the therapeutic experience. However, for reasons discussed above, they have been found too hazardous for the alcoholic patient, in spite of the alcoholic's crucial need to experience continuity. Therefore—particularly when the therapist must be absent for an extended period—other means of promoting a feeling of continuing interest and concern must be substituted. Letters, for example, sent during the therapist's vacation period, reminding his patients of the resumption of meetings and including some personal note, can be very meaningful—both to the impoverished "Skid Row" group member (who has long ceased to get mail or be remembered) and to the alcoholic (in better circumstances) who is, in any case, so highly sensitive to abandonment (15). Many such letters, creased and worn, are still carried in wallets and purses months after they have been received; and, in one group at least, the therapist's letters aroused a great deal of emotion and discussion. Many members could not remember the last time they had sent a greeting card. Encouraged to communicate with each other by mail, all kinds of questions arose: How should their names be signed? Why were they unable to address each other as "dear" or close with "love?"—all issues that become meaningful in the therapy.

REFERENCES

1. Allen, D. W., and Houston, M.: The management of hysteriod acting-out patients in a training clinic. *Psychiatry, 22*:41-49, 1959.
2. Wolf, A. et al.: Sexual acting out in the psychoanalysis of groups. *Int. J. Psychother., 4*:369-380, 1954.
3. Murphy, G. E., and Guze, S. B.: Setting limits: The management of the manipulative patient. *Amer. J. Psychother., 14*:30-47, 1960.
4. Bird, B.: A specific peculiarity of acting out. *J. Amer. Psychoanal. Ass., 5*: 630-647, 1957.
5. Johnson, A.: Juvenile delinquency. *American Handbook of Psychiatry.* New York. Basic Books, 1959.
6. Johnson, A., and Szurek, S.: Etiology of antisocial behavior in delinquents and psychopaths. *J. A. M. A., 154*:814-817, 1954
7. Scher, J. M.: Group structure and narcotic addiction: notes from a natural history. *Int. J. Group Psychother., 11*(1):88-93, 1961.
8. Battegay, R.: Group therapy with alcoholics and analgesic addicts. *Int. J. Group Psychother., 8*(4):428-434, 1958.
9. Osberg, J. W., and Berliner, A. K.: The development stages in group psychotherapy with hospitalized narcotic addicts. *Int. J. Group Psychother., 6* (4):436-446, 1956.
10. Mullan, H., and Sangiuliano, I.: *The Therapist's Contribution to the Treatment Process: His Person, Transactions and Treatment Methods.* Springfield, Thomas, 1964.
11. Bird, B.: One aspect of causation in alcoholism. *Quart. J. Stud. Alcohol, 9*: 532-543, 1949.
12. Bateson, G., Jackson, D., Haley, J., and Weakland, J.: Toward a theory of schizophrenia. *Behav. Sci., 1*:251-264, 1956.
13. Jackson, D., and Weakland, J.: Conjoint family therapy. *Psychiatry, 24*:30-45, 1961.
14. Mullan, H., and Sangiuliano, I.: Group psychotherapy with the alcoholic. Summary of a Workshop (#19), American Group Psychotherapy Association's 6th Institute and 19th Conference, 24-27 Jan. 1962, New York.
15. Tarleton, G. H., and Tarnower, S. M.: The use of letters as part of the psychotherapeutic relationship. *Quart. J. Stud. Alcohol, 21*:82-89, 1960.

CHAPTER XII

DREAM PROCESS
IN GROUP PSYCHOTHERAPY
WITH THE ALCOHOLIC

IRIS SANGIULIANO, Ph.D.

(The dream, and particularly the dreaming process (dreaming, recalling and reporting), are considered significant in facilitating and directing treatment in alcoholic patient groups. The dream is selected for discussion since it most usefully illustrates the depth and intensity of the group psychotherapeutic process, as well as the intent of the professional leader. In addition, the phenomenological use of the dream distinguishes the aims and methods of group psychotherapy from the goals and means of other groups of alcoholics concerned only with sobriety. The dream is a communication which not only identifies the manner in which the patient presents himself in his treatment group but also his way of existing in life. The phenomenological approach to dreaming in the alcoholic group suggests that this process, common to patient and therapist, must be mutually engaged in to promote therapeusis. The therapist's use of his own dreams is another means to reach the alienated alcoholic, to lessen this patient's unbearable isolation and to disrupt his destructiveness to himself and to others.)

INTRODUCTION

The Importance of the Dreaming Process

The use of dreams can be of considerable value in the group psychoterapeutic process. Particularly is this true in the alcoholic group where the patient's resistance frequently takes the form of super-rationality. If the response to the dream is properly directed by the psychotherapist, not only are the intrapsychic dynamics of the dreamer revealed but also the depth of communication is intensified and relevant interaction increased within the group. The therapeutic function of the dream rests upon its dual communication to the dreamer and to the others. The dream expresses the intrapsychic struggle of the dreamer, and once it is told to the group, it becomes an interpersonal communication as well. As a result, both the dreamer and his conflict become more accessible to the group and therapist.

The dreamer's struggle, which was previously only partially conscious, is now made more fully available for treatment. Moreover, the use which the group makes of the dream becomes a valuable measure of therapeutic engagement. The way in which the group responds to the dream and the dreamer, that is, the way it uses the dream's themes and symbols to describe current behavior are thus a direct index of the depth and intensity of the therapeutic involvement within the group. The change in the manner of reporting and in the content of the alcoholic patients' dreams from the initial to later sessions reflects a general change in the group members' involvement with therapy.

Dream analysis is part of the traditional armamentarium of most psychotherapies, although the way a dream is used in therapy is very much a function of the particular theoretical orientation of the therapist. The patient's dream, when presented to a group, should be considered to be more than a product to be analyzed (1). Like the group experience itself, dreaming, and the recalling and reporting of the dream, are all part of an individual's life process, meaningful in and of themselves. The very fact that a dream is related to a group of peers makes the dream process a very different phenomenon from that involved in a dream which is related to a single authority figure for "analysis." The experience of relating a dream in a group is much more vital than telling it to a single person, and carries with it greater risk of revelation accompanied by a greater intensification of feelings. Basically, then, the dream is a communication that has two levels. It is a self-communication: as one aspect of the self communicates a feeling, thought or action to another aspect. Once the dream is related, it becomes a communication of another order between self and others. In group psychotherapy therefore it is not only the content and structure of the dream that are significant; but also the fact that the dream is recalled and reported to a *group,* which in turn responds spontaneously to the dreamer and his dream.

The dream process with all the risks involved for the dreamer and

the untutored responder is the critical element in the group psychotherapy of the alcoholic. Empirically, this emphasis has been found
to be extremely worthwhile in breaking through the initial resistance
to psychotherapy manifested in the early quasi-group cohesion with
the alcoholic, and to deepening the group interaction. In this chapter,
therefore, the content of a particular dream is not fully explored for
its diagnostic implications or causal origins. This is not to say that this
might not be helpful. The content of the alcoholic's dreams deserves
further research and discussion since at the present time there is a paucity of information on the subject (2). However, for the purposes of this
chapter, the use made of the dreaming process outweighs, at this time,
other ways of using dreams in heightening and intensifying the group
experience for the alcoholic patient. The manner of relating a dream,
the moment selected to relate it, and the one to whom the dream
is related are all part of the dream process and point to its importance.
When a dream is recounted to a group, the group members—who
are deeply engaged in a therapeutic process—more than the therapist
schooled in a certain theoretical framework, respond to the dreamer
as a total person, rather than to a universal dream symbol. For example, one group member responded to another's dream, seemingly
ignoring the content, by stating: "Last time you were terribly angry
at Iris (the therapist); I think you're jealous of her." Because the
group has this relative unconcern for the dream content *per se,* the
dream becomes another vehicle for more authentic communication.

The therapy group, through the dream, becomes engaged in the
nonrational aspects of the dreamer's and the therapist's lives, thus
circumventing the patient's penchant for abstractions and rationalizations. The dream discloses why the person is in the group, how he conceives of the group, and how he relates or will relate to the group.
In essence, the dream exposes the dreamer's life theme. As the play-
wright Ionesco points out: "The dream is not the means of exploring
a world *divorced* from waking reality; it is a means of discovering
truths *about* waking reality" (3, p. 36) (italics the author's).

Phenomenological Approach to the Group Dream

The dream process, like any creative process, requires a translation
of its symbols: in this case, from the realm of the dream world or

unawareness to the realm of waking reality, or awareness. After it is translated, the dream genuinely becomes a "creative act of discovery about reality" (3, p. 37). How a dream symbol is translated and utilized, is one of the characteristics that differentiates various schools of analytic practice, each of which labels or fixes the dream production in its own way. At the beginning, however, the dream phenomenon, regardless of the therapist's orientation, is the same. The dreamer presents the therapist and group with an emergent—that is, the manifest content. Much like a child's first drawings, what emerges is essentially "unlabeled." The therapist originally, and then the others, begin the process of selection that leads the patient to certain specific perceptions. The therapist as he draws attention to certain aspects of the dream production, the manner in which he draws attention, and what he chooses to attend to, will reflect his theoretical orientation, and his values, as well as the stage of the therapeutic engagement. The very fact that the therapist is conducting a group and that the patient relates the dream in a group alters the dream process and its therapeutic utilization (4). In relating a dream to the group, the intrapsychic phenomenon becomes an interpersonal experience as the therapist and other group members respond to the dreamer and his dream.

The intense and involving experience which can follow the reporting of a dream, when therapist and patients respond directly to the phenomenon, is unlike the usual superficial interaction of alcoholics, for it is rooted deeply in the therapist's and group members' inner fantasies. Moreover, when the translation of the dream experience keeps close to the language of the dream itself, the group member, together with the others, has an opportunity to develop his own symbolic, meaningful vocabulary with which to communicate his intrapsychic struggle, and to better understand both himself and the others.

The following dream was reported by a periodic drinker and vividly depicts his struggle with repeated drinking bouts. His feeling of being "shackled" to another self, which is destructive and uncontrollable, was a significant experience for all the group members and the term became a meaningful reference in describing their struggle with whether to drink or not.

I am shackled to another man on a boat and being taken to prison. He was sentenced to six months once, and this time to twelve years. He was envious of the other man whose sentence was only two years. He was a regular jailbird.

The therapist who is conducting a group emphasizes the immediate interaction and the affective involvements which result from it. Consequently, the manner in which the group therapist treats a dream must be such as to enhance the immediate, experiential impact for all the group members. As the dream becomes a real and meaningful experience—a unique presentation of the dreamer's self—the dream and the dreamer begin to merge. The dream is no longer a dissociated emanation to be "analyzed"; it is a vital part of the individual. In a very direct sense also, the dream presented to a group of patients, all of whom respond differently, offers the dreamer the opportunity to experiment with many different ways of being and many different solutions to his struggle. Although this experimentation in fantasy may be limited at first, the use of the dream as a point of departure for mutual fantasies involving dreamer and group allows the dreamer a myriad of diverse possibilities and likely solutions, many otherwise unavailable chances to act out identifications and test various ways of handling his real-life problems. (See The Experiential Response to the Dream, p. 291.)

As the patient recalls and relates his dream, he is forced to acknowledge at least some responsibility for, or ownership of, the nonrational aspects of his self characterized in the dream. This is verbalized by such introductory comments to the dream as: "this dream is crazy," "this dream makes no sense." In relating a dream, however, the dreamer usually feels less responsible for his product than he does when relating a fantasy. This is why a dream may be given more readily by a beginning patient than a fantasy, for it can be more readily disowned. One of the first tasks for the therapist and group therefore is to identify the dreamer with his dream. In ordinary patient groups this identification occurs more readily than with the alcoholic patient. It is quite another matter to get the alcoholic patient himself to integrate his dream with his conscious feelings and actions. The alcoholic's sober waking behavior many times can be a total denial of his dream. The very act of dreaming, recalling and reporting the dream, however, serves a valuable end by bringing to light a struggle within the dreamer which has not been sufficiently acknowledged, experienced, or accepted by the patient. In addition, the dream material indicates the areas of conflict, prepares the dreamer for the possibility and need for change, and sets the example for the others in the group to consider their dreams also.

THE UNIQUE USE OF THE DREAM PROCESS

Introduction

When the dream is used as described, it becomes central in directing the alcoholic group away from a superficial orientation which only considers the symptom of alcoholism, toward a concern with intra-psychic and interpersonal conflicts. This development is particularly necessary in this kind of group which at first makes such a strong stand for its homogeneity, and uses the mechanism of denial to an extreme. The relating of a dream can be used to bring out the fundamental heterogeneity of the group by focusing upon the uniqueness of each dreamer. Although the alcoholic exhibits a great tendency toward denial, the relating of a dream permits him to acknowledge, at first tangentially, the many constructive and destructive aspects of himself other than his drinking symptom. The use of the dream certainly affords one way that the alcoholic's conflict, which he so readily externalizes in his acting out, can begin to be internalized, with an increasing awareness of anxiety and possibilities for changing his way of life.

The Alcoholic Dreamer

It is important to consider and understand the general atmosphere of the alcoholic group when the therapist esteems and uses the dream process. Initially, particularly in a newly formed alcoholic group, the alcoholic will treat his and the other members' dream as he does everything else in his life, by denial, by generalizing, abstracting, intellectualizing, and looking for universalities in it. It is up to the psychotherapist of a new group to alter these attitudes. In an already-functioning therapy group, the group milieu should serve to discourage any superficial party-game atmosphere of dream reporting. For example, at the beginning of one group, the therapist requested dreams, and was as a result deluged with "drinking dreams" (see Chapter IX); however, rather than respond to the content of these dreams, the thera-

pist chose to respond to the frivolous manner in which they were related. To one group member she said, "You tell your dreams rapidly
and vaguely, so that I won't have any feelings for you." About another
dream, she commented, "You're just telling me that all you are is
alcoholic and all alcoholics are alike. Maybe you're protecting me
against being hurt by you." By the thirteenth session of this newly-
formed group, the dreams were reported in a more individualized, less
vague manner, and in a way that more fully identified the dreamer.
These later dreams also centered less on alcoholism *per se* and more
on their total life struggle. Initially, too, the patients often stated that
they don't dream, that they "forget" dreams, or they tend to withhold
all or part of the dream. Later, as patients feel more secure in the
group, dreams are spontaneously given.

The Therapist's Response to the Dream in an Alcoholic Group

The attitude of the therapist toward dreams and the use which he
makes of them therefore will do much toward molding the group
atmosphere. The therapist begins to indicate in a variety of ways that
he values dreams, not only by the things he says but also by what he
does. In a beginning alcoholic group, he may explain the importance
of bringing in fantasy material. The therapist continues to show his
interest in the nonrational aspects of his patient when he asks for the
patient's dreams; when he responds to the patient's dreams; and when
the therapist dreams himself, and admits it. He may volunteer the
information, "I had a dream last night and I think that it's about the
group." From time to time he may turn to one member who seems
particularly silent and ask, "What is your dream?" If the patient
persists in maintaining that he does not dream, the therapist may
reply, "Perhaps you will have a dream for us next time."

The therapist may thus facilitate the reporting of dreams very
directly. The crucial point, however, is his response to the dream and
dreamer, for this will do much to encourage or deter the use of fantasy
material in the group. If the therapist sets himself up as the expert, the
decoder of mysterious symbols, much that is of value in the dream
process will be lost. It is more effective if the therapist can respond to
the dream as an immediate event. Depending on the context, he may

state, for example, "That is a good dream, I like it. I'm glad that you've finally included me in your dream." Or, "Your dream upsets me and makes me angry. Why do you always leave women out?" This kind of interpretation also frees the group members to spontaneously express their reactions and feelings. The dream then becomes a group experience rather than something to be scrutinized and puzzled out by an "expert." The use of dreams in group therapy with alcoholics does not imply that the group therapist's function is to analyze a single patient's dream in the presence of an audience of the other six or seven group members. Rather, "the dream in the therapeutic group must be used as the symbolic frame upon which rests the genuine meaning of the interactional component of therapy."* This is especially the case in the alcoholic group in which the therapist must make every effort to develop a deeply therapeutic group milieu and interaction.

The Experiential Response to the Dream

What the therapist chooses to respond to in the dream is very much a function of who he is, what he believes to be significant, and his degree of involvement with the dreamer. Dr. Mullan has characterized three primary channels of communication in the group dream which are particularly pertinent for the alcoholic group: (a) the dream as allegory; (b) the dream as paradox, and (c) the dream as experiential contagion (5). These three elements may be found in any dream, but when they are used in the group, they are especially relevant avenues of communication within the dreamer himself, and between the dreamer and the other group members and therapist.

The Dream as Allegory

The description of one thing in terms of another thing is the simplest definition of an allegory. To maintain the communication in the patient's unique idiom the therapist may respond to the dream in terms of the patient's own symbolic language without any translation or interpretation of those symbols. In other words, the therapist or group may continue the patient's dream fantasy using *his* terms, although at the same time offering other possibilities or perceptions of

---

*The author is grateful for the use of Dr. Hugh Mullan's paper, "The Process on the Utilization of Dreams in Psychotherapy, National Psychological Association for Psychoanalysis, January 1962.

the dream content. As the dream is responded to in this manner, the allegorical reference is brought into the present and becomes an integral part of the group's interaction and communication.

The following dream was the first dream reported by William, a new member in an already functioning alcoholic group.

> I had a dream. It was a dream like the Spanish Civil War. I was there with my family, we were at one side just watching. Everyone was tugging at each other, war, war, pulling at each other.

Through this dream, William describes his initial feelings of apprehension, discomfort, and distrust specifically about the therapy group and more generally about his life. The group is seen as a family divided in internecine warfare with conflicting and destructive loyalties rampant. He is also communicating his own family experience. The therapist and group members responded to this dream by saying, in effect, "Yes, we are tugging and pulling at each other; but we are also involved with each other and trying to work something out." The paradoxical nature of the relationship was voiced in one remark by another group member: "All you see is the tugging. What about the fact that we need and want to be here and come here every week?" Responses like these put the symbolic content in a more relevant perspective taking into consideration the new influence in the patient's life, his treatment group. These responses further suggest that there are other interpretations to his life than just the old way in which he experiences it.

Another example of the allegorical communication is a beginning dream brought in by Diana. Diana had a long history of drinking and A.A. membership. She was quite concrete and defensive in the group, spoke in clichés, and was prone to oratory. She brought in the following dream one session after the therapist had asked her for her dreams.

> I dreamt that I was with two women that I don't care for. It was confused. I thought that I was in a hospital on a job, working there. But one of these women was conducting a meeting. I was present, working there but the others thought I was *here at* the meeting. This woman looked pleadingly at me. I ran out.

In this dream Diana communicates her feelings about the group and the woman therapist, feelings which hitherto she could not expose directly to the group. It is significant that in the midst of relating the dream she shifted location and slipped into "I was *here* at the meeting." Through this dream, Diana identifies her resistance to group psychotherapy. (Diana was an active worker in A.A. The confusion between this role, and what is expected of her as a group therapy member, was depicted in the dream by her confusion about being either "a worker in a hospital" or "here at the meeting.") She also forewarns the therapist and group against getting too close to her; she will run out. The therapist responded to this communication by saying, "I wasn't aware that I was pleading but I must be. I'm concerned that you won't stay with us if we get too close to you." Other responses brought out Diana's dilemma in the group—her struggle between what she expected group therapy to be and how she actually experienced it. These responses included remarks such as, "Why can't you attend the meeting and also be a worker?" Another group member volunteered, "I go to A.A. and come here also." The therapist further commented, "It's true, Diana, that I assume you're here because you're struggling with your life, not only with your drinking." Diana responded with feeling, and said she considered herself understood by the group for the first time. She stated that her constant fear had been that group therapy would "unsettle my emotions. I must not get too sad or too happy, or I'll drink."

The Dream as Paradox

A paradox is an assertion or sentiment that seemingly contradicts or is opposed to common sense, but that may possibly be true. The therapist's response to the paradoxical elements of a dream is directed toward facilitating the patient's awareness of his conflicts and intrapsychic struggles.

The following dream was reported by an alcoholic group member, an overt Lesbian, who had attained several years of sbriety. Grace was a member of the original core group and quite committed to her therapy. She had been in the group approximately six months when she related:

> I dreamt that Alice (another group member) gave birth to a
> baby elephant and I wanted to buy a gift. I began selecting a gift

for the baby but couldn't find the right thing. I went on to select something for Alice. This ranged from slacks to something very feminine and frilly—but nothing fit.

Through the dream process, Grace describes her active struggle with her homosexuality. She had prefaced this dream by speaking of an affair she was having with a married man. The therapist responded to this dream in a number of ways. Since she accepted Grace as a woman, she stated, "I would like you to have a real baby of your own and someone to care for you both." Also, "You are searching, but nothing fits—it's either 'butch' or 'whorish'; try your own kind of clothes instead." For Grace, sexuality meant either a rejection of the male or being, like Alice, sexually promiscuous.

The Dream as Experiential Contagion

When a dream is reported it becomes the common property of the group. When the theme of the dream and its symbols are used spontaneously by the therapist and patients, these dream elements become a private language of communication and offer a way for the overrational and defensive alcoholic group to begin to deal with its inner fantasy life. The group can begin to shift from an exclusive concern with alcoholism and its concomitant "reality" problems to the deep experience of intrapsychic and interpersonal conflict.

The experiential elements of the group interaction are enhanced through the phenomenological use of dreams. For example, both William's and Diana's initial dreams expressed the fears and mistrust of other group members. In responding to William's dream of Civil War, the therapist turned to another member, Seymour, who had not as yet reported any dreams, and said, "That could be your dream Seymour; it certainly sounds like your home life." Similarly, Diana's struggle and conflict about A.A., and her fear that deep self-questioning might disrupt her life, because they are common themes among alcoholics, stimulated other members toward re-evaluating themselves. Her dream was countered by another patient who responded that he was able to participate in both A.A. and group therapy and get something from each.

The experiential contagion of a single dream may be observed in the greater number of dreams reported, in the more effective use which the group makes of their dreams and in their more active response. Through this new avenue of communication, group members are enabled to show concern, interest, and deep understanding for each other, both consciously—in responding to the dreams—and also unconsciously through dreaming about other members of the group as well as the therapist. For example, Grace's dream about Alice was a communication about herself, and it also pointed to Alice's confused identity. Up to the time of Grace's dream, Alice had conveyed an image in the group of an "extremely feminine" woman whose femininity, however, was exaggerated and overly sexualized. With Grace's dream, the therapist was able to stimulate Alice into self-questioning about her exaggerated need to convey this oversexualized image. Following this, Alice discussed, for the first time, her own feelings of inadequacy about being a woman.

Identifying the Therapeutic Relationship

Frequently dreams can also be used to clarify the nature of the relationship between the therapist and patient, and to thereby give an indication of transferential problems which may be causing difficulty. This is a special advantage, sometimes even critical, with the alcoholic patient who is so quick to terminate treatment with the arousal of even minimal anxiety. The following dream was related to the group by Nicholas at his first group session. It indicates the immediate transference bind which the patient brings to the therapeutic relationship. He explained that he had this dream following his initial evaluation interview in which he was accepted for group therapy by the therapist.

> I can't remember any of the details of the dream but I know that Iris (the therapist), Betty (a woman with whom he had been having a long-term affair), and Angela (the patient's mother, whom he referred to by her first name) were in it. I know that Betty and Angela kept getting mixed up as to who was who. I had a feeling of relief and euphoria after the dream.

Since this was the beginning of Nicholas' treatment, the therapist merely responded to the dream by saying, "I'm glad that you've joined us, and that you feel relieved in being with us. You seem to be searching for who Angela, Betty, and I really are. Maybe together we can find out." After these comments, Nicholas spoke freely about himself and his mother, who had died recently. This dream not only brought Nicholas into the group; it also forecast potential pitfalls in the therapist-patient relationship as it shows that Nicholas identifies the therapist with Angela and Betty. This kind of information is of particular value in the management and control of patients who may develop intense psychotic transference reactions.

The inclusion of the therapist in a dream is not always overt. Often the therapist may be referred to in a disguised symbolic form. For example, Diana dreamed of "a woman I don't care for." Or, the therapist may be represented by some authority figure. The therapeutic process is significantly facilitated and many times initial resistances are clarified when the therapist responds to such symbols as if he were being directly referred to. This is especially pertinent in the homogeneous alcoholic group which makes a point of excluding the therapist. For this reason, the therapist included herself in Diana's dream by interpreting it quite literally and responding directly to Diana.

Dreams reveal areas of *impasse* and also many conscious resistances. In one of Grace's earliest dreams, she described her life struggle with drinking, her fight for sobriety, and her initial response to group therapy. The impact that the therapist had made on Grace by questioning her many homosexual affairs was apparent in a dream about Governor Faubus. Faubus as a symbol for the therapist had particular meaning for Grace, who was a staunch believer in Civil Rights.

> I am so tired, I lay down in the rain, someone came along and helped me. I then joined the group and Governor Faubus was there. I resented having to listen to him, I didn't hear a thing.

In a very real sense the group interaction during this session, before and after the relating of this dream, served as an association to the dream. During the group session, it was mentioned that Grace was involved in a new homosexual affair. Grace had spoken of this at the previous alternate session* but was reluctant to speak in front of the therapist. This dream, however, was related by Grace during the regular group meeting and indirectly expressed her resentment against the therapist whom she construed as having hetereosexual values pre-

---

*An alternate group meeting is a session in which the group meets without the presence of the psychotherapist. This practice was used at one point and later discontinued (see Chapter X).

judicial to her own values. The therapist responded to the dream by saying, "I don't feel prejudiced against *you,* Grace. I'm not certain what homosexuality is for you."

The Therapist's Dream

Any discussion on the use of the dream in psychotherapy generally implies the patient's dream. For the therapist to dream, or to relate his dreams to move the treatment process, is highly suspect. The very fact that the therapist dreams about a patient or patient-group is usually considered as wholly negative, indicating an unwarranted involvement or strong counter-transference toward his patient. Further to reveal that dream is viewed by some as acting out on the therapist's part and, more strongly by others, as an exploitation of the patient.

However, in view of the fact that therapists also have an unconscious and they do dream, it is suggested that those dreams which are pertinent to any single patient or group of patients can be used to help facilitate, identify and intensify the psychotherapeutic relationship and group interaction. This is of special value in the alcoholic group who for a long time forms a quasi-cohesive unit which excludes the therapist.

The group therapist's use of his dream, however, does not imply by any means an impulsive or naive reporting of his dream, or a detailed intellectual interpretation or analysis. The therapist's dream is treated phenomenologically, without explanation of its genetic orgins, as a present experience in the group to which the members are free to respond. There is care in the selection of the dreams and also in the timing of the presentation. The experienced group therapist must be aware that his dream has to do with him, his unconscious struggle in the group as well as with the dynamics of the group. The dream can be used to identify a problem or *impasse* which exists in the group and used in this manner it moves the group. Rather than acting out on the therapist's part, dreams revealed in this manner, show the tremendous seriousness and devotion of the trained and experienced group therapist to his task. Thus, instead of facilitating acting out, a therapist's knowledge and acceptance of his dreams can clarify the acting out impasse (see Chapter XI).

A retrospective analysis of this therapist's dreams in relation to three alcoholic groups revealed some significant developments. The therapist's dream behavior, like that of the patients', also underwent a change. The therapist's dreams relevant to the group paralleled the group's growth in involvement and interaction. Initially the therapist had no dreams either about these particular groups as a whole or about any specific member. By the fourteenth session of one group, however, at a time when there had been a change in the group milieu, the therapist reported one dream which seemed to epitomize her feelings about each member of the group. The group became quite involved with this dream and responded to it as though it were a current happening in the group. The therapist then had other dreams, some quite specifically concerned different members of the group, and others dealt more generally with the "alcoholic" grouping.

Interestingly enough, there was also a change in the ease with which the therapist reported dreams to each of these groups. Unquestionably, the degree of group maturity influenced the ease with which a dream could be related, and indeed, the very fact that a dream was related at all. This fact was made obvious, moreover, when one group remained on a superficial level over an extended period of time, and the therapist continued to feel a real reluctance to reveal any dreams. It seems that the more immature or lacking in therapeutic involvement the group is, the more anonymous and professional must the therapist remain.

The Therapist's Utilization of the Dream

To sum up, the psychotherapist uses the dream to enhance the immediate, affective meaning of the group experience, so that the associations to the dream make up the content of the entire group session just prior to, and also after the reporting of the dream. Dreams do more than identify a patient's past and present intrapsychic struggle; they also forecast future developments. By using the dream fantasy, the patient, the group, and the therapist are enabled to experiment with other ways of being and other possible solutions to their conflicts. Alcoholics are rigidly fixed in one manner of response to the world; nonetheless utilization of the dream process can add immeasureably to free them and give them other avenues of expression, communication, identification, and belonging.

REFERENCES

1. Mullan, H.: The nonteleleological in dreams in group psychotherapy. *J. Hillside Hosp., 5*(304):480-487, 1956.
2. Moore, R. A.: The manifest dream in alcoholism. *Quart. J. Stud. Alcohol, 25*:583-589, 1962.
3. Coe, R.: *Eugene Ionesco.* New York, Evergree Pilot Book, Grove Press, 1961.
4. Chalfen, L.: The use of dreams in psychoanalytic group psychotherapy. *Psychoanalysis, 51*(3):125-132, 1964.
5. Mullan, H.: The process-oriented use of dreams in the therapeutic group: Symposium on the utilization of dreams in psychotherapy. *Nat'l Psychol. Ass. for Psychoanal.,* January 1962.

CHAPTER XIII

LEAVETAKING
FROM THE ALCOHOLIC GROUP

IRIS SANGIULIANO, Ph.D.

(Leavetaking, so characteristic of the alcoholic, is a main ob-stacle in the group treatment of this patient. Treatment cannot continue if the patient does not remain in his therapy group, and all the theoretical discussion on the nuances and the subtleties of psychotherapeutic methods are of no avail. Leavtaking in the alcoholic group occurs at any stage of treatment. This chapter differentiates among the early drop-outs who leave after a few group sessions, the abrupt terminators who leave prematurely at a mid-phase of therapy, and those who remain in treatment working toward some resolution of their problems, designated as "remainers." An attempt is made to identify those patients who tend to leave treatment prematurely, and those who tend to stay on. The impermanence of the alcoholic as far as remaining in treatment, or for that matter, remaining permanently out of treatment, places a greater demand for flexibility on the group therapist. These unique aspects of the group treatment of the alcoholic are described.)

INTRODUCTION

The Tendency to Leave in the Alcoholic

For the alcoholic, leavetaking or the abrupt severance of ties, activi-ties and interests, is a way of life. More specifically, it is his way of coping with the world which he construes as hostile, or at best un-sympathetic. It is usual for an alcoholic, within the span of a few years, to have changed his job, his financial status, residence, career plans, marital status and treatment plans. Leavetaking, in this last instance, particularly when the form of treatment is group psycho-therapy has other ramifications. This seeming impermanence is deceptive. Although the alcoholic always appears to be in the state of separating from any meaningful relationships, he actually shows himself to be unable to *ever* completely separate from certain significant persons.

This tendency, perceptively designated by one alcoholic group patient as "separation allergy," does not however, hold the alcoholic physically in the therapy group. Rather, through a kind of self-deception the alcoholic conceives of the therapist or a fellow group patient in a fantasized way as an omnipotent "helper," always present and always available. This enables him to leave abruptly and yet not separate emotionally.

The alcoholic who cuts ties in this fashion isolates himself from others and causes a state of continuing impermanence. His relationships exist essentially in fantasy where he can direct and control them. However, to counterbalance this continuous instability he requires an unswerving permanence in others—if any significant relationships are to develop. The one he selects as "helper" must be devoted, interested, sympathetic and understanding. If he is married, for example, the spouse generally is this figure, all-giving and unchanging, from whom he momentarily separates only to return each time. If the alcoholic is in group therapy, the therapist or an important group member becomes this figure and is made to assume the role of an all-giving, omnipotent "helper." This kind of distortion in the ordinary patient might be a desirable step in making the group more cohesive. But with the alcoholic, who uses this fantasy relationship to abruptly leave and yet remain dependent, this step is hardly beneficial. The therapist, then, who treats alcoholics in groups must come to understand this kind of departure and prevent it if possible. He must be able to tolerate this unstable relationship with the compulsive drinker and continue to treat him even after extended breaks in treatment.

In this chapter, those who prematurely take leave of their treatment group are designated as "drop-outs," or abrupt terminators, while those who remain in treatment are called "remainers." More specifically, the "drop-out" leaves the group shortly after placement and his departure is usually based upon: (1) poor selection; (2) insufficient preparation; (3) incorrect timing in group placement, and (4) placement in an inappropriate group. The abrupt terminator leaves early in the cohesive phase of group treatment, possibly during the first six months, when the group has shifted from the quasi-cohesive phase, and is genuinely beginning to change. The remainers terminate when the group is more truly cohesive, after the first six months, and their general approach to leavetaking is much like the nonalcoholic patient. These patients probably have undergone more permanent psychological change and when they leave therefore have less need to depend on the fantasized "helper" although this need does continue to some extent.

The question of early termination in psychotherapy is necessarily related to the therapist's treatment values and goals. If these goals are to be relevant to particular patients, however, they cannot be formulated in the abstract. They must evolve and change in relation to the person the therapist is with; and they must be real rather than ideal. The alcoholic challenges the therapist most, perhaps, in this area of goals (see Chapter III) for frequently he enters therapy offering much reassurance, promise and resolution to change, so that the psychotherapist becomes mistakenly optimistic. Initially, the patient is totally dependent upon the therapist for guidance, and endows him with omnipotent powers. This honeymoon, however, is shortlived: Sessions are missed, lateness recurs, alcoholic acting out begins, and the therapist finds himself put in a situation where he feels quite powerless. The psychotherapist's methods and goals therefore must be modified at least to some extent and come to rest somewhere between a total omnipotence or abject impotence. Despite the individual differences among alcoholic patients, neither differences in native endowment nor in other indices of growth potential can alter the therapist's limited treatment goals, unless the patient's compulsive drinking and resultant noncommitment change.

The alcoholic's "unusual vulnerability to stress and challenge" referred to by Dr. Wolfson in Chapter VI, makes the course of psychotherapy with the alcoholic at best tenuous. In general, as with any patient, the therapist attempts to undermine the alcoholic's fantastic life theme (1); when this occurs, the alcoholic patient's depressive tenor begins to lift as a more realistically-based sense of self emerges. However, the patient's fantasies cannot be interrupted, unless he can achieve an increase in control of and tolerance for frustration and its accompanying anxiety. Which happens first is a moot question. The fact is that the alcoholic's very low frustration tolerance which moves him out of treatment makes him a special treatment problem. The question of drop-outs and premature terminators therefore is critical if any hope is be held out for the rehabilitation of the alcoholic.

The alcoholic rates poorly, according to various predictive indices for continuance in therapy. It has been observed that the patients who are most likely to remain in treatment have "a history of less impulsive and less antisocial behavior, admit more anxious behavior, are more critical of themselves, and are less likely to endorse rigid, irrational beliefs" (2, p. 13). However, the personal equation cannot be ignored. It is also likely that the more experienced and interested therapists retain a higher proportion of all patients, good and poor risks (3).

It may well be that the high incidence of drop-outs and premature terminators among the alcoholics in group therapy is attributable in part to inadequate selection procedures (see Chapter VIII). Certainly if the psychotherapist is able to set up a group in which a core membership of four to six individuals could begin to participate seriously and with commitment for several months, the introduction of new patients, and therapy in general, becomes much easier. It is good practice for the therapist to select from among alcoholic referrals, those individuals who could most benefit from psychotherapy. This core group of more-committed patients could shorten the quasi-cohesive phase and also permit the addition of the less motivated patient without undue disruption to the group as a whole. This way of starting an alcoholic group is more easily achieved in a treatment center than in private practice, because of the large number of referrals; however, the alcoholic population in treatment, even in clinics, is noted for its high rate of atrition, regardless of the greater selection possibilities.

KINDS OF LEAVETAKING

Drop-outs

In our experience, alcoholic group members, compared with other patients, may drop out of treatment after attending only one or two group sessions. Alcoholics seem to require a longer preparation before group placement if they are entering an already functioning group (see Chapter VIII). One reason for this may be that the alcoholic patient seems more vulnerable and threatened by spontaneous group interaction. If, for example, his initial response to the therapist is negative, his tolerance for his hostility is so low that it is very likely that he will not return.

The following case material illustrates how a beginning negative transference toward the therapist affects the alcoholic group patient.

Richard attended only two group sessions and then dropped out. Efforts to reach him proved to no avail. At the time Richard joined the group, the group was in the midst of being reorganized. In his first session, only one woman group member, and the therapist, also a woman were present. In his second session, there were two women members, plus the woman therapist. Richard's behavior was very "proper," reticent and tight. This small group accepted him but it also made an effort to encourage him "to loosen up." In the second session, Richard reported the following dream: "My aunt was running a supermarket. None of the help showed up. I was a clerk there and I had to get the figures from the cash registers from the night before. She was checking the people out and giving me the wrong figures. I got angry. She then accused me of using bad language, like *hell* and *damn*. I hadn't though. She told me not to use that kind of language in the store." With this dream Richard recalled his hatred of his aunt whom he described as a "domineering, executive type, a personnel manager. I felt she pushed people around."

The dream gives evidence of the developing negative transference to the woman therapist and perhaps the group as a whole, together with his disappointment in the group membership ("none of the help showed up"). Interestingly, the group's permissiveness in the use of "bad language" was too threatening for him to tolerate.

Moreover, should the group interact more intensely, by expressing hostility or reporting fantasy material, the challenge to a newly-arrived alcoholic patient may be too great for him to continue. This marked vulnerability to the group atmosphere is the reason why selection for the alcoholic treatment group is so crucial. Initially, during the quasi-cohesive phase, the group is too poorly integrated to contain any new member who is disruptive (see Chapter IX). Psychopaths and others who monopolize the group to the detriment of all, for example, cannot be readily integrated into a group, and the psychotherapist must remove them from group treatment. The alcoholic's inordinate demand for the therapist's exclusive attention will also move some to leave a group on the basis that it is inferior treatment. The referring agency can help immeasurably in the initial success or failure of the therapy if they have oriented the patient to group treatment. Undoubtedly, the manner in which the patient is referred and selected does much to influence the necessary initial positive relationship to the institution, therapist, and group.

Proper selection is also important for the development and use of effective group interaction. Mindlin mentions four critical areas which she believes relate directly to therapeutic outcome: "socio-economic resources; past adjustment; gravity of the diagnosis; and motivation" (4). Precipitous drop-outs militate against an effective group functioning. Great care should be taken to select patients who are more likely to remain in treatment. If the therapy group is to become more than an open meeting for the superficial airing of common symptoms, the group therapist must be adept at selecting alcoholic patients who can tolerate at least minimal anxiety.

Abrupt Terminators in the Early Cohesive Phase of Group Psychotherapy

Those patients who terminate in the early cohesive phase of therapy require far more attention and consideration than those who drop out early, since they are individuals, who after all, have stayed in therapy for several months. This midphase is the time when premature terminations are very apt to occur. As the transferences within the group begin to develop and intensify, the problem of alcoholism *per se* becomes less and less the main focus of the group's interest. With the intensification of the transference, distortions are awakened and more deeply experienced. If these distortions arouse hostile and angry feelings, they may be too much for the patient to tolerate and he leaves. Also should his presence in the group be based solely on his identification as an alcoholic, he may terminate at that point in which the group members become less identified with alcoholism and more concerned with themselves as conflicted human beings. Acting out and anxiety may increase at this time and fear is expressed that their sobriety is in jeopardy.

Dolores was richly endowed intellectually but prone to universalizations. The psychological examination indicated that she was overabstracted and inclined to project her problems. She had been sober for more than a year when she began group therapy. Dolores had remarried a few years before starting treatment to an alcoholic much below her intellectual and social level. However, she stated that it was through him that she had attained and maintained her sobriety since she had to keep sober so that he woudn't drink. Moreover, his "bovine-like" existence offered no challenge and made no demand on her. Initially, Dolores was very verbal in the group, overrationalized, and replete with clichés and psychological jargon. With considerable effort on her own and the group's parts, this attitude gradually diminished and she became deeply involved. Her dreams, for example, reflected a shift from preoccupation with "transcendental" feelings to very intimate and personal strivings. Dolores' womanly strivings and competitiveness were first acknowledged when she related a dream in which she was "flashing a mink coat." Her work aspirations at this time gradually became commensurate with her capacities; she also began to take greater care of her person. As her intellectualizations crumbled, there appeared an open hostility—first toward the men in the group and later the women. Joseph, another group member, responded to her hostility by fantasizing how much freer he would feel in the group if three of the members were not present, among whom he mentioned Dolores. Dolores retreated to her former defensiveness and pointed out, "Oh, it's nothing *personal* with Joseph." However, after this session she refused to return to the group and, despite the therapist's efforts to reach her, she remained adamant. Dolores explained that she feared that Joseph's and her "serenity" might be disrupted and that she might resume drinking if she remained. Her parting words were, "I don't want that mink coat."

Dolores was too threatened by her hostile and competitive strivings, especially in relation to the woman therapist. In addressing the therapist during their last phone conversation, she became confused and referred to the therapist by Joseph's surname. With Dolores' growing involvement, she also seemed to fear the rise of her strong passive-dependency needs which she now realized could never be fulfilled. Nevertheless, she had been roused from her "bovine" existence with her spouse. Despite the tremendous rage with which she abruptly terminated, two years later she wrote to the Center to tell of her greater well-being and an increasing sense of accomplishment.

Another factor which may act to precipitate a premature termination is the characteristic kind of relationship between members that many times forms in a homogeneously symptomed group. This homogeneity, as indicated earlier (see Chapters IX and X) has both its merits and serious drawbacks. Because of the symbiotic nature of the group patient's relationships and their close symptom-identification, a change that occurs in one group member may strongly affect the others. The effect, however, is not always saluatory, as it may perematurely challenge and thus threaten another member.

Grace and Leslie were original members of a beginning group; both were involved in the group and seemed to have a genuine concern and regard for each other. Both had previously attained many years of sobriety. Both were overt Lesbians. Leslie presented a flip and brassy exterior which she used to defend herself against intimate contact and possible hurt. Behind this facade, however, was a very sensitive, dependent and easily wounded individual. According to the psychological examination, her "urge to childish dependency, narcissistic self-display, and sexual curiosity seem to weaken her defenses drastically." Over a period of months, the nature of Grace's relationships changed and in one session, Grace reluctantly spoke of her new heterosexual interests, adding that she had feared revealing this in the group in front of Leslie. Leslie seemingly ignored her, and went on to discuss her homosexuality, but ended the evening in a rage against the entire group. Her feelings toward the therapist had become strongly ambivalent. She related that she had a dream about the therapist but refused to reveal its content. In recent months Leslie had come to openly experience her dread of men and sexual intercourse, and was reaching a point where she would have to reevaluate her homosexual relationships. Grace's change left her unsupported and threatened. Leslie terminated abruptly in anger, and all efforts to reach her proved fruitless. Leslie wrote a letter in which she curtly expressed her desire to leave the group and asked that she not be contacted ever again.

The awakening of intense positive or negative feelings is very threatening for the alcoholic patient and leaves him quite vulnerable. If these feelings occur before the patient is firmly entrenched in the therapeutic treatment process, he may leave precipitously. A group which has a good therapeutic climate, however, can do much to support the patient at this moment and extend his stay in treatment.

Joseph had a difficult struggle in the group. Initially, he was verbose, intellectualized, and somewhat pompous, all behavior that seemed to be an attempt to mask deep rooted feelings of inadequacy. His psychological examination appropriately described him as a "sentimentalist who poses as a rationalist." His role in the group was similar to that of a master of ceremonies. With the support and stimulation of an evolving group, Joseph also began to change. Strong crosscurrents were aroused in his relationship to the various group members, through which he began to re-experience his marital failure and deep seated fear of impotence. He began to face his rage toward his wife, who had "abandoned" him for another man; more important still, he was confronted with his own isolation and inability to relate intimately to any woman. His relationship to the woman therapist was positive and sexually-tinged. Joseph reported, "I have so many inner strivings now, I feel more screwed up than when I came, and I feel worse too." However, his compulsion to drink subsided and he stated that he felt less compulsive in his life in general as well. As the group interaction intensified, Joseph became visibly disturbed. At one point, one of the men in the group responded to Joseph's strong positive feelings toward the therapist and related them to Joseph's feelings of impotence in the face of the "unattainable." Joseph then became ambivalent toward the therapist. He openly expressed anger that she had not been able to prevent the sexual acting out which had taken place between one group member to whom he was attracted, and a new member. During this period his behavior became defensive, hostile, and withdrawn. As the group asked him to relinquish his over-rationality, by focusing on what he really felt and not how he *ought* to feel, Joseph retorted, "I don't believe in God, therefore I have to establish a rigid code of rules for myself and I don't intend to relinquish it." A few weeks later, after considerable upheaval in the group, Joseph stated that he was leaving. This announcement took place the last ten minutes of one session. Joseph explained that he had gained "more confidence" in his life; that he was no longer afraid of psychotherapy; but that he had reached a "plateau" and had decided to leave. Joseph could not be dissuaded from his decision and left with a tearful good-bye.

In a retrospective analysis of these and other abrupt terminations in the early phase of group cohesion, several common characteristics appear which permit of some generalization. One of the most critical similarities in each of these terminators is the nature of the motivation which originally moved these patients to seek treatment. In each patient described above, the original reason for seeking help was a desire to have the symptom relieved, plus a desire for counsel and "how to" advice—not psychotherapy. Leslie had agreed to group therapy since she hoped that she would get a vocational evaluation which would help her find a suitable job. Joseph came for advice: He feared he was becoming an uncontrollable drinker and his job and promotion were in jeopardy. Dolores also sought advice: She was alarmed at the thought that after one year of sobriety she would resume drinking, since she was withdrawing more and more from all activity. Of much more significance, moreover, each of these alcoholics admitted little dissatisfaction with himself personally* or his way of life.

Regardless of their initial motivation, however, once these patients entered a therapy group, they inevitably became interested and involved with the other group members. A moment of decision came as the group became genuinely cohesive and involved in a therapeutic process. They then had to decide whether to participate genuinely in the psychotherapy group, or to leave. All three reached a point where it became apparent to them that psychotherapy was more than symptom-relief, and that they had to make a basic change in themselves if there was to be any change in their manner of coping with the world. Dolores tacitly acknowledged this in her parting words to the therapist: "I don't want a mink coat." Joseph spoke of a "plateau," and his unwillingness to relinquish his "rigid code of rules." Leslie was threatened by another member's re-evaluation of her homosexuality. Each had reached the threshold of intensive group interaction, each terminated.

Another similarity among these three terminators was first described in the psychological examination and later corroborated in the group interaction. All three seemed markedly reactive to their passive-dependency needs which involved their wish for an omnipotent and omniscient figure that would take care of them. As these feelings began to come to the surface, their defenses appeared to weaken drastically;

---

*This paradoxical attitude has also been observed in an experimental study on defensiveness in alcoholics, which suggests that a number of alcoholics, in this instance A.A. members, although they admit to the problem of alcoholism and suicidal behavior, resist the implication that they are unhappy with life as a whole (5).

there was also the fear that they would be either disillusioned or completely enveloped. Significantly each presented a superrational sophisticated facade which gave them an air of self-sufficiency and impenetrability. Perhaps these very dependency needs and sensitivity permitted them to form an initial strong positive bond that also ultimately caused the therapeutic relationship to break. Their leaving seemed to express an inner sense of futility at the idea that their needs could ever be fulfilled and the subsequent development of negative feelings toward the therapist proved unsupportable. One can theoretically surmise that had these patients developed sufficient inner support in their preparatory group phase, they would have stayed.* In other words, had these critical periods come later in their therapy, they may not have felt as threatened. This surmise is difficult to prove; however, in life as in the therapy group, the timing of events cannot always be controlled.

In our discussion of the premature terminator, the issue of goals, particularly with the alcoholic patient, once again arises. Certainly the individuals described had not fulfilled the therapist's predetermined goals. However, these patients were selected as illustrative since they were part of research project** that permitted follow-up study. Two of the three patients cooperated in the follow-up interviews. These two patients were leading a less precarious existence than previously; and the label, *alcoholic,* no longer appeared to be the only way that they identified themselves. Although it is easy to rationalize one's failures, it may be that the gain from such a brief group experience was not sufficiently acknowledged since it did not coincide with certain of the therapist's goals.

Treatment for the Terminators

A word should be said at this point about methods of treating terminators. All efforts must be made to keep the alcoholic patient in treatment. If the patient absents himself from group meetings, the

---

*These patients took part in the New York Alcoholism Vocational Rehabilitation Project. Because of the experimental design of this study, these patients were given only one preparatory individual session prior to group placement.

**New York Alcoholism Vocational Rehabilitation Project of the National Council on Alcoholism in cooperation with the Office of Vocational Rehabilitation, U.S. Dept. of Health, Education, and Welfare, Project # 418.

therapist may phone to inquire about him. Telephoning is especially important at the beginning of treatment; also after a particularly upsetting group session. When the patient leaves abruptly, an effort should also be made to have him come in and discuss his decision to leave. The social worker can be of considerable assistance in contacting the patient and also in directing him to other sources of help if he refuses to participate further in the rehabilitative program (see Chapter IV).

Unlike other patients, an alcoholic's leavetaking, whether his is a drop-out or abrupt termination, is never considered as the final decision. The patient is always offered the opportunity to return at a later date when he is better able to undertake treatment. This isn't meant as an avoidance of the therapeutic process but rather as a recognition of the alcoholic's markedly low tolerance for frustration and his inability to withstand stress.

REMAINERS

Is there any fundamental difference between those alcoholics who remain in treatment and those who terminate therapy either immediately or after a period of a few months? All that can be offered at this point in answer to this question are some hunches based on the group experience.

For comparative purposes, histories of three members of the same alcoholic group as the three terminators discussed above will be given. These three are *remainers,* since all either stayed in therapy whenever feasible, until the termination of the research project, or continued treatment in another setting. In describing the variable that may possibly differentiate between these two populations, it is, unfortunately, easier to describe the similarities rather than the dissimilarities. For instance, the severity of the underlying psychopathology barring overt psychosis or psychopathy, does not appear to be a differentiating variable between those who continued therapy and those who left. Some who left after a short while were verging on psychosis; but others equally as disturbed remained in therapy.

Nicholas came to the initial interview while in a depression. Diagnostically, the psychological material described him as latently psychotic. He was unmarried and his mother had died recently.

He spoke of feeling lost. He had been actively drinking up to a few hours before the interview and reported that he acted out in a bizarre fashion when inebriated. He was moved to seek treatment because of a continuing depression after his mother's death. In the group he felt compelled to perform. He was very glib, witty, and astute in discerning the irrationalities of the other group members. However, his glibness and pseudo-sophiscated repartée did not cover his dependency needs; rather, they were used to seduce and entrench himself with the therapist who now in his fantasy took "mother's" place. He perceived the therapist as an omnipotent and beneficent mother figure and openly accepted her as such. Fantasy material was too easily accessible and what was worse, readily acted out. His treatment was directed toward greater structuring and containment of his many scattered impulses. Up to the time he went into therapy, Nicholas' life was characterized by a lack of commitment and impermanence: his work, for instance, rarely kept him in one city for any period of time. Fortunately, the nature of his job was such that it allowed him the freedom to move about. His work history, however, was good; he had worked from an early age and been self-supporting. Nicholas' commitment to therapy soon became evident in his readjusting his work schedule in order to remain in the city for treatment. His drinking ceased entirely after a few sessions and it has presented no problem over a period of two years; however, the bizarre acting out which took many different forms recurred in periods of stress, and he at length began to acknowledge these episodes as coincident with, rather than as caused by the excessive and compulsive drinking. Nicholas is continuing in therapy privately.

Another problem that sometimes arises in the treatment of the alcoholic, which is unique to him, is a division of loyalties between membership in A.A. and membership in a psychotherapeutic group. Concomitant membership in A.A. and group psychotherapy cannot be said, on the basis of our recent experience,* to be a determining factor between those who leave therapy and those who remain. Membership in Alcoholic Anonymous is in many instances undoubtedly used as a resistance to beginning or continuing group psychotherapy. In many cases also, these patients find support for their resistance to

*New York Alcoholism Vocational Rehabilitation Project.

treatment among the members of A.A. However, like any other resistance, if this is effectively responded to by the therapist, it can be
used to facilitate rather than deter therapeutic process.

Seymour seemed confused and ill at ease in his initial interview.
He spoke about his homosexual affairs, his separation from his
wife, and his confused feelings regarding her. Seymour was still
actively drinking; and while drunk, he abused his wife, and
accused her of illicit love affairs. The psychological examination
described him as a man with good potentialities who, however,
was verging on psychosis. From the beginning Seymour made a
great effort to stop drinking. He was encouraged in the group to
become an active A.A. member. His attendance in the group
therapy sessions was constant. In the group, Seymour was at first
withdrawn. As he entered more spontaneously into the group
interaction, it became apparent that his incestuous familial relationships were continuing to adversely affect all his relationships.
Seymour's father was a shadowy figure. The patient knew no
bounds; his sense of self was as amorphous as his sense of limits.
His infantile omnipotence had yet to be challenged. In the pro-
jected version of this, he sought the ultimate authority, and the
wisest gods, finding them in turn in religion, psychotherapy, and
A.A. Seymour attained several months of sobriety and in these
months his confusion and disorganization came more actively
into focus. At this point, he decided that he should leave group
therapy since it might conflict with A.A. and jeopardize his newly
attained sobriety. Seymour was distressed but believed that he
had to choose between the two. The therapist intervened. She
experienced his relationship to group therapy and A.A. as being
much like his early relationship to his parents. One parent always
had to be in the shadows. Seymour felt torn in his loyalties; he
didn't know to whom he belonged; and he despaired of ever
finding himself. The therapist pointed out that rather than having
to choose between the two, he was able to have both, and should
continue both in A.A. and group therapy. Seymour seemed to
sense the significance of this possibilty and chose to continue.
Undue marital stress and a growing inner turmoil finally produced
a psychotic break. Psychotherapy was continued in a hospital
setting and later, once again, extramurally.

Although sobriety is a *sine qua non* for psychotherapeutic treatment, it cannot be designated in itself, as a differentiating factor between those who remain in therapy and those who terminate. The attainment of sobriety although essential to treatment, is no panacea. The "pink cloud" feeling described by the alcoholic after the attainment of several months of sobriety is ultimately followed by a deep sense of futility, especially if the alcoholism has been used to avoid his inner struggle and deep despair. "What percentage is there in being sober? Nothing is any better really; maybe it's even worse."

A good number of alcoholics either begin or continue in therapy even after several years of sobriety.

> Grace had attained five years of sobriety. She had begun individual therapy three months before joining the group. Grace explained that she had become upset and terminated individual therapy when her therapist stated that since she had remained dry for five years, she was not an alcoholic. Grace sought psychotherapy again because of a deeply-rooted inertia and depression. During the initial interview, she spoke freely of her homosexual attachments, which began when she was eighteen. She appeared more disturbed about the general nature of her relationships than about their homosexual aspect. Grace was particularly upset by the possessiveness and jealousy which were always a part of these affairs. The psychological examination depicted a dependent, withdrawn woman, immature in her relationships, and with a problem about her identity and self-integration. Grace became a staunch group member and remained for the full two-year term in the group treatment project and then continued therapy privately. At the end of this two-year period, Grace showed definite change. Her behavior was much more spontaneous and she was considerably more self-aware. She dared to hope for many things now and to express her ambitions. Her inertia seemed considerably diminished. On retest, the psychological report described a greater surfacing of Grace's original frigidity and sexual confusion, with an evident wish now to be more femininely creative. With this, Grace showed signs of definite heterosexual involvements.

If the severity of the underlying pathology, membership in A.A., or the attainment of sobriety in themselves alone, are not the critical differentiating variables between those alcoholics who remain in group therapy and those who leave abruptly, what, if any, are important vectors that possibly contribute to continuing therapeutic participation? These factors described above, seem to be important only insofar as they contribute to a characterization of a more complex variable, the nature of the patient's motivation (see Chapter VIII). For all three cases of remainers cited, the stated motivation for beginning therapy appeared to be basically different from the stated motivation of the terminators. Each remainer had come with a complaint about himself as a person and a sense of dissatisfaction with his life as a whole. Moreover, this dissatisfaction was at least in part acknowledged as coincident with, rather than attributable to, the alcoholism. For example, Nicholas spoke of his depression, Seymour, his homosexuality and unhappy marriage, and Grace, her inertia and depression. The initial trusting relationship which formed between the therapist and these patients did not hold the potential threat of an intolerable self-revelation. These patients seemed more able to accept their passive dependency needs. If anything, they welcomed the existence of someone to whom they could turn. Moreover, they were initially less defensive and more inclined toward self-evaluation. Whatever transpired between these patients, therapist, and group, the therapist found himself able to support them when their self-esteem was threatened. This was only partly true with the three alcoholics described who left abruptly, for in these instances sudden threats to the patient's self-esteem could not be deflected. A recent investigation lends support to these clinical impressions (6). It suggests that those patients who possess a high need for approval terminate therapy much earlier than those with less need for approval. The terminators, moreover, were characterized as being more defensive, with a strong need to avoid anticipated threats to self-esteem.

Although the length of stay in therapy is an important factor with all patients, with the alcoholic patient it is particularly significant in determining the possibility of a successful outcome. A prolonged stay in treatment for the alcoholic patient, however, does not necessarily mean that he is deeply involved in the therapeutic process. The resistive alcoholic may have to be exposed to a therapeutic group climate for many months before he actually begins to participate effectively in the group. However, the longer he does remain in therapy, the greater the possibility for a therapeutic experience leading to change.

THE ALCOHOLIC'S LEAVETAKING
CHALLENGES THE GROUP THERAPIST

Values, expectations and goals which apply in the general practice of psychotherapy cannot be maintained in the practice of group psychotherapy with the alcoholic. Like the infant whose intake capacity is so limited that he is placed on demand feedings, it may well be that the alcoholic who so totally resists change must be permitted greater latitude in entering and withdrawing from group therapy. The alcoholic is unlike the nonalcoholic patient in another important respect also. Even though he physically takes leave of his therapist and group, with seeming ease, the question arises as to the permanence of this separation. It is not at all unusual to receive letters or phone calls from a "terminated" patient two or three years after his withdrawal from group treatment, either indicating his wish to resume therapy or simply keeping in touch by reporting on his greater sense of well-being and continued sobriety. The importance of this limited tie, in which the alcoholic experiences the therapist's availability, even though there is no longer an active therapeutic relationship, is evident. It follows that the therapist must be willing to see this patient intermittently, should the need arise.

It seems appropriate to ask at this point what are the unique contributions of group psychotherapy to the alcoholic patient? The attainment of sobriety, which certainly is an immediate therapeutic goal, is not the answer. Sobriety alone can result from any crucial life experience that confronts the alcoholic with the cumulative effect of his self-destructiveness, and so profoundly moves him that he chooses to live (remain sober.) For example, when the alcoholic is directly faced with sexual impotence, the loss of his family through an impending divorce, or an irreversible physical damage, such as a peripheral neuropathy, he may choose to stop drinking. However, the attainment of sobriety, which may be enough to reverse the destructive physical process, does not eradicate the alcoholic's psychological plight. Group psychotherapy, through its methods and goals, contributes by diminishing the alcoholic's self-destructiveness and lessening his isolation, as it brings to light the core conflict previously masked by the alcohol. Included among the aims of group psychotherapy, then, for the alcoholic patient is his more creative participation in society with greater satisfactions accruing to him in his life. The alcoholic as he recovers must attain a greater freedom to choose his own fate. Group psychotherapy gives him a deep sense of belonging and identification beyond his symptom of alcoholism, enabling him to broaden his scope of positive experiences and encouraging him to risk new feelings and behavior. His previous detachment from the rest of society diminishes as he begins to participate first in his group and later in his community, facing and not denying the conflicts and struggles inherent in his being human. Perhaps it is at this stage that the homogeneous alcoholic group becomes truly heterogeneous, consisting of separate and different persons. It is at this point that the alcoholic patient no longer requires the support of an exclusively alcoholic treatment group.

The alcoholism must be focused upon first and then emphasized together with the other problems throughout group therapy until sobriety is attained. An effective approach to the problem of drinking, however, is not to be thought of as only patient-directed. The therapist must also re-evaluate his goals with this kind of patient. The therapist, accustomed to a general psychiatric practice, must also be influenced by the alcoholic's continuing struggle in his group and in his life. The therapist must learn to appreciate the frequent though limited success of transference cures, where patients still remain dependent and in need of occasional therapeutic sessions. The fact that the patient has stopped drinking, and has achieved some degree of self-awareness; and, in addition, has returned to his community as a productive and more satisfied member of society, should not be minimized.

Alcoholism, as discussed throughout these chapters, can only be tackled by a united front of interested and involved professionals and lay persons working together. To offset the penchant that alcoholics have "to divide and conquer" the group therapist in private practice and his colleagues or the staff members of the treatment center must be united in purpose and in easy personal communication, one with another. The therapist, conducting the treatment group, even though he relies on the other disciplines and approaches, attempts to bring together all the disparate elements of the alcoholic's life. For example, the group therapist should comply, particularly at first, when asked by the patient to call his physician for no other reason than to "talk to him," or to attend an A.A. meeting for no other reason than to "learn what it is all about." These requests made in a purely human context, have great symbolic implication as far as treatment is concerned. In addition, they offer the group therapist the opportunity to be in contact with every aspect of the patient's effort toward remaining sober.

There appears to be a dependence between the alcoholic patient and the group therapist despite the patient's lateness to sessions, frequent unexplained absences, and periodic disappearances. This bond, different from the usual transference, seems to be based upon the alcoholic's inability to completely separate first, not from his parents but from his fantastic image of them; and second, not from his therapist but from the fantastic image of that therapist. The alcoholic's need for permanence, in this unusual relationship, is reflected in his requirement that his therapist remain unreal and yet be available at all times. The group psychotherapist, treating the alcoholic, must develop a tolerance for this patient, who paradoxically establishes an extremely dependent and "permanent" relationship while at the same time, takes his leave of treatment with seeming ease.

REFERENCES

1. Mullan, H., and Sangiuliano, I.: *The Therapist's Contribution to the Treatment Process: His Person, Transactions and Methods.* Spingfield, Thomas, 1964.
2. McNair, D. M., Porr, M., and Callahan, D. M.: Patient and therapist influences on quitting psychotherapy. *J. Consult. Psychol., 27*:10-17, 1963.
3. Hiler, E. W.: An analysis of patient-therapist compatibility. *J. Consult. Psychol., 22*:341-347, 1958.
4. Mindlin, D.: Characteristics of the alcoholic related to therapeutic outcome. *Quart. J. Stud. Alcohol, 20*:604-619, 1959.
5. Palola, E., Jackson, J., Kelleher, D.: Defensiveness in alcoholics: measures based on MMPI. *J. Hlth. Hum. Behav., 2*(3):185-189, 1961.
6. Strickland, B. R., and Crowne, D. P.: Need for approval and the premature termination of psychotherapy. *J. Consult. Psychol., 27*:95-101, 1963.

INDEX

flexibility of, 152-153
individual, 212
needed revisions, 8-9
noninstitutional, 6-7
patient's self-interest in, 7
process of intake, 116-117
for terminators, 310-311
Treatment center, group-oriented,
39-40
Treatment group
abandonment of, 18-19
acting out in, 267-283
avoidance of reality, 18
avoidance of responsibility, 16-17
clinical psychological, 45
drop-outs, 303-305
dynamic, 44-45
early indices of concern for self and
others, 241-243
essential value in, 62-63
exclusion of psychotherapist,
243-244
exploitation of, 17-18
movement of patient from one to
another, 229-230
orientation, 45
over-all staff, 43-44
patients placement in, 225-233
psychotherapeutic, 44
remainers in, 311-316
self selection of, 214-215
sobriety in, 62-63
social case work, 45
vocational evaluation, 44
vocational counselling, 44
Twelve steps, list of, 57

V

Vocational change, indices of, 88-89

Vocational counselling, 79-89,
173-318
aims, 81-88
aspect of coalition, 180-181
choice of, 122-126
combined with group psychotherapy,
198-201
definition of, 190
difference between group psychotherapy, 189-191
evaluative function, 86-88
fields of endeavor, 178-179
formats of, 193-201
individual, 193-196, 197
social worker's conviction about,
126
therapeutic interventions, 189-190
overall purpose, 83-88
relationship with patient, 191,
194-196
Vocational evaluation, 78-89,
183-189
aims, 81-88
tests used in, 187-189
timing and method of, 185-187
Vogel, S., 62

W

Weakland, J., 283
What About Alcoholism? (film), 151
What About Drinking? (film), 150
Willmar State Hospital, 136
Wolfson, Dr., 302

Y

Yeshiva University Film Library,
147, 150

Z

Zax, M., 215

THE LIBRARY